ACES
IN COMMAND

ACES
IN COMMAND

★ ★ Fighter Pilots as Combat Leaders ★ ★

WALTER J. BOYNE

BRASSEY'S
Washington, D.C.

Library of Congress Cataloging-in-Publication Data

Boyne, Walter J., 1929–
    Aces in command : fighter pilots as combat leaders / Walter J. Boyne.
        p.   cm.
    ISBN 1-57488-310-0
    1. Fighter pilots—United States—Case studies.   2. Leadership—Case studies.   3. Command of troops—Case studies.   4. Fighter plane combat—United States—Case studies.   I. Title
        UG626 .B69 2001
        358.4'3'092—dc21

                                                                    00-049421

ISBN 1-57488-310-0   (alk. paper)

Printed in the United States of America on acid-free paper that meets the American National Standards Institute Z39-48 Standard.

Brassey's, Inc.
22841 Quicksilver Drive
Dulles, Virginia 20166

First Edition

10 9 8 7 6 5 4 3 2 1

★ CONTENTS ★

★ CONTENTS ★

★ PREFACE ★

Aces in Command is the story of four American fighter aces, one from each of the major wars of the twentieth century. The careers of the selected aces show the wide variety of skills, techniques, and personal attributes necessary to achieve that status.

Attaining the coveted title "ace" has always been a difficult task, fraught with danger and demanding the very most from those who aspire to the honor. In the most memorable instances, the pilot who becomes an ace also becomes a leader and an innovator. In modern terms, he becomes a "force multiplier," because his leadership multiplies the effectiveness of his squadron, and sometimes, of his entire air force. The aces selected here did just that.

Although the goal of scoring five victories and becoming an ace has been constant over time, the environment in which the attempts were made has changed continuously. Even within a particular war—World War I, World War II, Korea, or Vietnam—changes occurred rapidly. Becoming an ace—and staying alive in the process—demanded an incredible ability to adapt to changes in technology and tactics of air combat. The very essence of being an ace required the pilot to throw himself against the hard steel, sharp edges, and explosions of rapidly developing technology. Those who were able to master their own technologies, and counter those of the enemy, survived to become an ace. Those who did not often became the victims of aces from the other side. For this reason, each of the relevant technical developments affecting the ace are explained in detail, with emphasis on the human qualities required to use—or overcome—them. For clarity, the dimensions and performance characteristics of the planes the aces used are presented in an appendix.

Becoming an ace also required an Olympian effort to extract every ounce of personal courage and determination to close with and then kill the enemy. It is here where that outstanding personality, the ace-leader, further distinguishes himself by embracing danger and inspiring those who follow him to do the same. This is one of his most important challenges, for studies have shown that of all the pilots who have an opportunity to engage in combat, fully 65 percent manage to avoid doing so. Clearly there is something—a warrior gene perhaps—that separates the aces from the rest.

Aversion to battle—and often aversion to the idea of killing another human being—has been found in all services in every war that has been studied. Well-validated studies show that from Waterloo to Pork Chop Hill, men engaged in combat tend to shoot over their enemies' heads to avoid killing them. (This almost unexplainable phenomenon disappeared in Vietnam because of the training given and the weapons employed.) It is thus not surprising that the same phenomenon occurs in air combat, given the far greater ease with which combat can be avoided by those who wish to do so. The ace, in contrast, seeks out and embraces combat—he never tries to fire over their heads.

In *Aces in Command*, the character of each of the selected aces can be fully developed. The analysis will explain just what it was that allowed him to reach the elevated status of fighter ace and at the same time demonstrate the unique qualities of leadership that distinguished him from his fellow aces. Four outstanding individuals have been selected for analysis—Eddie Rickenbacker from World War I, Hub Zemke from World War II, Boots Blesse from the Korean War, and Robin Olds from the Vietnam War. Each one of these aces became an outstanding leader, and it is instructive to compare the similarities and the differences in their backgrounds, economic situations, and education as they wrestled with the changing technology of war.

★ FOREWORD ★

I t has been my good fortune to have been actively engaged in aviation from my days as an aviation cadet at Randolph Field to the present. I am in awe when I view with wonder the marvelous engineering triumphs that not only defend our country, but also provide us with swift, efficient commercial air transportation.

In the course of my long career, and, as a fighter ace myself, I have met the aces of several nations—some in combat, but most in the cheerful warmth of post-war associations. I have come to know many of the American aces, including the four fine gentlemen whose lives are charted in this book: Eddie Rickenbacker, "Hub" Zemke, "Boots" Blesse, and Robin Olds.

My association with these gentlemen is both broad and deep. "Hub" and I were fighter pilots together at Langley Field, during the 1930s, when the Air Corps was small, and Lieutenant Colonel Robert Olds was commander of the 2d Bombardment Group. His son Robin was a familiar sight on the field and gave early promise of his later success.

Fate dictated that Hub and I would have closely related careers for a number of years. We both became quite proficient in the Curtiss P-40, so much so that we were selected to go to the United Kingdom, landing in London the night of the biggest air raid of the war. Officially we were there as neutral "observers," but in fact our job was to instruct our colleagues in the Royal Air Force on the virtues (and there were many) of the P-40. It was a dream assignment. Two young Lieutenants with a terrific job that provided them firsthand insight into the German air assault on Great Britain! We also gained insight into problems the United States would face after Pearl Harbor.

To our amazement, Hub and I were then tapped to go to the Soviet Union, to do the same thing with the 200 P-40s the RAF had made available as an early form of Lend-Lease.

After many fascinating experiences, our paths parted there. Hub came back to become one of the all-time-great fighter group commanders. He introduced a new unit into combat, flying a brand-new fighter, the Republic P-47. He was a great leader who led from the front, not only in the air, but in withering ground attacks. Later in the war, the Mustang he was flying broke up in a violent thunderstorm, and he became a prisoner of war. As the senior officer of his prison camp, Hub demonstrated his leadership qualities again, under the most difficult circumstances.

In the meantime, my war took me from Russia to the Persian Gulf and finally to China, where I first flew with the 75th Fighter Squadron as part of the Flying Tigers. Later, with Colonel Philip Cochran, I was blessed to be able to both found and lead the 1st Air Commando Group—but that's another story.

It was in China that I first met Eddie Rickenbacker, in a none-too-auspicious manner. A Japanese Oscar had just finished placing all of his ammunition into my P-40, removing my rudder and rendering me helpless. The armor plate (which I had thought about removing) stopped the bullets from harming me, but the airplane was badly shot up, including my tires. When I landed, the tires came off and my poor old P-40 nosed over. I climbed out of the airplane, and to my great embarrassment, the first man I met was Eddie Rickenbacker, on tour of the Far East.

Rickenbacker was then in his fifties, but he was hale and hearty, and was a continuing inspiration to me and to my colleagues in the Flying Tigers. Rickenbacker, who, with twenty-six victories, was the American Ace of Aces in World War I, was the prototype of the most important class of aces—the ace who is also a leader.

Just as Rickenbacker was one of my heroes, so he was to Boots Blesse, who scored ten victories flying the great North American F-86 Sabre during the Korean War. While I did not serve in combat with Boots, I came to know him well and to admire not only his victory score, but also the leadership he showed in establishing what became the standard United States Air Force fighter tactics. Boots flew again in Vietnam, this time in a McDonnell F-4 Phantom, and once again, he initiated new tactics.

Robin Olds, the fourth ace discussed in Walter Boyne's fascinating book, had a most unusual career in that he served with Hub Zemke and became an ace in 1944, then returned to combat flying the F-4 in Vietnam in 1966. In Vietnam, he conceived and led the single greatest tactical fighter victory of the war, Operation Bolo, in which seven enemy aircraft were shot down.

Like Rickenbacker, Zemke, and Blesse, Olds was far more than an ace—he was a warrior who led his troops into combat with imagination and with concern for their welfare.

Aces in Command is the first book to examine the phenomenon of the fighter ace in its full context and to analyze exactly what it is that differentiates the ace from the ordinary fighter pilot, and more important, that differentiates the ace who is also a great leader from the ordinary ace. It is an epic story, one in which I was proud to have played a part, and one that should inspire a future generation of pilots.

Major General John R. Alison, USAF (Ret.)
Washington, D.C.

★ ACKNOWLEDGMENTS ★

Many, many people were involved in the production of this book, and I am grateful to them all. One of the amazing things about writing today is the number of people and organizations that use the Internet, and that are so willing to provide information and photographs at virtually a moment's notice. Even organizations as large as the National Archives have adopted the Internet as a tool and use it to make much more thorough research possible than ever before.

I am particularly grateful to two of the principals of this book, Major General Frederick "Boots" Blesse, USAF (Ret.), and Brigadier General Robin Olds, USAF (Ret.). Both of these distinguished aces gave me many hours of their time in interviews and in correspondence, and both were kind enough to review the finished manuscript in great detail.

Although I had met Eddie Rickenbacker on one occasion, I did not know him. However, I feel that I came to know him through the good offices of several historians who have so thoroughly researched his life. Professor W. David Lewis, Distinguished University Professor of Auburn University's Department of History, is presently engaged in writing what will undoubtedly be the definitive biography of Rickenbacker. Doctor Lewis was unstinting in his kindness, furnishing me with much material that a lesser person might have wished to retain for his own publication. He was also able to point out many errors I had made in my own research, and I am particularly grateful for this. In addition, he introduced me to Martin T. Oliff, Assistant Archivist at Auburn, who was also very helpful.

Another expert on the period, Peter Kilduff, gave me much information, many photos, and much good advice after reviewing the manuscript. Howard Fisher, another expert on World War I aviation, also provided me much information, advice, and exceptional insight into the period. Larry Ellman, another World War I specialist, reviewed the manuscript and was the source of much good information.

I had met Hub Zemke only once, in passing, and turned to his many admirers for assistance. My friend Roger Freeman had written an admirable book on Hub's days in the 56th, and was kind enough to offer me insights into Zemke's complex personality. Warren Bodie, a successful author and publisher, had known Zemke quite well and provided me some private papers that were very revealing along with some excellent photos. Peter Rausch, who is a historian of aces, grew to know Zemke in his later life and shared his knowledge with me. Major General John Alison, an ace in his own right, flew with Zemke for years and knew him well after the war, and in his usual gracious manner, told me story after story about their amazing adventures in England and the Soviet Union.

"Boots" Blesse has a host of friends and admirers, and I had come to know him quite well in the process of doing several lengthy television interviews with him. General Blesse generously shared his own writings with me and provided many photographs. One of his greatest admirers is Lieutenant General William E. "Earl" Brown, USAF (Ret.). "Brownie," as Blesse called him, gave me many an anecdote about their time together in Korea, and in the postwar years, and he, like many others, feels that Blesse was one of the all-time-great fighter-pilot-leaders.

I had also come to know the great Colonel Walker "Bud" Mahurin over the course of researching several books and conducting several television interviews. Mahurin, an excellent author in his own right, is one of the most indomitable men ever to fly for the United States Air Force, and over the years, he taught me much about Zemke, Blesse, and Robin Olds.

Olds is a towering personality who dominates every room he enters. He has a host of friends and admirers who were anxious to give their impressions of him as an ace and as a leader. Among these were Walter Radeke, Everett Raspberry, Mark Berent, Darrel Whitcomb, and Jack Broughton. Berent and Broughton were kind enough to review my material on "Going Downtown," so that I could be confident it was accurate.

Others who read the manuscript, or parts of it, for accuracy and content included Ned Jacoby, Cal Bass, Randy Sohn, Birch Matthews, and Henry Snelling. I want to thank Wally Meeks for many good suggestions and C. V. Glines for his excellent overview on what it takes to make an ace.

One always reads about problems with big government and the inability to get things done. It is all the more refreshing, therefore, to report on the swift, superb work done by a number of government offices in helping struggling authors. At the Air Force Office of History, Dr. George Watson was of immeasurable help, pointing out a number of sources I would never have found otherwise. Dr. Lynn Gamma, Archivist of the United States Air Force, provided terrific help on several occasions, as did Dr. Robert Lane, Director of the Air University Library. The Air Force Historical Research Center at Maxwell Air Force Base was equally helpful, with Ms. Pauline Tubbs giving me guidance. At the Air Force Museum, Jerry Rep and Sarah Sessions were quick to respond to my request for audio tapes.

The National Archives has moved in part to a large new building, but the excellent service, as provided by the legendary John Taylor and by Tim Nenninger, remains absolutely first rate. Greg Bryant, of the National Air & Space Museum, did some excellent research, for which I am grateful.

The Air Force Association has been extremely helpful as always, and I am indebted to John Correll for allowing me to use the reference facilities there. Librarian Pearlie Draughn was her usual cheerful, helpful self, and provided much material and many photographs.

There are many many web sites that were helpful, but two, one by Rocky Gooch, the Warbirds Research Group, and one by Sam McGowan, were particularly useful.

Of the many publications that were consulted, five stand out. These included the late, lamented *Cross & Cockade*, *Over the Front*, *World War One Aero*, *Air Power History*, and the *Journal of the American Aviation Historical Society*.

There were many others who helped by introductions and other means, including Bill Greener, Bill Jobes, and Gerald Horiuchi.

As always, I want to thank my agent, Jacques de Spoelberch, for his patience and persistence, and my editor at Brassey's, Don Jacobs, who shepherded me through many a change and who improved the book immensely with his editorial insight.

I undoubtedly and unconscionably have forgotten some people who were of great help, and to them I apologize and ask understanding.

And again, as always, my family and friends served as an inspiration and put up with my monomaniac work habits.

Walter J. Boyne
Ashburn, Virginia
2000

★ O N E ★
AIR WAR AND THE ACE MYTH

Over the years, three warrior symbols—the knight in shining armor, the laconic, gun-toting cowboy, and the cocky, aggressive fighter pilot ace—have captured the public's imagination.

All three are surrounded with myth derived from books and film, but they have a vital conceptual difference. While there were individually famous knights and individually famous cowboys, there was no standard hierarchical ranking system that cut across time and national borders. With fighter pilots, however, a definite hierarchy was established, with the magic figure of five victories separating the ace from the mass of aspirants. The respect the ace has earned results in no small part from his rarity.

Hundreds of thousands of men have trained to be a fighter pilot but fewer than 1 percent of these ever entered combat. Of those few who entered combat, only 5 percent became aces. Thus, of all the many people who have trained to be a fighter pilot, only .0005 percent (five ten-thousandths of a percent) have become aces. They are a true elite.

Although the fighter ace is a contemporary icon, less is known about him than is known about knights and cowboys. The first aces were recognized in 1915, and the last official American pilot ace—Steve Ritchie—scored his fifth victory in 1972, just fifty-seven years later.

The term "pilot ace" is used to distinguish those individuals who were at the controls of the aircraft engaged in combat from those who flew as observers, gunners, or weapon systems operators and shared in the victories. There is no question that the "guy in back," the so-called backseater, was vitally important, but for the purposes of this book, we will be concerned only with the men who did the hands-on flying to become aces.

In that fifty-seven-year period, only a relatively few young men practiced one of the most challenging and difficult professions, air-to-air combat. Of these, only a very small fraction became aces. Just to be politically correct, it should be noted here that virtually all aces were men except for a very few, very courageous, Soviet women during World War II.

The original driving force in selecting a totally new type of hero and raising him to celebrity status was not simply recognition of the fighter ace's daring or his skill. It was instead an almost convulsive reaction to the abysmal horror of World War I trench fighting.

It became impossible to raise morale at home with uplifting stories about trench warfare—the utter misery could not be disguised nor could the somber casualty lists that filled columns in the newspapers and were plastered in serried rows on public squares. But combat in the sky, clean, sporting battles between the flower of each nation's youth—there was a story that could be told—even if the reporter had to fiddle with the facts.

Although the first pilots to score multiple victories were French, the passionate celebration of the successful fighter pilot began in Germany. This was somewhat surprising, given the almost monastic Prussian tradition that forbade officers from seeking personal publicity. But the need was great. Two young Lieutenants, Oswald Boelcke and Max Immelmann, were selected to fly the Fokker E I *Eindecker* (one wing, i.e., a monoplane), the very first purpose-built fighter plane placed in series production. Sometimes flying together, but most often going on solo patrols, the two young officers would score a series of victories to earn the highest decorations and endear themselves to the German public. They were deluged in fan mail that asked for everything from signatures to sex, and their names and portraits were instantly commercialized by tobacco firms, newspapers, greeting card manufacturers, and anyone else who could come up with a way to exploit their new-found fame. (The original German term for ace translates as "star turn." Initially, the Germans required seven victories to earn this title, but this was later reduced to five.)

It was both a propaganda triumph and a great incentive program, and other pilots sought to follow their lead. The idea caught on at once in France, but was for a time cold-shouldered in England, where it was felt the pilot was no more exposed to danger than a Tommie in the trenches, and deserving of no more honor.

Yet in time even the British had to come around and celebrate their own heroes. When that time came, they would do so with a vengeance, in some cases going so far as deliberately awarding confirmation for unsubstantiated claims. Predictably, when the United States entered the war, it embraced the concept, cheering its pilots just as it cheered George M. Cohan or Ty Cobb.

As would be the case for many future aces, Boelcke and Immelmann secured their initial successes by exploiting a technical innovation. In many respects, the Fokker E I was a relatively primitive aircraft for the time. Instead of using ailerons for lateral control, its wings were warped just as those of the Wright Flyer had been. The E I's performance was mediocre, with a top speed of less than 90 miles per hour and an endurance of just over one hour.

The E I would be progressively modified with more guns and bigger engines, with only incremental gains in performance. Only about 350 of the little monoplanes were built, but they built up so fearsome a reputation that Royal Flying Corps pilots were termed "Fokker Fodder" in Parliament.

The distinguishing characteristic that made the E I such a lethal weapon, was a machine gun aligned with the axis of the fuselage that fired forward through the propeller. This idea, so obvious now, was revolutionary when the E I was introduced in 1915.

A whole series of "pusher" aircraft (propeller in the rear) was developed. These provided a good field of fire, but most pushers were too slow to catch, much less attack, an enemy aircraft.

Other methods were tried, including firing forward with a gun fixed at a forty-five-degree angle and crabbing sidewise to fire at the enemy, an almost hopeless endeavor. The best compromise was the installation of the gun on the upper wing, where it fired over the propeller—but was very difficult to load.

Ironically, the solution to the problem—synchronizing the gun so that it could only fire when the propeller was not in front of the muzzle—had been patented by a Swiss engineer, Franz Schneider, in July 1913. Similar work had been done in Great Britain, France, Germany, and Russia. There is strong evidence to believe that the French were the first to use the idea in combat, fitting an interrupter gear to a Morane Saulnier Model L monoplane flown by the famous pioneer aviator Roland Garros. The interrupter gear was not perfected, and the blades of Garros's propeller were fitted with steel deflector plates to prevent their being shot off if the interrupter gear failed to interrupt. (Most accounts refer only to the deflector plates and ignore the possibility of the interrupter gear being fitted.)

Garros tested the concept at the front and shot down three German planes in

April 1915, before a chance rifle shot from the ground ruptured his fuel line and forced him down behind enemy lines. His plane was captured, and the brilliant young Dutch stunt pilot turned manufacturer, Anthony Fokker, was tasked to adapt the idea for German use. His engineers did so in short order, probably because they were familiar with Schneider's work. Their invention was a simple linkage of cams and push rods between the oil-pump drive of the rotary engine and the gun trigger. Its operation was timed so that the gun could not fire when the propeller blade passed in front of the muzzle. Fokker, as was his wont, subsequently claimed that the invention was his alone.

The synchronizing gear, far less complex than the suspension system of a modern car, revolutionized air combat and set the stage for the appearance of the fighter ace. Oddly enough, the chosen fighter, the Fokker E I, had many shortcomings. Its landing gear was weak, it had a low rate of climb, and its performance fell off rapidly at altitude. Nonetheless, it had two essential qualities: an adequate degree of maneuverability and a machine gun that could be aimed by aiming the airplane.

That was more than enough for Boelcke and Immelmann, who began their scoring streak in the summer of 1915 and who soared to the heights of popularity in Germany. Though it would have been unseemly for either man to admit it, they were as much rivals as Sammy Sosa and Mark McGwire.

Immelmann scored his first victory on August 1, 1915, knocking down a Royal Flying Corps BE 2c biplane near Douai. A contest soon developed between Immelmann and Boelcke to become the top scoring pilot. The German public followed the race closely, and both men became celebrities, a fact not much appreciated by other young Germans fighting their war from the trenches.

Both received the Kingdom of Prussia's highest decoration, the coveted *Orden Pour le Merite*, on January 12, 1916, by which time each had scored eight victories. Affectionately called "The Blue Max," the *Pour le Merite* was reserved for officers only and corresponded in prestige to the American Medal of Honor. It differed in a significant aspect that affected the lives of German aces.

The Blue Max became an immediate object of competition, and scoring levels were set for its award, eight at first, then sixteen, and then twenty. As German pilots approached the award level, they became increasingly bold, and often even reckless. American pilots competed with equal intent for scoring honors and the decorations that went with them, but *not* directly for the Medal of Honor, which had particular restrictions. It could be awarded only to someone who accomplished a heroic deed at great risk to his life, and the danger of which act he could have avoided honorably. The Medal of Honor was all too often awarded posthumously.

The competition between the two friends also serves as a symbol for the wide variety of personalities who would later become aces, for they were very different types. Immelmann was a teetotaler and a vegetarian, which may account for tales of his being moody and often ill-tempered. He was a loner, intent on his personal war with the enemy. Boelcke, in contrast, was even tempered, and while reserved with subordinates, could be charming in social situations. The greatest difference between the two men was in their penchant for leadership. Immelmann fought his own war, while Boelcke carefully selected and nurtured pilots for his fighter unit, *Jagdstaffel 2*, the first of its kind. He was a teacher and a tactician who set down the "Boelcke Dicta," a set of rules for air fighting that have resonance today. (See appendix 6.) Boelcke serves as the paradigm for the later ace-leaders of every air force.

The two men were similar in one respect. They pushed themselves to the limits of their ability and beyond, wringing the utmost from the weapons they had at hand. Both were ultimately lost in battle.

Immelmann, called the "Eagle of Lille" for his fights over that city, had achieved fifteen victories when he was killed. The cause of his death is disputed, as it is with so many aces. The British claimed he was shot down by one of their F. E. 2b two-seaters. Somewhat ironically, the Germans insisted that his synchronizing system had failed, and he had shot off his own propeller, resulting in an in-flight structural failure and a fatal crash.

Boelcke, the first architect of fighter tactics, had scored forty victories when one of his protégés, the very capable but much older Lieutenant Erwin Boehme, collided with him in the midst of a dogfight. Boelcke was killed in the crash of his Albatros fighter. A badly shaken and deeply depressed Boehme survived the collision to go on to a successful twenty-four-victory career before his own death a year later at the age of thirty-eight.

The competition between Immelmann and Boelcke signaled the beginning of the evolutionary process by which young fighter pilots would adapt to the ever swifter changes in technology. It took all of Boelcke's and Immelmann's considerable skills to master the slow Eindecker and its single forward-firing machine gun. In the next six decades, well within an ordinary human's life span, future aces would have to master an absolute avalanche of technological advances.

The pilots of each nation and in all wars had to take full advantage of each opportunity when they flew the best aircraft, and they had to devise strategies for survival when the aircraft they flew were not the best. As we'll see in later chapters, the man with the best aircraft did not always win.

The war-induced changes in technology brought improvements in performance that were incredible. Aircraft speeds would advance from the SPAD XIII's 130 mph maximum of World War I to the sleek, twin-jet Messerschmitt Me 262's 540 mph by the end of World War II. In Korea the North American F-86 and the MiG-15 would duke it out at speeds just under the sound barrier, while their Vietnam counterparts would have the capability of going twice the speed of sound (even though maneuvering combat still took place at subsonic speeds). Aces had to contend with closing speeds of 250 mph in World War I. The ante was raised to 800 in World War II and by Vietnam had reached 1,500 mph. Decisions that had to be made in thirty seconds over Verdun had to be made in split seconds over Vietnam.

Armament would also advance, from the simple twin .30-caliber weapons of 1918, to the multiple heavy machine gun and cannon batteries of 1945, to the heat-seeking and television-guided missiles of 1972. The difference in killing power was dramatic. The typical twin machine gun armament of 1918 poured out .303 ammunition at the rate of 600 rounds per minute at any enemy that had better be no more than 100 yards away to get a hit. In contrast, in Vietnam the Sparrow missile could send a six-pound warhead out for up to twenty-five miles to home on its target with radar guidance. Such growth in weapons capability required extreme adaptation in both offensive and defensive tactics.

All of the advances required adaptation on the part of all of the pilots of each period, but it was the special qualities of the aces that enabled them to adapt more swiftly and to use the technological advances more effectively. It took great courage to fly combat in any of the eras; as we will see, the aces went well beyond sheer courage in their process of adaptation. The aces adapted best because they shared certain fundamental physical, mental, and spiritual qualities that allowed them to be among that top 1 percent of fighter pilots. As Korean ace "Boots" Blesse puts it: "No Guts No Glory."

The demands on the ace varied over time, so that the ace of World War I might not have met the situation found in Vietnam—and vice versa. The aces of each generation went to war as products of their contemporary culture. In World War I, pilots on both sides entered their training with an enormous idealism. They believed deeply in the justice of their cause and accepted the possibility of their death as the simple "price of honor."

It was somewhat different during World War II. On the Allied side, the men who entered World War II as pilots had been exposed to a generation of the anti-war sentiment that pervaded films and books. They were patriotic, but they were also more sophisticated and saw "their" war as something that had to be fought because the enemy was so demonstrably evil. For many, it was a great adventure, a chance to escape the Depression. In contrast, young Luftwaffe pilots were far less sophisticated and much more fanatically devoted to their cause, having been fed Nazi propaganda on the iniquities of the Versailles treaty and the German right to *Lebensraum*. In Japan the indoctrination had been even more intense, giving the Japanese pilots a religious fervor about their profession. They were taught that death in battle was a desirable end, one that would see them enshrined in the Yasukuni Shrine in Tokyo, gods to be worshipped.

By the Korean War, American pilots were competent professionals, confident that they would prevail in combat against any adversary. Their opponents were almost always Russians, also competent professionals but somewhat less confident, having seen the great masses of superb American equipment in World War II. The greatest operational difference was that the Russians fought under complete ground control, while the aggressive, well-trained Americans could make their own combat decisions within their fairly restrictive rules of engagement.

A totally new situation had developed by the Vietnam War. U.S. pilots were still competent professionals, but were shackled by irrational, politically dictated rules of engagement that forced them always to fight on enemy terms. By mid-1967, it was far worse, for the pilots had to fight a very difficult, dangerous war with the knowledge that they had lost the backing of much of the American public.

But regardless of changing technology or the variability of warfare, there was a constant factor, and that was the leadership quality that went hand in hand with being an ace. There have been exceptions, but for the most part, aces almost always carried with them the mantle of leadership.

Despite being the richest country in the world, the United States Congress always manages to find ways to reduce the military budget in peacetime. As a result, the military is often sent into war with inferior numbers and equipment. In the past the public forced Congress to make huge appropriations during wartime that allowed for a significant buildup of excellent equipment. While appropriations were being adjusted in Washington, the leadership and training of the regular components of the armed services struggled to fight the enemy and overcome the odds. Thus it was with the aces, who fought tough battles, took their squadrons into combat, taught newcomers the ropes, created new tactics, and, always, inspired aggressiveness.

Given the speed of modern warfare, future wars will not allow for such a lengthy buildup. Today it is more important than ever to give our leaders the equipment they need now—for there may be no tomorrow.

THE ACE MYTH

One aspect of the ace myth is the fictional ace, created in novels and films in a process that goes on to this day. The classic fictional ace is always a maverick loner, alienated from his squadron mates à la Tom Cruise in *Top Gun*. He gets in fights and is generally an outcast, except when in the air, where only his super-human talents enable him to save the situation. In most cases, the ace is a tragic figure who must die to tidy up the plot as Dick Arlen did in *Wings;* less often, he lives and wins the girl.

From the very beginning of the ace phenomenon, far better myths were generated about real-life individual aces. No matter which country was involved, reporters inevitably found their aces to be modest, good humored, patriotic, and convinced of the righteousness of their cause.

The media did not have its present destructive bent in the early years of the ace, and any eccentricities or imperfections of character in the ace were ignored. Albert Ball, the British "boy ace," was a recluse who built bonfires and walked around them playing his violin, traits that today would get him on Ritilin. The most famous World War I ace, the Red Baron, Manfred von Richthofen, was fascinated with shooting and killing and considered a day wasted unless he had assassinated some wildlife, the larger and rarer the animal the better. Richthofen scored eighty victories, while his younger brother Lothar scored half that amount. Lothar conducted himself on a much more human scale, preferring drinking and women to stalking elk in the woods. His peccadilloes were ignored, by both the press and his superiors.

By World War II, everything was in place for a wild expansion of the cult of the ace. The media was ready, the public expected it, and the pilots were anxious to take part. Each nation followed its own path in doing so.

The beginning of the war had gone badly for the United States, and aces were exceptionally welcome heroes. As time passed and the situation improved, the press kept careful tabs on individual aces. The World Series of aces was the competition for the most coveted title of all, "ace of aces," meaning the ace with the most victories of all. This resulted in several neck and neck races in both the European and Pacific theaters that gave the media more grist for their mill.

When an American ace had completed a tour of combat (often reluctantly, if he was in competition to be the leading scorer), he was brought home to be lionized at war bond rallies, factory tours, and indoctrinations of new pilots. It was the exception, rather than the rule, that the high-scoring ace would return for another combat tour.

The Germans had a much grimmer, thoroughly Teutonic, approach. They celebrated their aces even more than they had done in the last war, for Josef Goebbels's propaganda machine was effective in exploiting their fame. The German aces ran up incredible (but confirmed) scores, with two men, Majors Erich Hartman (352) and Gerhard Barkhorn (302), scoring more than 300 victories and twelve scoring more than 200. Their level of success was so great that new decorations had to be created for them. Under the German system, aces would fly until they were killed in combat or until the war ended.

Other countries had different systems. The British pattern was a compromise between the German and the American. The aces were lionized and given rest between tours of duty, but were returned to combat again and again. The Soviet Union awarded its aces with medals and a degree of publicity, but kept them firmly in combat. The Japanese aces were the least lionized. They received no decorations while they were alive, and only a few received even the distinction of a citation. There were no "tours of duty" for them; they fought till the end, and most died in the process.

THE ESSENCE OF THE ACE

Despite hundreds of studies and many books on the subject of the makeup of the ace, there is still no predictor, no test by which future aces can be selected from the mass of pilot applicants. In the following pages, we will study the careers of four American aces. They are Edward Vernon Rickenbacker, ace of aces of World War I; Hubert "Hub" Zemke, a great leader from World War II; the irrepressible Frederick C. "Boots" Blesse from Korea; and Robin Olds from World War II and Vietnam.

Their lives will depict the full anatomy of an ace, the essence of what makes up a warrior, and they will show how far removed they are from, and how superior they are to, the popular media concept of the fighter ace. Each one of them was a true leader, a man who made his unit more effective, and thus contributed far more to his cause than the destruction of five enemy aircraft. Each one did so in his own distinctive way.

★ T W O ★

THE RAW MATERIAL OF AN ACE

On September 25, the newly minted Captain Eddie Rickenbacker crammed himself into the tiny cockpit of his SPAD. As always, he had carefully checked the ammunition belts for his machine guns personally, even though he knew they had already been physically checked by the armament people.

At idle, the Hispano-Suiza had the sibilant purr of a high-powered automobile. As he moved the throttle forward, his experienced ear could tell by the sound that his engine was in perfect tune.

Rickenbacker flew toward the front lines, passing over the churned earth of Verdun. He sighted two L.V.G. two seaters, efficient German observation planes, protected by a flight of five Fokker D VIIs, the best fighter aircraft of the war.

Despite the formidable seven-to-one odds, Rickenbacker was determined to attack and stealthily maneuvered above and behind the Fokkers. He planned to make a diving attack, pick off one of the fighters, then use the speed in his dive to climb back to altitude. Rickenbacker believed air combat to be simply scientific murder—and he was skilled in the science.

The wind whistled, tugging at the SPAD's wires as it plunged in a headlong dive, controls stiffening under the pressure of the speeding air. Rick began firing as he closed on the nearest Fokker, killing its pilot. The remaining four fighters split up, diving away to the left and right. Rickenbacker immediately decided not to pull up, but instead carried on hell-for-leather dive to attack the two L.V.G.s.

The German observation planes were obviously manned by veterans, for they flew in parallel, about fifty yards apart, and soon had Rickenbacker sandwiched

in fire between the two backseat gunners. Rick maneuvered to one side and, calculating the flight path of the nearest L.V.G., fired ahead of it. He had the duck
hunter's satisfaction of seeing the German plane fly directly into his stream of
gunfire then burst into flame.

By then the four Fokkers had almost reached the scene of action; Rickenbacker
applied full power and dove for his lines, more excited about setting an example
for his squadron than winning the two victories.

On May 6, 1930, almost twelve years after the event, Rickenbacker was awarded
the Medal of Honor for his bravery in attacking a formation of seven aircraft
and shooting down two. The citation did not note the most important victory
Rickenbacker had scored in the process, over the blue bloods in his squadron
who had previously held him in contempt.

YOUNG EDD

Edd, as his family called Rickenbacker in his youth, was a bit of a layabout, not
holding a steady job until he was ten. Getting up at 2:00 A.M. every morning, he
would walk two miles to pick up his newspapers, then deliver the Columbus,
Ohio, *Dispatch* to houses on his route, each week adding another cool $1.00 in
hard cash to the family coffers. He had previously held many part-time jobs,
including planting vegetables in the family garden that fed them with plain, substantial food and selling goat milk at five cents a quart to his neighbors. Basic
economics ran the Rickenbacker household, and goats were cheaper to feed than
cows.

Edd was also a small-time thug. He ran with the Horse Head gang at a local
racetrack, and both his mother and his father worried that he might wind up in a
reformatory. He was not above stealing something that he wanted, and was very
quick to use his fists. He was a hard worker, but often worked at being a rotten kid.

Born on October 10, 1890, Edward was the third of eight children, one of
whom died in infancy. They lived in a small frame house on Livingston Avenue
to which their father, William Rickenbacher, had added a small loft. (Edward did
not change his name to Rickenbacker until World War I forced the issue. For
simplicity, it will be spelled in that manner throughout this book.) William had
apprenticed in the construction trade in his native Switzerland. Of German
descent, a fact that would later cause his son problems, the father had a strong
independent bent that he passed on to Edward. A skilled laborer, he provided

a barely adequate income for his family by doing small construction jobs. His wife, Elizabeth, took in laundry to help out. It was far from an easy life and they lived frugally.

Like many immigrants then and now, they found that neighbors were not always kind and rarely were politically correct. Young Rickenbacker wore ill-fitting hand-me-down clothes and spoke English with a German accent. At one particularly humiliating period of his life, his only pair of shoes was terribly mismatched. One shoe was tan, with a turned-up toe like a jester might wear; the other was an ordinary black shoe. The combination led to much jeering on the part of his schoolmates, but those who were unwise enough to taunt him with cries of "Kraut" or "Dutchy" usually did it only once, for that was enough for Rickenbacker's fists to fly. Later, as a young racing driver phenomenon, he'd wear better shoes and have more admiring nicknames thrust on him by the press, including "Baron" and "the Dutch Demon."

Discipline at home was of the period, strict and quick. By today's standards, the father abused the children with his whippings, a fact that the mature Edward Rickenbacker would both resent and conceal. Yet William was smart enough to turn his back on some of their activity, and his children enjoyed the usual youthful misdeeds of the time, including playing in forbidden quarries and smoking roll-your-own corn-silk cigarettes.

William had a strong work ethic, both in laboring jobs and around the house. He taught his children how to use tools, and Eddie was particularly adept, learning how to repair shoes at an early age. William also taught the importance of getting things done *now!* His strict discipline was balanced by the grace and goodwill of the mother, Elizabeth, also Swiss but of French ancestry. Edward received his often-overlooked artistic ability from her. She was a devout Protestant, who took her children to the daily services and inspired Edward's genuine faith in a personal God, a faith that would carry him through many more life-threatening situations than most men experience.

EARLY DAYS

The stark reality of an immigrant family's struggle for survival in America at the turn of the century took a grim turn when Edd was still very young. There was no employee compensation for injury in those days, and insurance was too expensive even to consider. Edd's father became engaged in a lunchtime argument with an itinerant, William Gaines. Gaines smashed William's head with blows from a metal spirit level. His skull fractured, William lapsed into a coma and lingered for several days before dying on August 26, 1904.

The incident devastated the family and transformed Edd from a troublemaker into a breadwinner. Not yet fourteen, Edward asserted himself as the head of the house, with his mother and his six siblings, including his older brother, to provide for.

Edd Rickenbacker, scrawny and always hungry, stopped attending school in the seventh grade to take a job at the Federal Glass factory in Columbus, working the night shift from 6:00 P.M. to 6:00 A.M. six days a week. The work was hard and hot, and Rickenbacker walked to and from the job to save the nickel carfare.

Young Rickenbacker would do well at work, in part because of his excellent hand-eye coordination that would stand him in good stead all his life, from driving race cars to shooting down Germans to grabbing a seagull from his head when adrift on a raft in the South Pacific. Further, he was doubly blessed with his father's skills with tools and his mother's artistic ability. He combined these attributes with a pragmatic youthful confidence that allowed him to quit one job as soon as he sensed a better one in the offing, and he rose up in the harsh world of Ohio business with remarkable speed.

He moved on, swinging Tarzan-like from one job to the next, usually at an increase in pay, but not always. He wanted interesting work, and as he would often do later in life, he would take a pay cut if it led to a more challenging job. Rickenbacker graced his strong work ethic with considerable chutzpah and could talk his way into jobs that were well beyond his reach in terms of his experience and education. Rick, as he now preferred to be called, obtained such a job at the nearby Evans Garage, where he bootlegged driving experience in customer's cars when the boss had gone home.

There's not much time left for school when you are working a six-day week, but he managed to invest sixty dollars in mail-order courses. Like so many men who would become well known in industry, including Walter Chrysler, these courses were with the justly famous International Correspondence School of Scranton, Pennsylvania. Rick took courses in mechanical engineering so that he could work in the automobile industry. He willingly accepted a low-paying janitorial job at the Oscar Lear Company, which made the Frayer-Miller automobile.

As unlikely as it seems, this became the literal road to riches. Within nine years, he had gone from pushing a broom to being a star racing driver, earning $60,000 a year, the rough equivalent of a million dollars today. There was luck involved, as well as skill and hard work, but Rickenbacker would always have more than his share of luck, both good and bad.

The correspondence courses had tipped the scales for him. His boss, Lee Frayer, was a capable man himself, and when he took a new position with the Columbus Buggy Company, he brought Rick with him. Frayer was hired to develop a new gasoline-powered car for Columbus, a large organization that had previously built only electric cars. He helped Rickenbacker develop his capabilities and moved him into successively more responsible positions.

Frayer had faith in his judgment, and brought him into racing as a "riding mechanic" for the big Vanderbilt Cup race. The riding mechanic is no longer used today, but was indispensable in the early days of automobile racing. The job was also extraordinarily dangerous, for the driver had at least the steering wheel to grip.

Just a growing boy of sixteen, Rick had three essential duties as riding mechanic: watch the fuel and oil pressures, check the rear tires for wear, and signal if another car was going to pass. The risks were enormous. Although relatively advanced for the time, with wire rather than wooden-spoke wheels, the Frayer-Miller racing car was little more than an engine and a chassis with two steel bucket seats mounted on it. There was no safety equipment—seatbelts, shoulder harnesses, helmets, and fireproof suits were all well in the future. The suspension was primitive, and the brakes, bad to begin with, rapidly grew worse in the course of the race. Steering required much more muscle than brain, for the virtually springless cars were used on rutted tracks that tried to tear the steering wheel from the driver's hands.

Driving or even just riding in the Vanderbilt race was sheer physical torture. On the first day, Rick was thrown head-over-heels out of his car when it missed a turn and hit a sand dune. Rick and his driver hastily repaired the car and sought to qualify it again the following day, only to smash into an unfortunate guinea fowl. On the third day's trials, the engine simply overheated and seized, possibly still suffering from an overdose of guinea hen.

Over the crackling of cooling metal and the smell of burned oil, Frayer turned to Rickenbacker and said only, "We're through." They were out of the race—and out the $50,000 he had spent preparing for it. Frayer's casual acceptance of a major disappointment impressed young Rickenbacker and taught him a lesson that would come in handy in war and peace. He resolved then and there to always try hard to win—but never to complain when he lost. He never did, not when he was refused pilot training, nor when his Rickenbacker Automobile Company went belly-up, nor even when he ultimately lost his pride and joy, Eastern Air Lines.

Eddie came away with a taste for speed that he would satisfy a few years later as a driver, not a riding mechanic. In the meantime, however, he continued his fast-paced ascent in the world of business. Frayer put the seventeen-year-old Rickenbacker in charge of the experimental engineering department, supervising the work of more than a dozen professionals. It is a tribute to them that they permitted a young uneducated kid to be their boss and to him for having the maturity and the ability to carry it off.

Part of his success came from his physical demeanor. He was growing fast, and his sharply angular face was severe—until he broke into a grin. The strong facial features added to a natural gravitas that gave him presence. In time, he consciously adopted a smiling persona that today would be called "charismatic."

Frayer's confidence in Rickenbacker was soon matched by that of the head of the company, Clinton Firestone, who immediately began using him as a troubleshooter, sent to solve dealer's problems with the new car. These problems were many and varied, and it took all of Rick's ingenuity to solve them and keep the dealers happy. His skill with tools, his correspondence course training, and an almost preternatural common sense enabled him to get balky cars back on the road. More important, his solutions were usually applicable to the cars yet to be built, preventing future problems. In this troubleshooting process, he began to establish a pattern of leadership that would later resolve some sticky personnel situations when he entered army aviation.

With a monthly salary of $150—far more than the average lawyer or doctor made at the time—Rickenbacker was in relative clover. He had paid off the mortgage on the family home, saw to it that his family was comfortably provided for, and managed to have a good time himself. But he missed the thrill of racing.

Automobile dealerships, struggling for existence, often depended on racing for recognition and sales. Nothing spurred a buyer's interest more than a triumph on the local dirt track. Rickenbacker, with his racing experience, factory backing, and large number of dealer friends, was able to enter racing in March 1910. He was nineteen years old and now stood a full six feet two inches tall and weighed 165 pounds. He began spending his summers racing and his winters selling cars.

There were uncanny parallels in the manner in which Rickenbacker prepared for his racing career and the way he later prepared for his career as a fighter pilot. In both cases, he learned all he could from a mentor. In racing it was Frayer; in piloting it would be Raoul Lufbery, star of the French Lafayette Escadrille and the leading American air ace at the time. In both cases, he paid meticulous attention to his equipment, personally inspecting it before use.

Although he practiced a Dale Carnegie approach to the men he worked with, Rickenbacker acquired a reputation for being a "mean" racing driver, one who took advantage of every mistake of competitors, and who never permitted anyone to take advantage of him. If he was in the lead on a dust-laden track, he was not above swerving slightly to raise a larger dust cloud to blind those behind him. Nor did he attempt to avoid slinging chunks of dirt rearward into the windshields of following cars. This was simply adaptive behavior, enabling him, usually the youngest man on the track, to survive against older, more experienced drivers. He had to push himself to the limits to extract the most from his usually under-powered cars.

Nevertheless, races were not won by dirty tricks but by discipline. It was far more demanding on his inner resources to follow a game plan in a race, going only so fast in the turns to avoid wear and tear, and then revving the car to its very lim-its in the straightaways. Innovation was also required, and Rickenbacker created a screen to protect the driver from the clots of mud flung up by other cars.

Rickenbacker quickly became a "hot property," attracting offers from major racing organizations around the world and becoming a national sports figure. His success did not go to his head. Aware of his lack of education, he continued his self-improvement practices, constantly trying to expand his vocabulary. He took advantage of the elevated circles in which he was traveling and noted carefully how leaders in business and politics comported themselves. It was a technique that would stand him in good stead in later years.

While Rickenbacker was proving himself as a racing driver, the air war in Europe was swiftly changing. The first U.S. taste of this aspect of the war would come with a glamorous volunteer squadron, the Lafayette Escadrille.

FLYING FOR FRANCE

In April 1916 a squadron of volunteers was formed as the result of long efforts by a group of seven idealistic Americans who were already serving in the French air service. Of these seven, five were from aristocratic and wealthy American families, while two were from ordinary circumstances. Fate—and the press—would con-spire to have the five set the tone for the American concept of combat flying on the Western Front, one that would have important implications for men of humble origin, such as Edward Rickenbacker.

The new unit was initially called the *Escadrille Americaine*—the American Squadron. Five months later, the incensed German ambassador in Washington would protest, and the name was changed first to *Escadrille de Volontaires* and then to the more poetic *Lafayette Escadrille*, on December 6, 1916.

The Lafayette Escadrille would never be a potent military force, but it was of incalculable morale and propaganda value for the Allied side. The press was eager to report on the handsome young American pilots, for as the squadron grew in size, it attracted candidates of the same caliber as its founders. Most had college degrees and many of them came from distinguished families. Those members of the Escadrille who had a lesser pedigree were quietly tolerated if they behaved and shunned if they did not. A few "commoners," such as Raoul Lufbery, did so well in combat that they had to be accepted. Eddie Rickenbacker would benefit from this, for he and Lufbery were kindred souls.

The Ivy League mind-set of the majority of the members of the Lafayette Escadrille led to a lifestyle that inspired many legends. They devised an inspiring Indian head insignia for their aircraft, adopted two young lion cubs, "Whiskey" and "Soda," as mascots, and most important of all, fought bravely when the chips were down.

The French government valued the Lafayette Escadrille's propaganda value more than its combat potential. It delayed the unit's entry into combat by various administrative devices, then for the most part kept it deployed in relatively quiet sectors. Yet there were casualties enough; over two years of service, eleven pilots were killed, eight in combat and three in accidents. The unit was credited with fifty-seven victories, and it had kindled sufficient enthusiasm for an expansion.

The original Lafayette Escadrille had thirty-eight members. The Americans who served with the French in other units became known collectively as the "Lafayette Flying Corps" and counted 267 members. Of these, forty-three washed out; five died of illness; six died in accidents; fifteen were taken prisoner; nineteen were wounded; and fifty-one were killed in action. A total of 180 served in combat roles with the French.

The Lafayette Escadrille would be both of immense value and a definite handicap to the American Air Service when at last it went into combat in 1918. The value would come from the combat training it had experienced and the leaders it would furnish. The handicap would come from its being schooled in French strategy and tactics, which did not keep pace with those of the British or the Germans.

The failure of the U.S. Army to learn anything about air warfare on the Western Front would have a calamitous effect in procurement. By failing to develop indigenous aircraft equal to the combat conditions on the Western Front, the

United States was forced to scavenge aircraft from its British, French, and Italian allies. These allies were grateful that the United States had entered the war, but, for the French and Italians at least, they were not happy to the extent that they let their gratitude interfere with business.

The French were particularly difficult to deal with. They would supply aircraft and engines only at nonnegotiable prices. The books of French manufacturers were not open to audit, not even by their own government. They were not disposed to make concessions to the rich Americans.

The aircraft that were released for sale to the United States were for the most part obsolete, like the lumbering Caudron or Dorand observation planes. Others, like the Nieuport 28 fighter, had been refused as unsuitable for combat by their own military services. In fairness, the Breguet and Salmson observation planes released for U.S. purchase by the French were good performers, as was the SPAD XIII when it finally became available.

The first all-American pursuit unit, the 95th Aero Squadron, entered combat on March 15, 1918, equipped initially with unarmed Nieuport 28 fighters. It was an unfortunate coincidence that, just over one month later, the Germans would introduce what is generally conceded to have been the best fighter of the war, the Fokker D VII, a plane that would provide Rickenbacker with some of his greatest challenges.

RICKENBACKER GOES TO WAR

By 1916 Rickenbacker was an international celebrity in racing circles and his fame would both get him into trouble and bail him out of it. He was approached by Louis Coatalen, a brilliant but eccentric engineering genius for England's Sunbeam Company. Coatalen's Sunbeam racing car had spurred sales, reviving the almost moribund automobile company. He wanted to recruit Rickenbacker as a driver for the Sunbeam team, which was still racing in America despite the war.

Rickenbacker went to England in December of 1916, where he was promptly accused of being a German spy and kept under close surveillance until his departure the following February. Rick took it with good humor, despite the inconvenience of having to report to the police on a weekly basis. Far from being pro-German, Rickenbacker returned to the United States with a mission: to create a special aviation unit composed of racing drivers. Rick felt that their experience with high speeds and complex machinery would make them good combat pilots.

Several prominent racing drivers responded to his call, but the U.S. Army was not interested. The racing drivers had three strikes against them. They lacked a college education, they were over twenty-five, the maximum age for applicants to the Air Service, and worst of all, they knew *too much* about engines and "might be hesitant about going into combat" if the engine was malfunctioning.

In the end, Rickenbacker, patriot that he was, agreed to join the Army and go to France as staff driver, trading $60,000 a year for a sergeant's pay. As soon as the word was out, the world's press immediately announced that Rickenbacker would be General John "Black Jack" Pershing's personal driver. He was not, and never would be, but he went to France with the conviction that he could switch jobs as he had done so often in the past. This time, instead of looking for more money, he wanted to trade a steering wheel for a joy stick.

★ THREE ★
CAPTAIN EDDIE TRIUMPHS

lying was a rich man's sport in 1915, and it was only natural that combat flying should be quickly claimed as a gentleman's prerogative by the old school
elite. We have seen how other patrician idealists had already responded to the
Allied call and enlisted in the French Foreign Legion (so that they did not have to
give up their American citizenship) before creating the Lafayette Escadrille. This
same spirit was demonstrated in the 1916 formation of the First Yale Unit, which
was termed "a millionaires club" by the newspapers. Created by two men whose
names would be extraordinarily influential in aviation, F. Trubee Davison and
Robert Lovett, the First Yale Unit would form the nucleus of American aviation
forces in Europe during World War I. Backed by the financial power of Rodman
Wanamaker, they purchased aircraft, established training bases, hired instructors,
and in general prepared themselves as best they could for war in the air. One of
those who rallied to the cause was Kennenth MacLeish, brother of the famous
poet, Archibald MacLeish. It happens that MacLeish personified the patrician
proprietary patriot with whom Rickenbacker would have serious problems.

Ken MacLeish was apparently a natural pilot and was eager to get into combat. He was also an excellent administrator, and held a number of responsible
jobs before finally wangling his way to the front with the Royal Air Force No. 213
Squadron. Flying a Sopwith Camel, he scored two victories—and was himself
killed—on October 14, 1918, his first day of combat.

The night before he left for the front, MacLeish had written his mother as
follows:

If I find it necessary to make the supreme sacrifice, always remember this—I am so firmly convinced of the ideals I am going to fight for are right and splendid that I am happy to be able to give so much for them. I could not have any self-respect, I could not consider myself a man, if I saw these ideals defeated when it lies in my power to defend them. So I have no fears; I have no regrets. I have only to thank God for such a wonderful opportunity to serve Him and the world. No, if I must make the supreme sacrifice I will do it gladly and will do it honorably and bravely, as your son should, and the life that I lay down will be my preparation for the grander, finer life that I shall take up. I shall live! You must not grieve. I shall be supremely happy—so must you—not that I have "gone West," but that I have bought such a wonderful life at so small a price and paid for it gladly.

This was the noble side of the generally aristocratic crew with whom Eddie Rickenbacker would go to war. Sadly, there was another side to elitism, also illustrated by MacLeish. The Navy had trained enlisted personnel for flight duties. MacLeish disliked them intensely, and was openly contemptuous of their lack of education and refinement. He railed against these "roughnecks" in many of his letters, and in one murderous mood wrote that if he had his way, he would line them all up in front of a machine gun, "kiss 'em goodbye, and let drive."

MacLeish and his collegiate colleagues were not immune to human nature. As much as they hated the idea that roughnecks like Rickenbacker aspired to fly, they found that they could be his friend when the car salesman from Ohio became an ace.

ON THE WAY TO WINGS

Rickenbacker had accepted his position of chauffeur to senior officers good-naturedly, confident that he would ultimately earn a flying job. Rick did well at his job, not only driving swiftly, but attending to the protocol of opening doors, hanging around outside while meetings—or parties—took place, and generally being a good chauffeur. But he wanted to fly in combat, and what he wanted, he usually got.

Given his celebrity and his skills, it was inevitable that he would be tapped to be the personal driver of Colonel William "Billy" Mitchell. Mitchell, who is today best remembered as a true pioneer of air power, the rascally rebel who sank the captured German battleship, was then a flamboyant young officer given to wild trips around France in his Packard Twin Six. Mitchell had talked and worked his way into the position of Chief of the American Air Service, Zone of Advance, in France, and he understood Rickenbacker's similar methods.

Mitchell was taken with Rick's rare ability to diagnose and repair engines. In one instance, circumstances forced Mitchell to accept a lowly Hudson as a staff car. It burned out a connecting-rod bearing far from any repair shop, leaving a furious Mitchell stranded. Unperturbed, Rick diagnosed the problem and did some on-the-spot repairs. He formed a makeshift mold with sand and water, melted Babbitt metal into the mold with a blow torch, and then filed the resulting lump down to serve as a replacement bearing. As the Hudson got under way again, Mitchell was clearly impressed, as most people would have been.

One afternoon in Paris Rickenbacker met a friend from his racing days, Captain James Ely Miller. Miller was a prominent banker who came from a wealthy family and had earned his *Federation Aeronautique Internationale* Flying Certificate No. 548 long before the war. Miller had been in charge of recruiting in New York City before going to Europe. There he was assigned the command of the brand-new American advanced flying school being established at Issoudon, and he asked Rick to become his engineering officer. The engineering officer is a critically important person in any aviation squadron, and never more so than in the process of forming up.

Rickenbacker immediately agreed, with the proviso that he be allowed to go to flying school. Miller made a formal request for his services, and bowing to the inevitable, Colonel Mitchell agreed. Rick had to lie about his age, claiming that he was only twenty-five rather than twenty-seven. He was worried about the flight physical. Years before, a hot cinder from a railroad train had landed in his eye and had to be removed by a physician. It had left him with a small blind spot and a "floater," a bit of matter within his eye that would intermittently flash by. Fortunately, he took the flight physical from a friend, who passed him without difficulty, and entered the French primary flying school at Tours.

LEARNING THE HARD WAY

The French had an unusual approach to flying training. In addition to giving dual instruction, as was the case, before and since, in all other countries, they employed a unique combination of ground instruction and self-help flying.

Rickenbacker's class began instruction on the penguin, a version of the Blériot. It was a tiny monoplane powered by a tiny three-cylinder Anzani engine and equipped with wings so short it could not fly. The idea was to learn how to guide the penguin back and forth across the field in straight lines, using the normal stick and rudder aircraft controls. It was not easy, for an airplane's rudder pedals were totally different in response than a racing car's steering wheel. It took some practice, but Rick mastered it.

The next aircraft in the instruction series was the *rouleur*. It had slightly more power and wings large enough to permit short, straight-ahead flights. This was followed by an aircraft with still more power and larger wings that was actually capable of flight, and in which short, low-altitude circles of the field could be made. In many instances, the student soloed without ever having had an instructor in the plane with him. It was tough on students, because accidents were rife, but it saved the lives of the militarily more valuable instructors.

Rick went on to complete twenty-five hours of flying in seventeen days, graduating as a pilot with a commission as a First Lieutenant in the Signal Corps. He was officially an officer and a gentleman. In the next few months, not everyone he encountered would agree with this. In many ways, it reminded him of the days when he did not have matching shoes to wear to school.

TROUBLE AT THE ISSOUDON CORRAL

To borrow a term from World War II, the scheme for training American combat pilots was completely SNAFUed. The response to the call for flyers had been tremendous, and the Army had not been able to provide adequate training bases in the United States. To ease the stateside crowding, a decision was made that after July 1, 1917, about 100 aviation cadets a month would be shipped overseas for training.

Unfortunately, the continuous demand by the British, French, and Italian air forces for replacement pilots meant that not enough training slots were available in Europe. As an interim solution, the French turned over a primary training school at Tours to the Americans on October 1, 1917, and gave permission for the construction of an advanced training base in a huge empty field about seven kilometers from the tiny town of Issoudon. Construction of the 3d Aviation Instruction Center began on August 18, 1917, but a lack of materials and equipment inhibited training for weeks.

The aviation cadets sent from America had expected to go immediately into flight training. Instead, they were put to work constructing roads, buildings, and hangars. Their already high resentment was inflamed when their erstwhile colleagues from the United States began arriving in France as commissioned officers.

By January 1, 1918, there were 1,060 cadets in Europe, all awaiting training, most of them mired in the sucking sea of mud that was Issoudon. All were furious with the system.

The mud at least was familiar to Rickenbacker, for it resembled the infamous "gumbo" of the racing tracks. Composed of a rough soil that retained water in a viscous compound, it resisted every attempt to dig drains. Well studded with rocks, the gumbo tended to capture and hold spades, shoes, boots, and feet within its grasp.

It was into this hotbed of mucky discontent that Rickenbacker was thrust. He later commented that he understood how these highly educated young men from good families resented that he, "a Swiss German engineer with a grammar school education," was in a position of authority over them. He contrasted their beautifully tailored uniforms and handmade boots with his own rough-and-ready appearance, and ruefully admitted that their sarcastic remarks, made both behind his back and to his face, caused him to burn with a desire to get even.

He did so by assigning them necessary, if unpleasant, tasks. Latrines had to be dug, barracks and mess halls built and hangars erected—all work the cadets considered far beneath their dignity (and some were jobs that German prisoners of war had refused to do). With French help, they even built a seven-mile-long railway spur from town to the camp.

Not unnaturally, Rick took some pleasure in finding special mission-oriented "treats" for his gentlemen rankers to do. The training airplanes were throwing up rocks from the rough field and breaking propellers (we'd call it FOD, or foreign object damage, today). Rickenbacker sent the Ivy League cadets out on the airfield with buckets to pick up the rocks. They particularly resented this, calling it "coolie work" because of the Annamite (Indochinese) laborers who collected the filled buckets from them. They were not bashful about letting Rick know their anger, much to his pleasure. But with the rocks picked up, fewer propellers were damaged. Rick also reprised one of his racing coups by fashioning a mudguard to attach to the trainers' undercarriages, preventing "gumbo" from being thrown into their propellers.

If the cadets had been more mature, they would have seen that however rough-hewn he was, Rickenbacker drove himself harder than he drove anyone else. He was a key man in taking Issoudon from vacant fields to a huge enterprise with many flying fields in just a few months. More important, his desire to fly in combat was every bit as deeply rooted as theirs, and was no less worthy if it stemmed from his stern upbringing and his profound gratitude for his success rather than from a patrician background. The cadets had much time off, including evenings in town and football on Sundays. In sharp contrast, Rick did his full-time job and boot-legged both ground school and advanced flying training at Issoudon between his regular tasks.

His boss was now Major Carl "Tooey" Spatz, a tough, no-nonsense leader, who focused on getting the job done. (Spatz changed his name to Spaatz in 1938. In World War II, he would be the United States Army Air Forces' main combat commander. Later he was the last commanding general of the USAAF and the first Chief of Staff of the United States Air Force.)

Spatz initially turned Rickenbacker's requests for a flying job down with the usual withering "you'll do what I tell you to do" rigor of a regular Army officer. But Rick persisted, getting Spatz's attention by mixing minor disciplinary infrac-tions with exceptionally fine work. He knew and admired the way Rickenbacker was doing his flying on the side, but one weekend the ex–race car driver turned pilot went too far.

The cadets liked to relive their Ivy League days by holding football games every Sunday. They were talented, many of them having played varsity, and the games attracted high-ranking personnel from as far away as Paris. Rickenbacker had just taught himself how to recover from a tailspin, then as now one of the most frightening maneuvers in flying. On a Sunday afternoon, he expressed his contempt for Army regulations and his football-playing subordinates by cross-ing the field at 500 feet and putting his plane into a tailspin. (Most pilots today would not enter a spin below 5,000 feet, devoutly intending to recover by 3,000 feet at a minimum.) Rick pulled out of the spin just above the ground, frighten-ing himself and sending the crowd diving for cover.

Spatz immediately grounded him for thirty days—but Rickenbacker had made his point. He was flying while the college kids were playing. Spatz knew that he was serious about going to war, and finally gave in, allowing him to go to the gun-nery school at Cazeaux to polish off his training.

He did well at Cazeaux, given that he had only shot a gun twice before in his life. At the end of the course, he was assigned to the 94th Pursuit Squadron—and to his rendezvous with history.

THE AIR SERVICE GOES TO WAR

It was fortunate that the men of the American Air Service went to war with a youthful, almost joyous, naivete. Had they assessed the situation accurately, they could not have been blamed if they had declined to go at all.

The war they were entering was far different from that fought in the early days by Immelmann and Boelcke. Since 1915, aircraft had improved tremendously, training standards had gone up, effective tactics had been devised, and the air forces on both sides had become professional combat arms.

The Germans had become particularly adept in the use of their air arm. Always inferior in numbers, the Germans also lacked the resources to match the wide variety of powerful engines that the Allies had developed. They compensated for their deficiencies by developing specialized aircraft optimized to obtain the best performance from the engines available to them.

In terms of strategy, the Germans had always employed their aircraft defensively, fighting behind the front wherever possible. In *Freiherr* Manfred von Richthofen's words, they "preferred to let the customer come to the shop." ("*Freiherr*" was a rank just a step below that of baron, but "Red Freiherr" just doesn't have the ring of "Red Baron.") This tactic also allowed the prevailing west wind to help them and hinder the Allies, by blowing always into German territory.

An excellent early warning system was developed. When an Allied aircraft crossed the front lines, its progress was monitored visually and relayed to reporting centers that had direct telephone access to the German flying fields. Their strategy allowed the Germans to use their limited numbers to defend the most important sectors of the front. A system of quick deployment had been developed by which they could mass their aircraft at particular points if they wished to gain temporary air superiority. The Germans also tended to use larger formations than the Allies, the show of strength often intimidating opposing patrols and accomplishing the mission without a fight. The combination of using trains for deploying forces and employing larger squadrons of colorfully marked aircraft led to the popular term "the flying circus" to characterize the German air arm.

The advantages conferred by the German strategy were somewhat offset by several factors. The first of these was the practice of grouping the best pilots in elite units. These units always did well, but "lesser" units, lacking the leadership and the example of an ace, tended to be less aggressive and were far less successful. The loss of a great ace, as with the death of Richthofen on April 21, 1918, had a much more adverse effect on their morale than did a corresponding loss by the British or the Americans. The second was the general decline in the quality of materials available to the Germans as a result of the Allied blockade. By the summer of 1918, parts and materials salvaged from downed Allied aircraft were often used. In some instances, the Germans were reduced to rolling their fighters around on wooden wheels, saving the rubber-tired wheels for actual flights.

Despite the defensive strategy, there were inevitably casualties from combat and accidents, and even the generally good German flying schools could not fill the gaps and keep the squadrons up to strength.

On the whole, however, the Germans were able to use their air forces effectively. Their system of training, while different from that of the Allies, worked well, and they had learned how to improvise. German logistics were as good as could be expected, given the pervasive shortages of material caused by the Allied blockade.

In short, Rickenbacker and his colleagues were about to be plunged into combat against a seasoned opponent, just being equipped with technically superior weapons. By chance, the Americans would go to war synthesizing the worst of their British and French allies' techniques.

THE U.S. APPROACH TO ALLIED TECHNIQUES

The British strategy was the polar opposite of the Germans'. General Sir Hugh Trenchard, who headed the Royal Flying Corps, demanded continuous offensive operations without regard to the quality or quantity of aircraft or the state of the pilots' training. The result was tremendously heavy losses without accomplishing much more than establishing a moral ascendancy over the Germans. The British also used single-seat fighters for close support work, and suffered grievous casualties in the process. The routine British patrol formations, while not as large as the Germans' formations, did grow in size over time.

The French occupied a middle ground, neither so offensive minded as the British nor as defensive as the Germans. They continued to operate relatively small flights of aircraft, and many of their aces pursued the "lone wolf" tactics that the Germans had long abandoned. Like the Germans, they tended to group their best pilots in elite units, and this tended to cause the quality of individual squadrons to vary greatly.

In sharp contrast to the professional approach to the air war achieved by both their allies and their enemy after four years of war, the United States Army Air Service was sent to France without aircraft, pilots, or mechanics, armed only with the highest expectations from the home front. There was no training establishment, no logistics base, no procurement policy, and no research and development. There was instead a limitless supply of earnest goodwill and an enormous amount of money.

The Americans in the Lafayette Flying Corps formed the basis for the first officially constituted U.S. fighter unit to enter service on the Western Front. Commanded by Major William Thaw, a founding member of the Lafayette Escadrille, the 103d Pursuit Squadron was officially formed on February 18, 1918. It remained under the command of the French IVth Army.

Because the 103d's training and operations had all been conducted under French auspices, the new squadrons of the nascent 1st Pursuit Group came to be considered as the first "all-American" flying units in France. The group initially would be made up of four squadrons, given here in the order in which they became operational in 1918: the 95th (March 9), the 94th (March 19), the 27th (June 2), and the 147th (June 2). These squadrons would produce the most victories as well as the most famous names in the American Air Service, including Quentin Roosevelt, Douglas Campbell, Reed Chambers, Frank Luke, Harold Hartney, and, far from least, Edward Rickenbacker.

When the American units at last were equipped to enter combat, they pursued a combination of the British spirit of offense and the French sense of individualism. American patrols were typically made up of relatively small flights of aircraft, and voluntary solo patrols were not only not frowned on, but were admired and encouraged.

RICKENBACKER JOINS THE 94TH

Rick had played his cards well. He gained what he had sought by doing two first-rate jobs, one as engineering officer and the other as schmoozer of the brass. He saw to it that he was in the first class at Tours; he carefully built his flying time at Issoudon, and then made sure that he was selected for gunnery training at Cazeaux. As a result, he was among the first to be assigned to the 94th Pursuit Squadron, soon to be noted for its "Hat in the Ring" insignia.

The 94th and 95th Pursuit Squadrons shared the same heritage. They had been formed in the sweltering heat of Texas on August 20, 1917, crossed the Atlantic on the S.S. *Adriatic*, and slogged through the mud to help build Issoudon.

The 95th was the first to arrive at Villeneuve-les-Vertus, twenty miles behind the front lines. The squadron arrived by train and without airplanes, and found that the new location had much in common with Issoudon, most especially the mud. The 95th was commanded by Captain James E. Miller, who had accepted the job after it had been refused by Major Raoul Lufbery on the grounds that the 95th was merely a cadre unit. Lufbery would later be assigned to the 94th.

Nieuport 28 fighters began to dribble into Villeneuve, but they were in a sorry state. Of the fifteen that had left the depot in Paris, only six made it to

Villeneuve-les-Vertus, the others making forced landings for a variety of mechanical problems. Worse, when they did arrive, they had no weapons. Some sorties were flown over the lines without guns, a brave but pointless exercise. Miller was a man of action, eager to lead his squadron by example. On March 9, 1918, the very day his squadron became operational, Miller flew his unarmed Nieuport to Coincy, where he borrowed a SPAD and flew a volunteer patrol with two American friends from a French unit, Majors Davenport Johnson and Millard F. Harmon. Miller was shot down and killed in his first combat, the first American Air Service casualty of the war. It was a sudden, sharp lesson that the war was not an Ivy League sporting event, but a deadly serious business in which mistakes cost lives.

It was also a portent of things to come, as the war was heating up. On March 21, 1918, the Germans began a huge offensive designed to win the war before the American army arrived in strength. Before it was halted, the Germans would claw their way between the British and French armies and once again reach the Marne.

THE NIEUPORT 28

The Nieuport 28 was by far the most elegant and best performing of the Nieuport series of fighters. Its 160-horsepower Gnome 9-N Monosoupape (single valve) engine was neatly cowled, not so much for aerodynamic reasons as to contain the massive amounts of waste gasoline and castor oil lubricant thrown by the engine.

The Gnome was a nine-cylinder rotary engine. In a conventional engine, whether it is a radial or an in-line, the cylinders are stationary, and the propeller is connected to the crankshaft. In the rotary engine, the cylinders rotate around the crankshaft, and the propeller is connected to the cylinders. The benefit of such an arrangement is its light weight and excellent cooling. The drawback is the gyroscopic force involved in the combined mass of the rotating engine and propeller that had drastic and sometimes unexpected effect on the maneuverability of an aircraft so powered. The gyroscopic effect put an upper limit on the permissible size of rotary engines, restricting them to a maximum of about 230 horsepower.

Starting and operating the Gnome was a delicate process that some compared to the old parlor trick of rubbing one's head and patting one's stomach at the same time. The most difficult aspect was the pilot's operation of the "filter brake" to fine-tune the amount of gasoline flowing to the rapidly revolving mass of cylinders. Too much gas, and it flooded and quit; too little, and it starved and quit. Neither was a good option just after takeoff.

Nonetheless, the combination of the streamlined, lightweight airframe and the powerful Gnome engine imparted a remarkable performance to the Nieuport 28. It was nimble and very fast for the time, with a top speed of 122 mph.

The United States should have been concerned about the airplane simply because it had not been accepted for service by the French, who had instead opted for the SPAD XIII. The Americans chose to ignore the fact that they were receiving a rejected design for which they paid a hefty $18,500 each. They were in no position to argue and had reached the point that they would have accepted virtually any airplane if it permitted them to go into action.

The genuine virtues of the Nieuport—speed, maneuverability, and availability—concealed terrible flaws in its power plant and in its structure. It would be seen that Rickenbacker, more than any of his colleagues, was able to triumph over these obstacles and use the Nieuport effectively despite its handicaps.

Unfortunately, the Gnome engine had two flaming defects. The first of these was the rigidity of the connections of the lines between the fuel tanks and the engine. The tremendous vibration from the engine and from firing the machine guns rapidly caused these lines to crack and spew gasoline, causing many fires.

The second problem had to do with the operation of the engine itself. The Gnome rotary engine did not have a conventional throttle. It instead had a "blip switch," which allowed the engine to operate at less than full speed by suppressing the ignition to all or some of the cylinders. Using the blip switch to slow an aircraft down to land generated a characteristic rising and falling "buzzing" sound.

The almost absurd technical flaw in this approach was that gasoline was introduced into the cylinders at the full-speed rate, regardless of the position of the ignition switch. The result was raw gas being exhausted from the nonfiring cylinders into the cowling. If things went well, the gasoline was blown away harmlessly in the slipstream. Unfortunately, it often ignited instead, resulting in a fire. An in-flight fire was almost always fatal, given that the gasoline tanks were only a few feet in front of the pilot and the doped linen (and often fuel-soaked) fabric covering was highly flammable.

Despite these and other risks, Allied pilots were not given parachutes, although by 1918, many German pilots had them. Allied rear echelon personnel had decided that having parachutes might cause pilots to leave their aircraft "prematurely."

There were many inherent structural flaws in the Nieuport 28. These were less obvious than those of the power plant, but no less dangerous. The landing gear was weak, the fuel tanks were placed in dangerous proximity to the pilot, there were oil leaks, and the cowling was so lightly made that it tended to disintegrate. However, one structural flaw was more dangerous than all the others. In a dive, airspeed would build and the leading edge of the Nieuport's upper wing would sometimes tear off suddenly, allowing the fabric to balloon and leaving the wing devoid of lift. Depending on where and how this happened, the pilot had only a slim hope of nursing the crippled aircraft down safely.

The structural flaws caused Nieuport 28 pilots to fly more conservatively, making it more difficult to engage or disengage with the enemy as they might have in an airplane less given to structural failure. The delicate Nieuport 28s also tended to warp and lose their aerodynamic efficiency as they absorbed moisture.

Thus it happened that Rickenbacker and his colleagues would be going to war in an airplane in which they had never trained, one that tended to catch fire on short notice, and one that could lose its upper wing if maneuvered too strenuously. They could hardly wait to do so.

LUFBERY, THE MENTOR

It was almost inevitable that Rick would find a mentor in Major Gervais Raoul Lufbery, a man clearly after his own heart.

Luf, as everyone called him, had been the eighth man to volunteer for the Escadrille Americaine. Born in France on March 21, 1885, he was at heart a wanderer; at the age of nineteen he had drifted through Europe, North Africa, Turkey, and the Balkans before coming to the United States in 1906. Two years later, he was on the road again, visiting Cuba, New Orleans, and San Francisco before joining the U.S. Army. He served in the Philippines, then a hotbed of insurrection, and in doing so, secured his U.S. citizenship. He learned to shoot in the army, becoming a noted marksman.

Darkly handsome, Lufbery got into flying by his usual circuitous route. He had traveled to Japan, China, and India before meeting Marc Pourpe, who was at that time France's best-known exhibition pilot, his fame equal to that of Lincoln Beachey in the United States.

Lufbery became Pourpe's devoted mechanic, following him on tours through China and Egypt before returning to France, where in 1914 Pourpe enlisted in the French Air Service. Lufbery preserved his American citizenship by enlisting in the French Foreign Legion, and then pressed for a transfer to the air service so that he could continue serving as Pourpe's mechanic.

On December 2, 1914, Pourpe was killed landing at night, in fog. It was an accident, but Lufbery inexplicably took it as a personal affront by the Germans and swore vengeance. He entered flying training, where, somewhat surprisingly given his later success, he encountered some difficulties in mastering the airplane. He eventually succeeded, and ultimately was assigned to the Escadrille Americaine on May 24, 1916, where his aggressive ability as a pilot, his experience as a mechanic, and his language ability would serve him well.

Lufbery became the first American ace on October 12, 1916, with his fifth victory. He eventually scored seventeen official victories with the Lafayette Escadrille, rising to the rank of Second Lieutenant. This was a rare distinction, for most members of the Lafayette Flying Corps were promoted only to sergeant. Lufbery, introspective and moody, was noted for the meticulous care with which he maintained his aircraft and his machine guns. Many believe that his actual victory total might have been as high as seventy, for he frequently did not bother to report the results of his combat. He flew often and alone, deep behind enemy lines, always seeking revenge for Pourpe, and is said to have scored six victories on a single mission—without reporting them.

Lufbery was commissioned a major in the U.S. Air Service on January 10, 1918, and after a month of hated desk work, managed to get himself assigned to Villeneuve, where he would serve as an instructor to pilots of the 94th and 95th Pursuit Squadrons.

Rickenbacker and Lufbery hit it off from the start. Both were serious men, older than their colleagues, and completely devoted to their mission. More important, both were mechanics at heart for whom grease under the nails was a badge of honor, not a mark of shame. Rickenbacker sought out Lufbery and questioned him closely on every aspect of aerial combat. Lufbery responded in detail, giving Rick a crash course in survival. Lufbery, true to his experience with French units, extolled the solo patrol. His preferred method was to fly high, position himself in the sun so that the enemy could not see him coming, then make a single slashing attack that shot the enemy down. Most of his victims never knew what had happened to them; they were alive and flying one moment; in the next, he had killed them.

Their conversations ranged from the maintenance of the aircraft and their guns to the best methods of finding the enemy to whether or not to stay with a burning aircraft. Lufbery advocated riding a burning plane down, regardless of the pain. In a crash landing you had at least a chance of survival, but if you jumped, you had no chance at all. Lufbery also warned Rickenbacker that leading a flight of aircraft was difficult. A flight leader had to be concerned with his wingmen in regard to both their ability and their safety. The flight leader had to be sure not to take them into situations that might cost them their lives—but playing it safe cost many opportunities to score.

Rick and Luf engaged in very little small talk; both were focused on scoring victories, although each had different motives. Lufbery flew for revenge, while Rickenbacker flew to be the best. Rick would later write, "everything I learned, I learned from Lufbery." Two loners, they flew in spiritual formation when it came to aerial combat.

VISION IN THE AIR

The 94th Pursuit Squadron's first official combat patrol took place on March 28, 1918, and was led by Major Lufbery. Lieutenants Rickenbacker and Douglas Campbell flew on his wing. On paper it was a routine patrol; takeoff at 8:15 A.M., climb to 15,000 feet altitude, cross the lines near Suippe, circle north of Rheims, and return. Rick found it to be anything but routine.

Lufbery did not wish to fall prey to his own tactics. To avoid being a victim, he flew a corkscrew flight path, constantly swiveling his head to check every bit of sky for the enemy. The white silk scarf, usually seen as the romantic emblem of the fighter pilot, was an operational necessity to prevent chafing the neck from the constant head turning.

Corkscrew flight was sound practice, except that, to his utter dismay, it made Rickenbacker airsick. Nauseated to the point of vomiting, he was suddenly jerked out of his illness by the rattle of shrapnel as a German antiaircraft battery bracketed his aircraft with exploding shells. It was his first time under fire, and he was terrified by the Germans and resentful of his comrades who had told him that "Archie," as antiaircraft was called, was a joke to be enjoyed. After they emerged from the antiaircraft fire nothing much else happened and the flight back home was uneventful—until after the landing.

Lufbery let the excited Campbell and Rickenbacker do the initial talking. They were both amazed at how quiet the front had been except for the short interval of heavy antiaircraft fire, all of which had missed them. There had not been another airplane in the sky—or so they thought. Luf let them rattle on, then confided that they had crossed over one flight of SPADs on the way to the front, come within five hundred yards of another formation of SPADs about fifteen minutes later, then had almost encountered four enemy Albatros fighters and a German two-seater.

Lufbery then walked over to Rick's SPAD and poked his fingers through three separate areas where shrapnel had riddled it, including one hole less than a foot from the cockpit. Rickenbacker was dumbfounded; there was clearly a lot to learn, especially about "seeing in the air."

He was very concerned about problems with his vision caused by the incident with the hot cinder years before. On the one hand, the floater could look distressingly like an enemy plane; on the other, a real Fokker might be obscured by his blind spot. A friendly doctor had allowed him to pass the flight physical, but he could not count on finding any friendly Germans to make a similar allowance for poor vision. In the end, he simply practiced seeing as Lufbery suggested—looking at every square inch of the sky in a systematic way, and searching in depth for the slightest dot that might turn into an airplane. In time he acquired the skill, just as in time he overcame being made airsick by the corkscrew maneuver.

ON BECOMING AN ACE

The first essential step in becoming an ace is surviving, and many studies have shown that pilots who live through their first five missions increase their chance of survival by a factor of twenty. In the course of those five missions, they have had a chance to make a few mistakes, but most important, they have a chance to learn to see. Not everyone succeeds, and those who fail often pay the price.

Yet as the missions mount, combat fatigue begins to set in. The life expectancy of fighter pilots in the First World War varied, but in the most heated periods of combat it was sometimes as short as three weeks. Those lucky souls who survived could expect to fly and fight for about six months before beginning to suffer extreme combat fatigue. When they began to tire, certain symptoms were common. Typically, they became irritable and far more reckless. Unable to rest or even to enjoy leave, they compulsively sought to fly more and more. They made stupid mistakes in flight, and particularly on landing. It took a good doctor—and a lull in the battle—to remove them from combat.

Rickenbacker would have the good fortune to survive a number of battles before he ever scored a victory. Then, later in his combat career, he would suffer an ear infection that, ironically, probably not only saved his life but permitted him to become the ace of aces. The illness allowed him to avoid combat fatigue and finish his tour with a long succession of victories.

THE 94TH SCORES ITS FIRST KILLS

Although recognizing that he was clearly regarded as an outsider by many of the young men assigned to the 94th, Rickenbacker made plans for himself and for the squadron. He wanted to make the first kill, become the first ace, and have the highest victory score. However, he also wanted to lead the squadron to the same level of excellence so that it would have more victories than any other American unit at the front. Given the social dynamics of the situation, the probability of his gaining the most victories exceeded the probability of his leading the squadron.

Much to his dismay, Rick was flying an uneventful patrol on April 14, 1918, when the 94th's first victories were scored by Lieutenants Douglas Campbell and Alan Winslow.

Campbell and Winslow were on the 6:00 to 10:00 A.M. alert shift at the 94th's new airfield at Gengoult, about two miles east of Toul. The weather was misty, with a ceiling of clouds at about 1,500 feet. At 8:50 they took off to attack two German aircraft reported to be about fifteen miles away and heading in the direction of the airfield.

Each pilot probably had less than 100 hours total flying time when he took off. They had no instruments for flight in weather, no radios, no radar to guide them to the enemy, and no instrument landing system to bring them back if they became lost. It was a game of aerial blindman's bluff, where a collision in the clouds or a moment's spatial disorientation could be equally fatal.

By pure chance, they encountered the two wandering, equally ill-equipped German planes of the *Royal Wuerttemburg Jagdstaffel 64* over the airfield. Winslow attacked an Albatros D V just as a Pfalz D III began firing at Campbell. After a brief flurry of dangerous low-level maneuvering, both German aircraft were shot down. The Pfalz fell within 100 yards of the 94th's home field, and the Albatros crashed a half mile away. One of the German pilots was seriously burned, but both lived. They had been lost and had ducked below the clouds to pick up a landmark. Instead, they picked up Winslow's and Campbell's bullets. The stunning dual triumph had taken only four and one-half minutes from takeoff to landing. It was a tremendous tonic to the 94th's morale, and was duly celebrated in dispatches and with decorations.

RICKENBACKER BREAKS THE ICE

Late in the afternoon of April 29, Rickenbacker took off with Captain James Norman Hall, the thirty-fourth member of the Lafayette Escadrille. Hall would later team with another pilot, Charles Bernard Nordhoff, to write the history of the Lafayette Flying Corps, as well as a monumental series of novels that included *Mutiny on the Bounty.*

The mission proceeded in what had become a routine manner for Rickenbacker—he once again left formation to pursue what turned out to be an Allied aircraft. Hall patiently waited for him to rejoin, alerted him to a German fighter below them, and circled to place the sun behind them.

The enemy was flying a Pfalz D III, a beautifully sleek and streamlined aircraft that was stronger but less maneuverable than the more numerous Albatros. Slower than the Nieuport and outnumbered two to one, the Pfalz pilot tried to escape.

Hall fired first, and when the Pfalz turned to dive away, Rickenbacker attacked. The two Americans followed the Pfalz down. Rickenbacker closed to within 150 yards and fired; the airplane went down. The possibility of killing the pilot did not bother him, then or later; it was war, and his job was to down enemy aircraft. Killing pilots just happened to be part of the job.

French observers saw the crash and telephoned the 94th even before Rickenbacker and Hall had landed. The two men initially were each given credit for a victory.

At the time, Rickenbacker had no doubt that the Pfalz had fallen to his guns alone and apparently Hall felt the same way. Far more important to Rickenbacker than his victory was the abrupt change in attitude that he experienced in his squadron. In his words, "There is a peculiar gratification in receiving congratulations from one's squadron for a victory in the air. It is worth more to a pilot than the applause of the whole outside world." It was especially important to Rickenbacker, who now no longer could be considered an outsider and apparently was forgiven for not being born a gentleman.

As he was given increasing responsibility, his poor grammar and his rough manner would still cause some comment, but for the most part he was now accepted—his shoes now matched. It meant much to him, and it helped him in his drive to excel and to become an ace.

His scoring partner, Jim Hall, was one of the most well-liked men in the 94th. Rick and Lieutenant M. Edwin Green flew with him on May 7. They encountered German fighters, and Rick shot down what he took to be a Pfalz but actually later proved to be an Albatros.

During the fight, Hall's Nieuport experienced double trouble. First, its upper wing failed, then, as Hall attempted to nurse it back to Allied territory, an anti-aircraft shell smashed into the engine. The shell was a dud, or Hall would have been killed instantly. As it was, he managed to crash-land behind enemy lines and was captured and entertained by his captors, who confirmed Rick's victory before sending him off to prison camp. Many years later, Hall's testimony would result in the kill being awarded to Rickenbacker.

The generally low level of American experience was spotlighted by Rick being named to replace Hall as a Flight Commander. At the time, Rickenbacker had been at the front for less than two months and had engaged the enemy only a few times. His total flying time was less than 150 hours. Yet he was now tasked to lead men into combat, the very thing that Lufbery had warned him against.

Rickenbacker devoutly wished to be an ace, but he also wished to live, and he began to apply the wisdom he had learned in racing cars to the problems of air combat. He knew that experience was the key, and he flew as often as he could, learning all there was to learn about his aircraft. Some things he learned the hard way. On May 17, he and Reed Chambers had gone far over the enemy lines on a voluntary patrol, flying at 20,000 feet. It was bitterly cold, and the Nieuports were not equipped with oxygen.

About twenty miles behind the lines, he and Chambers became separated. Rick continued patrolling and spotted three Albatros fighters far below. He turned behind them to stalk them as they flew toward the front. His judgment possibly impaired from the lack of oxygen, he put his Nieuport in a headlong dive that brought him within firing range of the rear enemy fighter over Montsec. At about 14,000 feet, he fired, killing the pilot, and sending the plane in a long glide to the west. Anxious to maintain his advantage over the other two Germans, Rick pulled up too sharply. With a tremendous boom his upper right wing failed, throwing him into a swiftly turning tailspin. The enemy planes followed him down, firing alternately at his helpless aircraft.

Nothing he did could stop the spin until, just 4,000 feet off the ground, he at last applied full power to the Gnome engine. It caught with a roaring blast of flame and pulled the nose of his Nieuport up. Rickenbacker pushed the rudder pedal hard and found that he could maintain flight in a straight descending line. The Nieuport 28's ailerons were on the lower wings, giving him just sufficient control so that he could keep the battered aircraft airborne all the way back to his home field. He had been lucky, but he had also demonstrated the same cool, calculating bravery that had made him a racing star. Just as he had used engine power and brakes to take turns on the track at the fastest possible rate, so did he use the full 160 horses of the Gnome to offset the asymmetric loss of lift. He grazed the 94th's hangars as he landed hot, his engine full on. His wheels touched down at high speed, and of course, without any brakes, but he managed to stop safely.

His second victory was confirmed by the French. The German pilot was apparently killed instantly in Rick's attack, but had fallen on his controls in such a way that the Albatros glided a long distance and crashed behind French lines. Rick was now three victories away from his next goal: becoming the first American ace.

THE DEATH OF LUFBERY

Besides being Rick's mentor, Lufbery was also a symbol of invincibility to the young American pilots of the 1st Pursuit Group. On May 19, 1918, word was received that a German Rumpler observation plane was heading toward the 94th's field. It happened that the one pilot on alert, First Lieutenant Oscar J. Gude, was notorious for his extreme caution. Gude had somewhat ingenuously admitted he enjoyed flying but did not care for combat, and now proceeded to demonstrate his sentiments.

Gude was dispatched to shoot the Rumpler down. Instead, he made a series of ineffectual, long-range attacks that left the enemy aircraft unharmed. (His persistent cowardice led to Gude's being kicked out of the 94th. He ultimately deserted to Switzerland.)

Lufbery watched Gude's fainthearted fiasco from the ground, then leaped on a motorcycle and raced to the 94th's line of hangars. His own aircraft was down for maintenance, but he climbed in another and took off to attack the Rumpler.

He caught up with the enemy plane, but apparently had difficulty with his machine guns, as he made several attacks, breaking away each time. On his final attack, the Rumpler's observer put a bullet in Lufbery's fuel tank, setting the Nieuport on fire.

Two stories evolved. In the first, Lufbery was driven out of the cockpit by the flames and jumped, apparently aiming for a small stream that ran around the small village of Maron. He missed the stream, impaling himself on a picket fence. In the second, Lufbery is supposed not to have deliberately leaped. It was presumed that in his haste he had not fastened his seat belt, and simply fell out. Lufbery was given a funeral worthy of a reigning monarch, and Rickenbacker led his flight across the grave site, dropping flowers.

In the end, it didn't matter which story of Lufbery's death was true. The 94th had lost its hero, and Rick had lost his mentor, just as he began to be engaged in a race with Campbell to become the first "all-American" Air Service ace.

THE MAY RACE TO BE AN ACE

The desire to become the first ace in the American Air Service was implicit, but neither Rickenbacker nor Campbell admitted to it. Both flew all routine patrols and many solo missions, hunting for the enemy. Rick's efforts were inhibited by his new role as flight leader. He took his responsibilities seriously, giving newcomers much ground instruction and always accompanying them on their first flights over the lines. This sounds as if it should have been routine, but it was not in the First World War, particularly in the fledgling American Air Service.

After his first victory on April 14, Campbell received confirmation for victories on May 18, 19, 27, and 31, the last one bringing him acclaim as the first all-American Air Service ace. He would score one more victory before being wounded and sent home.

Rickenbacker's April 29 kill shared with Hall had been followed by a series of confirmed victories, the first of these on May 17 when the wing failed on his Nieuport. On the 22d, he was flying with his friend Reed Chambers and a new man, Lieutenant Paul B. Kurtz, on a patrol near St. Mihiel. They attacked three Albatros fighters. Rick was immediately engaged in a protracted dogfight with a first-rate German pilot. He shot the Albatros down about six miles behind German lines and was strongly tempted to follow it down, to make its confirmation more certain. Instead, he complied with his own rules of combat, and climbed back to altitude—and safety. Sadly, Kurtz crashed to his death on his return to the field when his Nieuport caught fire in the air.

On the 28th Rick and Campbell flew a patrol together, during which they sighted two Albatros two-seat reconnaissance planes protected by a flight of four Pfalz D IIIs. Veterans now, the two Americans maneuvered with the Germans until they were at last in a position to shoot down one of the Albatros two-seaters. Both men fired, but Rickenbacker received the sole credit for the victory, his fourth.

Rickenbacker had now mastered his trade. He "saw the sky" as clearly as any man and was able to identify enemy aircraft at great distances. Conservative tactics were his watchword, and he never entered an engagement unless he felt the odds were in his favor, nor did he hesitate to leave the scene if the odds tilted against him. He countered the enemy's technology by making use of the good features of the Nieuport while avoiding the bad. Rick had even overcome his most difficult challenge, coming to grips with his interpersonal problems with his colleagues, with whom he was increasingly popular.

On May 30, Rick made a solitary patrol of his own. After engaging in a long-running dogfight with several groups of aircraft, he shot down an Albatros two-seater near Jaulnay. Confirmation of this last victory, which made him officially an ace, was delayed by circumstance until after Campbell's fifth victory had been confirmed.

Rick had trained himself to be self-effacing as a racer, knowing that he would get more than his share of publicity. He had followed the same practice as his star began to rise as a fighter pilot. But in June, in Paris, he demonstrated just a touch of flamboyance by having a brand-new, strictly nonregulation uniform designed for himself. Patterned after the flamboyant uniforms of Billy Mitchell, Rickenbacker created a new look for himself with a tailored tunic that featured huge patch pockets, a cap modeled on Royal Air Force practice, whipcord riding breeches, and beautifully polished high boots. He topped it off with a Malacca cane. It was an indulgence totally unlike him—but it perhaps compensated in part for the bitter poverty he experienced as a boy.

RICKENBACKER'S ABSENCE AND THE FATE OF THE 94TH

The summer of 1918 was one of utter misery to Rickenbacker, yet it would have as profound an influence on his career as a fighter pilot as the death of his father had had on his youth. Rick had become an ace, but all of his other plans were going awry. Even worse than his failure to score any new victories was the poor performance of the squadron as a whole.

In the first months of its existence, the 94th Pursuit Squadron had compiled a distinguished record. It had shot down the first German planes and was home to two of the first aces. By the end of May, it had scored sixteen victories, more than any other American unit. Then it seemed to disintegrate under the force of circumstances.

The 1st Pursuit Group had been moved to a quiet sector of the front, operating out of Toquin, a small airfield twenty-five miles south of Château-Thierry. Late in June, the Germans launched another huge offensive, forcing a deep salient between Soissons and Rheims. As was their custom, the Germans had massed their premier aviation units behind the offensive.

Instead of a quiet sector, the 1st was now facing the best the Germans had to offer. In three months, it suffered heavy losses—forty-one pilots were captured or killed out of a normal complement of about eighty for the Group. Among them were Lieutenant Quentin Roosevelt, the former president's son, killed in action, and Alan Winslow, who had won the 94th's first victory. Winslow survived his crash and imprisonment, despite having his badly shattered left arm amputated.

Against their forty-one losses, the four squadrons of the 1st claimed forty-four victories. The casualties were certain; the victory claims were almost certainly inflated, as all victory claims of all air forces tend to be. The 94th Pursuit Squadron received official credit for only three and a half victories, against eight losses!

In Rickenbacker's eyes, this was infamous, but he was almost helpless, confined to bed for most of the long hot summer with a recurring fever. Grounded for weeks at a time and periodically hospitalized, he nonetheless insisted on flying whenever he could drag himself to the airplane. This naturally aggravated his condition, because even in the summer, at 20,000 feet, the 120 mph air streaming into his open cockpit brought wind-chill temperatures far below zero. Combat required steep climbs followed by swooping dives, and the swift changes in pressure played havoc with his ears. The pain also prevented him from swiveling his head to check for enemy planes.

Hospitalized in July to have an abscess in his ear lanced, he returned to flying duty only to suffer a relapse that resulted in a mastoid operation in August. (An infected mastoid was then a life-threatening illness, but is rarely seen now because of antibiotics.) His doctors assumed he would never fly in combat again.

Rick used the hospital stay to his advantage. Unlike the popular concept of the dashing fighter pilot, he was basically introspective. Although he was chafing to get back to flying, he spent his time analyzing all that he had done right, and all that he had done wrong, so far in his combat career. He realized that flying when he was not well, unable to even swing his neck to check the sky, was dangerous to the point of being foolish. Rick went on to analyze each of the fights and was appalled to see how many times he easily could have been the victim instead. He reexamined his tactics and established new standards for his operations. Rickenbacker looked closely into his own personal habits to see how they might have affected the way he performed in combat. He never took alcohol when he was a racing car driver, but had begun to drink a little socially in the air service. He resolved to make sure he didn't drink at least twenty-four hours before flying.

Rick decided that in the future he would be much more cautious in planning his attacks but become even bolder in their execution. As knowledgeable as he was about his planes, engines, and machine guns, he swore to learn even more. And he saw that he had to constantly evaluate his own performance, reviewing everything he did so that habit would not dull his technique. In many ways, the effect of his stay in hospital transformed him from pilot to ace of aces just as his father's death had transformed him from street hoodlum to the man of the family.

The stint in hospital effectively broke his combat tour into two distinct elements. The first tour was his time to learn. The second would provide him the opportunity to run up his score and become the American Ace of Aces. Unlike many others, he was able to return to the fray refreshed, without the combat fatigue that continuous battle brought.

During his confinement, he attended to another personal matter, solidifying the change of his name from Rickenbacher to Rickenbacker. He had toyed with this previously, but now the subtle difference emphasized his desire to be even more an American than ever. He was not yet aware that his smiling visage next to an airplane had already become an icon. Like Ted Williams in a later war, he had become the premier American expression of patriotism, the sports champion as warrior-hero.

Rickenbacker took little comfort from the lack of activity at the 94th Pursuit Squadron while he was sidelined with his illness. Many serious factors were adversely affecting the performance of the 1st Pursuit Group as a whole, and the 94th in particular. One of these, the changeover from the Nieuport 28 to the SPAD, would precipitate a brewing leadership crisis within the 1st Pursuit. One of the unintended consequences of the crisis would, quite by chance, benefit him directly.

On July 5, still convalescing from his fever, Rick went to the huge aviation depot at Le Bourget outside of Paris where the new aircraft for his unit were being readied for pickup. SPAD XIIIs had at last been made available by the French, and, without any paperwork, he talked his way into flying the very first one back to the 94th. The plane he picked up already bore the large number 1 on its side, and Rickenbacker would fly it (and a similarly marked sister ship) to fame.

The casual pickup underscores the informal nature of flying and flying training at the time. While it is reasonable to assume that Rickenbacker was at least familiar with the SPAD, he almost certainly had never received any training in it, and it was a far more fractious mount than the relatively docile Nieuport.

Its predecessor, the SPAD VII, had appeared on the Western Front in the fall of 1916, and it was so effective that it was also adopted for use by Great Britain, Belgium, Italy, and Russia. It was much less maneuverable than the Nieuport scouts, but, powered by a 180-horsepower Hispano-Suiza V-8 engine, it was stronger and faster.

The SPAD XIII was a slightly scaled-up version of the VII and was equipped with the 235-horsepower geared Hispano-Suiza. It was faster than the Nieuport 28, and you could dive it to hell and gone without anything breaking. Far less maneuverable, it "glided like a brick" in the terms of the time.

The SPAD XIII became the standard French fighter, with about 8,500 being built. Unfortunately, the larger Hisso, as the engine was called, had grave mechanical problems with the gears that connected crankshaft to propeller, affecting both safety and serviceability. It was also more difficult to maintain and took many more hours to overhaul than the Gnome engines of the Nieuport. For the duration of the war, it was not unusual to have 50 percent or more of the SPADs simultaneously unavailable because of mechanical problems.

An open rebellion broke out among the 1st Pursuit Group's squadron commanders over the change in aircraft. Like most rebellions, the overt cause masked an underlying discontent.

The 1st Pursuit Group had been formed under the leadership of Major Bert Milton Atkinson, a former infantry officer, who learned to fly in 1915 and had campaigned with the 1st Aero Squadron against Pancho Villa in Mexico. Now only twenty-nine, he was a serious career officer who would distinguish himself later in the war in the St. Mihiel campaign.

In July 1918, the fateful month when the SPADs began to arrive, Atkinson supervised four squadron commanders, each with a different personality. Major Kenneth Marr commanded the 94th. He was unpopular in part because of his personality and in part because he had replaced the well-liked Major John W. F. M. Huffer as commander. Marr knew that he was on thin ice and behaved accordingly, becoming very conservative, an undesirable characteristic in a fighter squadron commander.

The 95th was commanded by the able Captain David McKelvey Peterson, who was extremely well liked by his men. The 27th was led by an experienced ace of the Royal Flying Corps, a Canadian, Major Harold E. Hartney. The 147th was commanded by another RFC veteran whose career had paralleled Hartney's, Major Geoffrey H. Bonnell.

Both Hartney and Bonnell were professionals, well aware of the adverse impact the SPADs would have on their war-making capability. They vehemently protested the arrival of the new plane. They knew that their mechanics had neither the experience nor the equipment to service the Hispano-Suizas properly and anticipated that there would inevitably be an ever higher percentage of aircraft out of commission. Not having sufficient aircraft to mount patrols hindered their mission and it was dangerous, for the enemy often appeared in large numbers.

Hartney was by nature more tactful than Bonnell. Savvy in the ways of the military and good with words, he not only survived, but would be promoted. Despite an impeccable combat record, Bonnell was fired, replaced by a veteran of the 94th and a friend of Rickenbacker's, Captain James A. Meissner. The summer of 1918 thus found the 1st Pursuit Group with as many as two-thirds of its aircraft out for maintenance and rent by internal dissension. The month of June had passed with virtually no contact with the enemy. The tempo picked up in July, but fell back sharply in August, as secret preparations were made for the offensive at St. Mihiel.

THE ILLUSORY BATTLE OF ST. MIHIEL

The Battle of St. Mihiel was the first battle in France in which an American army fought under the American flag and the first time that air power had ever been used en masse. It would prove to be a turning point for Rickenbacker.

The St. Mihiel salient, about twenty-five miles wide at its base and fifteen miles deep, had been created when the Germans had attempted to take Verdun in 1916. The terrain provided the Germans a naturally strong defensive position, which they had enhanced with a series of fortifications. On July 24, 1918, a decision was made to allow the American First Army to blood itself in combat by eliminating the salient.

Colonel Billy Mitchell was Commander, First Army Air Service, and he conceived an aerial battle plan unlike any in history. It clearly demonstrated how far aviation had advanced since the almost casual early observation flights of 1914, and, equally clearly, forecast the future.

Using the greatest secrecy, Mitchell assembled some 1,481 airplanes in twenty-six American, sixty French, eight British, and three Italian squadrons. The extent of Mitchell's personal influence with the Allies is confirmed by their willingness to place so many of their assets under his direction. Intelligence reports indicated that just over 200 German aircraft opposed them in the sector, but that would change.

The ground assault began on September 12, 1918, in heavy rain that kept all the aviation units grounded. On the 14th, Mitchell was able to get his air units into action, by which time the Germans had reinforced the front with some of their best units, including *Jagdgeschwader II*, operating the infamous Fokker D VIIs. Some 500 Allied aircraft attacked frontline positions, while the remainder alternately attacked supply and communication centers behind the lines.

In the end, the ground battle proved to be a bit of an anticlimax; the Germans were prepared to surrender the salient, pulling back to shorten their lines. By September 14, the Allies had gained complete air superiority, but at tremendous cost. American losses were far higher than they should have been primarily as a result of the Americans' eagerness to engage despite their lack of experience. The young pilots threw themselves into battle with an ingenuous exuberance. The quality of the JG II pilots was high, and they quite literally slaughtered their inexperienced American opponents. A distinguished historian of World War I, Dr. Howard Fisher, has compared JG II's ascendancy to the so-called Happy Time of World War II, when German submarines wreaked havoc on American shipping.

The otherwise lackluster St. Mihiel offensive proved to be vitally important to Rickenbacker. In a fierce demonstration that he was not merely a hotshot seeking glory with aerial victories, Rickenbacker distinguished himself by engaging continually in the most dangerous work of the war: ground attack. As Flight Commander, he led his SPADs down to ground level, shooting up trenches, artillery positions, and supply lines. Danger was everywhere. The disciplined German ground forces put up individual and barrage fire from their rifles, machine guns, and antiaircraft cannons. The air was torn by hundreds of artillery shells, Allied and German, which continually permeated the airspace, and to which there was no counter but prayer. Finally, operating at low level, absorbed by the task, the SPADs were prey to any prowling Fokkers.

Scarcely out of his sickbed, Rick scored the first of his next twenty victories on September 14. The official report of this victory is worth reading, for it tells much about his straightforward nature.

Lieut. Rickenbacker reports:
Left at 7 h 30 A.M. Met one enemy biplace over Verdun. Looked like an L.V.G. [a German reconnaissance plane] Followed him about seven (7) kilometers, but it was too high to reach.

[A minor point, but the L.V.G. was probably a Rumpler, for the latter had a much greater altitude capability because it was lighter and had a more efficient airfoil. Aircraft misidentification was a chronic problem for both sides throughout the war.]

Then returned from the lines at 4000 meters. Met four (4) enemy Fokkers with red wings, light gray fuselage and striped tail over the towns of Villency and Wayville. They were flying at about 3000 meters. I piqued [dove down] on the upper man of their formation, fired apparently 200 rounds and saw him go down, apparently out of control.

[Given that the Fokker D VII was equal or superior to the SPAD XIII, this was an extraordinarily brave attack by Rickenbacker.]

Was unable to follow him on account of the other three who showed excellent fighting spirits [sic].

[Rickenbacker shows his common sense here—he'd scored at least a probable, and there was no point in trying to make sure with three D VIIs ready to attack.]

This took place at 8 h 10 and 8 h 15. I then returned over Lachausee, where, at 8 h 25, I noticed five (5) Fokkers with their regular camauflage [sic] crosses on the tail, apparently new men. I started to pique, but they immediately turned for home. Fired about 50 rounds without result.

Confirmation requested.

[The technique of selecting a victim, diving from altitude, firing, and then leaving the scene would be a useful one for aces in all wars. It was not the colorful, protracted aerobatic dogfight preferred by reporters and fiction writers, but it got the job done. It is worth noting that Rickenbacker, like Zemke, Blesse, and Olds, did not hesitate to point out his own mistakes.]

ACE OF ACES

Raoul Lufbery had been recognized as the first American Ace of Aces; his title had passed successively to Lieutenant Paul Baer (nine victories), Lieutenant Frank Baylies (thirteen victories), and then Lieutenant David Putnam (twelve victories). Each of these men in turn had been shot down and killed or captured. The title had passed briefly to Lieutenant Edgar G. Tobin, who had six victories when Rick resumed his scoring streak. Rickenbacker added two more to his score on September 15, becoming the American Ace of Aces for the first time.

The way he had succeeded to the title gave him pause. Every previous Ace of Aces except Tobin had either been killed or captured. There would soon be another concern—the rise of Frank Luke, the Arizona Balloon Buster.

LUKE

Frank Luke was the polar opposite of Rickenbacker as an ace, although both had come from tough backgrounds. Born on May 19, 1897, Luke was one of nine children of his immigrant German mother. He was a natural athlete and an expert shot, learning the skill while working in the tough Arizona copper mines.

The war was an escape for Luke, who gladly enlisted in the Aviation Section and was commissioned a Second Lieutenant in January 1918. On July 26, he was posted to Hartney's 27th Pursuit Squadron.

A complete nonconformist who scorned formation flying, Luke managed to shoot down his first airplane and antagonize almost everyone within two weeks of his arrival. Like Rickenbacker, his personality did not suit most of his squadron mates, and he was widely regarded as both a braggart and a liar.

Luke responded by making a specialty of the most dangerous target at the front, the German observation balloons. The *"Drachen"* were vital because they controlled the fire of the artillery upon which the German defensive system had become dependent. As a result, the balloons were ringed by heavy concentrations of antiaircraft guns and machine guns able to put up a blanket of fire when enemy fighters appeared. The enemy gunners knew the height of their balloons and could bore-sight and fuse their weapons for that altitude. The balloons were also protected by patrolling fighters whenever possible. Attacks on balloons were not quite suicide missions, but they came close enough for most pilots.

Another pilot who had fallen into disfavor with the other members of the 27th, was Lieutenant Joseph Wehner, who, like Rickenbacker, had been under investigation because of his German ancestry. Wehner attached himself to Luke, and they began a spectacular series of attacks on the huge, sausage-shaped bags. The balloons, floating at the end of long cables at about 2,000 feet altitude, carried two observers. Equipped with parachutes, they were quick to use them, unwilling to chance being burned alive when the hydrogen-filled balloons were attacked. The balloons were difficult targets. When wet with early morning dew, they did not ignite even when the 11-mm "balloon gun" bullets pierced their hide. If there was any warning at all, the balloons could rapidly be brought back to their nests by engine-driven winches, making attacks virtually suicidal.

Luke shot down his first balloon on September 12 and with typical chutzpah landed in an open field by an American balloon company to see if they had confirmed his victory. Balloons were counted the same as a downed aircraft. They had confirmed his victory, but when Luke returned to his airplane to take off, he found it had been shot so full of holes during the attack that it was not flyable. In the next seventeen days, Luke would bring back five more aircraft in similar derelict condition; the sixth would be so battered that it could not bring him back.

On September 14, Luke began the first of his scoring sprees, shooting down six balloons in three days, while his sidekick, Wehner, downed three. On the 18th, Luke shot down three airplanes (two Fokker D VIIs and a Halberstadt) and two balloons; Wehner also got two balloons. In five days, Luke had accounted for nine balloons and three airplanes, while Wehner had five balloons to his credit. It was unprecedented scoring, and Luke found himself the fair-haired boy of the Air Service, having replaced Rickenbacker as the Ace of Aces.

The title had no meaning for Luke, however, for Wehner had been killed on the 18th, protecting Luke from an attack by Fokkers. It shook Luke to his very core, and he became even moodier. He now flew for revenge, as Lufbery had done.

Luke scored another victory on the 26th, but lost another wingman. He fell into a depressed state, and his behavior became more erratic, but he was allowed to continue his solo forays, shooting down a balloon on September 28, on the last mission from which he would return.

On September 29, Luke staged out of an advanced field, under orders from Hartney not to take off until 5:56 P.M. Hartney, knowing that he could not control Luke, wished to at least avoid opposing Fokkers, which usually went home by 6:00 P.M. Luke took off exactly on time, diverting his course to drop a note to the American 7th Balloon Company. It read, "Watch for burning balloons. Luke."

Precisely at 7:05, he exploded his first balloon, at Dun-sur-Meuse. Moments later, he flamed a second balloon at Briere Farm. Attacked by enemy aircraft, he reportedly downed two Fokkers before continuing on to Milly, where he shot down a third balloon at 7:12.

At some point, he had been badly wounded, but he strafed German troops before crashing behind enemy lines near Murvaux. According to a now disputed legend, Luke dragged himself from the aircraft and fought off German soldiers with his .45-caliber automatic until he was killed. The gunfight may not have happened, but it was entirely characteristic of Luke if it did.

The last two Fokkers Luke was supposed to have shot down were not confirmed, but even three balloons in seven minutes was a brilliant cap to his blazing career. Luke was awarded the Medal of Honor posthumously.

Yet as an ace, Luke epitomized everything that Rickenbacker condemned. He was a loner, the antithesis of the ace-leader. He was not interested in the success of his squadron, did not baby his aircraft, and took absurd risks, for which he paid the price. Luke's conduct was in many ways suicidal, and it cost the lives of two of his wingmen. This was reprehensible to Rickenbacker, however much he admired Luke's bravery. In essence, Luke had a fatal, losing formula for success.

THE ULTIMATE ACCOLADE

Despite the rumpus he had raised over the SPADs, the tiny, birdlike Hartney had been promoted to command the 1st Pursuit Group on August 21, 1918. Hartney, in appearance a miniature David Niven, had watched Rickenbacker operate and knew he had more to offer than just his qualities as a fighter pilot. He saw him as a leader of men. Hartney appreciated Rick's good rapport with the mechanics and his intimate knowledge of the damnable Hispano-Suiza engine. He decided to promote Lieutenant Rickenbacker to become the Commanding Officer of the 94th, despite two formidable obstacles he knew he had to overcome.

The first was within the 94th itself, where Rickenbacker had by now been accepted as a colleague, but would be resented as a commanding officer, especially as he would have to be promoted over some pilots who were senior to him in rank. The second was at headquarters, where the regular army staff officers did not regard Rickenbacker as "officer material" and felt that he would be hopelessly out of his depth as a CO.

With the same astute political maneuvering that had kept him from being fired over his protests about the SPADs, Hartney worked for more than a month to obtain headquarters approval to make the change. He knew that it would be up to Rickenbacker to make the change work in the squadron.

RICKENBACKER AS COMMANDER

On September 24, 1918, the operations of the 94th took a dramatic turn for the better when Rickenbacker assumed command. Feeling the full weight of his responsibility as commander, he proceeded to fly more missions and score more victories than anyone else in the Air Service.

On the night he was informed he was to command the 94th, Rickenbacker called two meetings. Significantly, the first was at 8:00 P.M., for the mechanics, with whom he had established a strong rapport. He told them that he knew of their problems with the SPADs and that they would have 100 percent of his support. They responded in kind, and immediately established the same sort of team spirit that had characterized Rick's racing crews. Within weeks, the 94th was obtaining as much as 100 hours flying time on the Hispanos before an overhaul was required, compared to thirty hours in other squadrons.

An hour later, he met with the pilots. He set forth his rules: there was to be no military nonsense, no saluting, and most especially, no taking care of oneself instead of taking care of the mechanics. Every man was to fly as often and as aggressively as possible. He made it known that his object was for the 94th to lead all other squadrons in victories, and that the only reason for their being there was to down Germans.

At this meeting, and in subsequent briefings, Rick's bad grammar, blazing profanity, and occasional malapropisms caused some of his more blue-blooded colleagues to cringe. He knew this to be the case but no longer cared, for he was now in a position to obtain the results he wanted. Just as he had done with his racing teams, he now dictated how the 94th would fight the war in the air.

RICK'S LEADERSHIP

In just two conversations, Rickenbacker had turned the 94th around. Scoring two victories on his first day as squadron commander showed that he could back up his talk with action. From that point on, it became the crack American unit of the war, with more victories and more flying hours over the line than any other.

The Great War had only forty-seven days to run when Rickenbacker scored his double victory. As squadron commander, he might have picked his missions carefully, but Rick was a true leader, and he flew exactly the same missions he assigned his men. His fourteen victories in October would include three balloons, still the toughest target of the war. They also included eight Fokkers and three two-seaters. One of the latter was a Hannover that was subsequently made flyable and appeared in a carefully staged propaganda film.

If there was ever a self-made ace, it was Rickenbacker. He had to fight to get into flight school, then fight to get into combat. Thrown into the fray against experienced adversaries, he, with a minimum of training and inferior equipment, not only survived but prevailed.

Like most pilots, and particularly most fighter pilots, Rick possessed good hand-eye coordination. He taught himself to "see in the air" and, although aggressive, knew when to attack and when to lay back. Luke's headlong style repelled him; it was not smart flying, no matter how brave it was. He was completely focused on his mission and did not let his ego interfere. And like some of the other great aces—Georges Guynemer, Richthofen, and others—he managed to fly and score while desperately ill, pushing himself beyond all ordinary human limits.

In doing so, he had to cope with two divergent kinds of technological evolution. The first was with his offensive weapons, for he had to learn how to fly the delicate Nieuport aggressively, to score victories without pulling the wing fabric off. Next he had to learn how to keep the stoutly built SPAD in the air, for he believed devoutly in Lufbery's maxim "You can't score victories sitting around in the hangar." It was undoubtedly more difficult for him to master the technological evolution of the enemy, whose transition from the lackluster Pfalz and Albatros scouts to the deadly Fokker D VII presented Allied pilots with a deadly danger.

Rickenbacker's real leadership was demonstrated not so much by his scoring the most victories—twenty-six—of all American airmen, but instead by his leadership of the 94th. He raised it from its summer doldrums to becoming the highest-scoring American squadron at the front, ending the war with a total of sixty-six and a half victories against eighteen casualties. He was truly the Ace of Aces, but he was also the CO of COs.

He forged his leadership at the anvil of combat. He not only sought battle himself, but also insisted that his squadron seek it out. His unique leadership abilities encouraged them to do this in a sane way, always taking advantage of the odds, and avoiding casualties wherever possible. Unlike some of the aces, for example, Britain's Albert Ball or the 94th's Frank Luke, who threw themselves into combat without thought of the consequences, Rick preferred to be conservative even as he was being aggressive. Most important, he did not see aerial combat as gallant. He termed it, accurately, "scientific murder."

AFTER THE WAR

Rickenbacker's celebrity as a war ace helped propel him to a roller-coaster business career. He helped found the Rickenbacker Automobile Company, which from 1922 to 1927 produced about 35,000 great cars but no profits. In 1935 he took over the stewardship of Eastern Air Lines, buying it in 1938. With his usual intense management style, he took it to the top of the airlines in profitability for many years, but, later in his life, made some errors of judgment in regard to equipment that ultimately forced him to retire.

Although a Lieutenant Colonel in the Air Corps reserve, he continued to prefer being called Captain, the rank he felt he had earned. He refused cabinet-level positions in the government as well as the offer of a major general's rank in the Army Air Forces. He served the government all through World War II and made headlines once again by surviving a crash in the Pacific. He spent twenty-one difficult days on a raft awaiting rescue, setting the example for his companions. Some resented his exhortations—but all but one survived the ordeal.

Rickenbacker was larger than life, and as he grew older he became a curmudgeon with a penchant for saying the wrong thing at the wrong time. His forthright manner had always created enemies, but he also had friends who were loyal to the end. His 1967 autobiography, *Rickenbacker—His Own Story,* was an instant best-seller. Not unnaturally, it was a somewhat sanitized version of his life, but it clearly revealed the moral and psychological fabric of his personality, the very fabric that had permitted him to become a true ace and a great leader.

Rickenbacker's example was strong enough to survive the decades of neglect endured by American fighter pilots, and to serve as an example for the next great ace-leader.

★ FOUR ★
HOW QUICKLY THEY FORGET—
THE PEACETIME DAMPER
ON PROGRESS

The country had been rocked by claims of waste and fraud in the creation of the American Air Service during World War I. Lengthy postwar investigations proved that while there had been a mindless optimism and many mistakes, there was little or no evidence of fraud or corruption.

The results obtained in World War I by the American Air Service were really quite remarkable, given its primitive origins in 1917. By the Armistice on November 11, 1918, it had risen from 55 noncombat aircraft to a force of almost 700 aircraft in the field. Some 13,000 aircraft had been either manufactured or acquired from foreign sources. If the war had gone on for another year, more than 200 American squadrons would have been at the front, most of them flying airplanes designed and built in the United States.

The Air Service's combat record was equally impressive. In action for just over seven months in 1918, it destroyed 776 enemy airplanes and 72 balloons. American bombers dropped 138 tons of bombs in more than 150 raids on German targets. Observation planes took more than 18,000 individual photographs of German positions. In the process, some 680 flying personnel of the Air Service were killed. Of these, 75 percent died in accidents, most in training.

Far more important than the statistics was the fact that it had become a battle-hardened professional air arm. From ground zero had been created the disciplines that made combat possible, including training, logistics, maintenance, procurement, recruitment, and many more.

AERIAL DÉJÀ VU

Rickenbacker's fighting style was passed on to those few pilots who remained in the Air Service after World War I had ended. They carried on for more than a decade in biplanes not too different from his SPAD. The best of them formed aerial groups such as the "Three Men on a Flying Trapeze" team that performed at air shows around the country. Seen by thousands every year, they were the best recruiting advertisements possible, inspiring many a ground-bound youth with the desire to fly.

One they did not inspire was a young Iowa lad, Hubert Zemke, the spiritual heir to Edward Vernon Rickenbacker. Unlike many future aces, Zemke was not bitten by the flying bug as a young man, but instead was preoccupied by school, work, and sports.

Rickenbacker and Zemke had much in common, from their humble origins to their views on life. Hub Zemke would learn to fly and fight, taking Rickenbacker's tactics as a benchmark, and going on to invent his own as he became a leading ace. Both men had strong feelings of inferiority in their relations with people of higher rank and social status. Rickenbacker was far more politically savvy than Zemke and handled his feelings of resentment with greater skill. Both were great aces and great leaders.

WHERE DID ALL THE ACES GO?

Rickenbacker led the list of thirty-one airmen who had achieved the rank of ace within the American Air Service. Another forty-four Americans became aces while serving with British or French units.

Rickenbacker could not afford to remain in the Army Air Service. Before the war, he had become accustomed to the lifestyle of a $60,000 a year race car driver, and his prospects were now brighter than ever, with dazzling offers from a variety of sources. As it happened, very few aces remained in the Air Service after the war. Of these, only two, Frank O'Driscoll Hunter and Clayton Bissell, became general officers. Bissell was Mitchell's aide and a lead pilot in the bombing of the battleships. Hunter, who had scored six and a half victories, became Commanding General of the VIII Fighter Command during World War II and would twice loom large in Zemke's career.

There were many reasons for the exodus of aces. The end of the war was also the end of appropriations, and the importance of the Air Service was quickly forgotten in the traditional budget battles. For the next twenty years, the Air

Service (after 1926, the Air Corps) struggled to survive on budgets that averaged about $13 million a year. The strength of the Air Service dropped from its peak of 195,000 officers and men to hover at about 10,000 for the next decade. Demotions rather than promotions were the order of the day, and even a bright officer could expect to spend ten or more years as a lieutenant.

Flying was the single great incentive that induced the pilots to remain in the Air Service, even though peacetime aviation was a far cry from the thrills of combat. Flying hours were limited because fuel was expensive, but you did get paid to fly, and if you were stationed at Dayton's McCook Field (later Wright Field), you got to fly the most advanced aircraft in the country.

MAKING THE MOST OF IT

Most pilots did not get to fly the advanced aircraft. As barely tolerated auxiliaries at artillery or cavalry posts, they endured the boring routine for the opportunity to fly obsolete Jennies and DH-4s. Hangars were jammed with World War I surplus airplanes and a frugal Congress made sure that these were used up before any more could be procured. The war surplus aircraft became increasingly dangerous over time, as their wood and fabric construction deteriorated rapidly.

Despite its difficulties, the Air Service had leaders who managed to hold the organization together by spending the limited funds in the wisest possible manner. They kept the force structure small and spent the money instead on training and research. Although the Army bought very few aircraft, it spread the purchases among the maximum number of contractors, trying to keep as many of them as possible in business. Aircraft engineers became some of the first migrant workers, as they followed contracts from one company to another.

Wherever possible, record flights were used to improve technique and raise morale. In the midst of the force stagnation of the 1920s, the Army provided funds for the first nonstop transcontinental flight (1923), the first round-the-world flight (1924), and the first flight to Hawaii (1927). Many speed and altitude records were set by pioneer test pilots, the 1920s equivalent of today's astronauts.

In the perverse way of most budgeting strategies, record flights actually proved to be counterproductive, for they made it reasonable for the public and Congress to assume that progress in aviation technology was on track despite the limited budgets. It was only when foreign dictators—first Mussolini, then Hitler—brandished their air power that the public began to be concerned.

THE BOMBER BOYS TAKE CONTROL

The single most important individual in American military aviation in the first five years after World War I was Billy Mitchell. Too flamboyant to be made Chief of the Air Service, Mitchell used his position as Assistant to the Chief to advance the concept of air power as articulated by Giulio Douhet and others. Mitchell wanted an independent air force, and he openly castigated the Navy for wasting funds on ships, raucously challenging them to a test of airplanes versus battleships.

The Navy tried first to ignore him and then to laugh him off. When ultimately forced to accept his challenge, it arranged a series of tests in which the cards were stacked against the airplane. The target ships were moored off the coast of Virginia, some sixty-five miles out to sea, almost beyond the extreme range of Mitchell's aircraft when loaded with bombs. The Navy crafted the ground rules for the test, limiting the number and size of bombs that could be used. The Navy also bent the rules to its own advantage whenever possible, with subterfuges ranging from providing bad information on weather conditions to diverting ships into the safety area around the target and disrupting bombing runs. It was dirty pool in the best traditions of interservice rivalry.

Mitchell quietly agreed to the rules and just as quietly violated them. When told that he could use only three of the huge 2,000-pound bombs that he personally had designed, he ignored the order and sent eight to be dropped.

The first tests were conducted in July 1921 and astounded the world. The major target was the captured German 27,000-ton battleship, the *Ostfriesland*. Heavily compartmentalized fore and aft and with four separate skins to protect it, the Navy considered the battleship "unsinkable," because during the Battle of Jutland it had survived eighteen direct hits from heavy British guns and a mine explosion.

After lighter bombs had done some minor damage, six 2,000 pounders from Mitchell's Martin bombers crushed the *Ostfriesland,* sending it in a rolling dive to the bottom of the sea. The drama off the Virginia Capes revolutionized air and naval warfare at home and abroad. It also put the proponents of bombers in control of air power policy for the next seventy years. Within the Air Corps, interest in developing fighters and fighter tactics waned until the initial years of combat during World War II.

FLYING THE FIGHTERS IN PEACETIME

For those few who remained in the fighter business, life was sweet, even though the pay was low, promotion nonexistent, and danger ever present. Peacetime fighter pilots flew only when the weather was good. A typical day began with role call at 07:30 and a scheduled early morning flight of perhaps one hour. An eager pilot could make another hour's flight on his own. At 12:30 everyone was released for the day. Nonflying duties were nominal, and there was plenty of time off for athletics and other recreation.

Training was totally deficient, with no instrument flying and very little night flying. No tactical doctrine was practiced. While there were always pickup "dog-fights" between individuals, there was no serious combat training in which one pilot was pitted against another and the results evaluated. (It would be called ACM, air combat maneuvering, today.) On weekends, the planes could be used for cross-country flights that ostensibly provided navigation training but that really took the pilots home to see their girlfriends. In many ways, it was a high-powered flying club whose members were paid to participate.

There was a curious dichotomy in the far-reaching research efforts by engineers at the McCook Field and Wright Field laboratories and the practical application of that research to the operational level. While the labs experimented with superchargers, pressurized cabins, all-metal construction, instrument flight, retractable landing gears, radio navigation, radio controlled operation, self-sealing tanks, autopilots, and other sophisticated equipment, only simple (read inexpensive) fighters were procured, and these in small number. The most sophisticated of these, the Boeing P-26, was a transitional aircraft, mixing its monoplane, all-metal construction with a fixed gear, open cockpit, and strut bracing.

Things were different in Europe, because 1934 was a watershed year in foreign fighter technology. Great Britain and Germany were going far beyond American aerial capability and would do so for the next eight years.

WAR CLOUDS

Just as human beings do, military services go into denial when placed in an uncontrollable situation. The budget constraints on the United States military leaders forced them to play down the rapid advances seen in European aircraft, often by claiming that they had "copied" American ideas.

The first of the new generation of modern fighters was the German Messerschmitt Bf 109. Built in Germany from 1935 through 1945, and continued subsequently in production in both Czechoslovakia and Spain, the 109 was one of the most important fighters of the century. It was of all-metal construction and featured an enclosed canopy, retractable landing gear, and heavy armament. The first prototype, powered, oddly enough, by a 695-horsepower Rolls Royce engine, was flown in September 1935, and more than 33,000 improved models were manufactured. The thirteenth prototype was fitted with a special 1,650-horsepower engine and set a world's land-plane speed record of 379.39 mph in 1937. Like all true classics, the Bf 109 would prove to be very adaptable to larger engines and a wide variety of missions. One of the last models, the Bf 109K, was powered by a 2,000-horsepower Daimler Benz engine and had a top speed of 452 mph.

The Messerschmitt was almost matched by the first of its English contemporaries, the Hawker Hurricane, first flown on November 6, 1935. A private venture of the Hawker Aircraft Company, the Hurricane abandoned the traditional British open-cockpit biplane formula for a design that would also be built in great numbers and serve all the way through World War II. Still of mixed metal, fabric, and wood construction, the Hurricane also had an enclosed cockpit and retractable landing gear. It would prove to be the most important British fighter in the Battle of Britain and then go on to star as a ground-attack aircraft in every theater.

Both the Messerschmitt and the Hurricane would be overshadowed by the classic British fighter of World War II, the Supermarine Spitfire, first flown on March 6, 1936. Like the Hurricane, a private venture, the Spitfire's lovely lines and outstanding performance made it an instant success. Its initial production models had a top speed of 354 mph, faster than either the Messerschmitt or the Hurricane. The Spitfire was built in more than forty variants and in greater numbers (some 22,000) than any other British fighter.

BEHIND THE SMOOTH LINES

All of the leaders of the Army Air Corps should have been shocked by the debut of these three foreign fighters, each one with a performance greater than anything in the U.S. inventory. Most of the leaders were not, for they were convinced of the superiority of the fast, well-armed bomber. A few, like the renegade Captain Claire Chennault, had long insisted that American fighters were falling behind in performance, but these naysayers were ignored. Chennault left the service an embittered man, and went on to become a legend as the founder of the American Volunteer Group, the Flying Tigers.

In effect, the argument between bomber and fighter proponents was as vicious as the interservice rivalry of the Army and the Navy. When Chennault attempted to demonstrate fighter capability in maneuvers, he was shackled with artificial restrictions. After 1936 the tactical school at Maxwell Field dropped fighter tactics from the curriculum.

It was politically correct to believe that the bomber would always get through, and the new Boeing B-17 seemed to lend credence to the concept. Called a "Flying Fortress" by an admiring press, the B-17 seemed to offer the speed and firepower necessary to fight its way through formations of any fighters in the world.

This idea was cherished, despite the fact that the Congress decided that the B-17 was not only too expensive, but also too large to be controlled safely by the average pilot, and bought only thirteen for service test.

The stunning advances in European aviation technology were somehow accepted and forgotten by the American military. The crisp, efficient lines of the Messerschmitt, Hurricane, and Spitfire were applauded and their speed admired, but the combat capability that those lines concealed was ignored. Production models of the foreign aircraft would have armor, self-sealing fuel tanks, efficient gun sights, and heavy armament, all essential for modern warfare, and all lacking in American fighters.

The fundamental bankruptcy of American military aviation was never more evident than in the series of design competitions beginning in 1935 for a new fighter to replace the obsolete P-26. At a time when foreign fighters were achieving speeds of 330 to 350 mph, it was hoped that the new Air Corps fighter could at least reach 300 mph, but it was not to be. Four aircraft competed for the contract, which was won by the Seversky P-35, a developed version of the noted Alexander P. de Seversky's 1933 floatplane—an ancestor of the plane Hub Zemke would fly to fame.

A long series of bitter wars followed in which aircraft were continually improved. Japan invaded China and backed into a rough fight with the Soviet Union in Manchuria. Italy bullied Ethiopia into submission. Italy and Germany allied themselves against the Soviet Union in the Spanish Civil War. Three years later, the Soviet Union molested Finland in an embarrassingly inept war.

The most incredible aspect of all these conflicts was that the air force leaders of the United States, France, and Great Britain learned virtually nothing from them in terms of the type of equipment, the training, or the tactics required for a modern war. It would mean that future aces like Zemke would start their war in the same relative position that Rickenbacker had been in, with inferior technology, inadequate tactics, and facing a skilled, well-equipped opponent.

FROM FORESTER TO FIGHTER PILOT

Hubert Zemke was born in Missoula, Montana, on March 14, 1914, to Benno and Anna Zemke. Both were German immigrants, although the father's naturalization papers indicated he was Swiss. Benno had lived an adventuresome life, having run away to sea to escape his father, then jumping ship to sample the delights of the United States. He was deported to Germany in 1902, and there served two years in the Kaiser's army. Benno returned to the United States as soon as he could. Frugal and hardworking as a locomotive fireman, he saved his money and by 1910 was able to visit his home in Germany in style. On the return voyage, he met his future wife. The indomitable Anna had, at age twenty-one, borrowed $100 in gold and set out by herself for the United States.

The two probably would not have been considered a suitable match in their native land. Benno was rough and poorly educated, while Anna was refined, with a taste for the arts. Yet in America like many another couple (including Rickenbacker's parents), they worked together to achieve the American dream. They had only one child, although, as an act of charity, they took in and raised the son of a divorced friend.

Young Hubert Zemke had to endure the same sort of ethnic taunts that Rickenbacker had experienced, and was insulted with exactly the same unimaginative names—"Kraut," "Dutchie," and "Square Head"—by his classmates. As the only child, young "Hoo-bart" (as his mother called him) was subjected to strict razor-strap discipline by his father and learned early on that an order was an order. His father, while gruff, saw to it that Hubert gained experience in life, taking him hunting, showing him how to use tools, and encouraging him to take tough jobs to earn money. On occasion, Benno would break down and show his soft side with an unexpected gift.

Unlike Rick, Zemke grew up in a protective family environment and was even given the opportunity to learn to play the violin. He was adept at sports, and soon became a strongly built young athlete, good in softball and track, but excelling as a boxer.

While Rickenbacker had largely given up fighting when he assumed the mantle of family leadership, Zemke enjoyed boxing and would not be reluctant to use his fists for many years. He twice was the Montana state middleweight champion, and a sportswriter gave him the nickname "The Hub" as a comment on the endless series of blows that poured out from his husky body. "Hub," as he was called thereafter, fought fifty-nine times, lost three bouts and knocked out twenty-seven opponents. Zemke retained a boxer's pugnacious attitude as a fighter pilot and as a commander. In the air, he devised tactics that took the war to the Luftwaffe, hitting the Nazis hard and often where it hurt. On the ground, he was said to have settled several incidents at the Officers' Club with his short six-inch right-hand punch.

Zemke studied forestry as he worked his way through Montana State University, where all male students were required to participate in the Reserve Officers Training Corps. The ROTC offered the opportunity to try for the Army Air Corps flying training program. Although Hub had never had any interest in aircraft, the chance for a trip to San Antonio, combined with the highly competitive nature of the testing, prompted him to try.

FLYING SCHOOL

When Zemke arrived at Randolph Field in February 1936 the Army Air Corps was at a low ebb in its budget and its power. It had some 1,200 pilots to operate its 900 first-line aircraft. The term "first line" was a misnomer, for none of them were equipped to fight a war, lacking armor, self-sealing tanks, and adequate armament. Funds were so limited that only three classes of flying school candidates were admitted, each class consisting of seventy people. Some were officers, graduates of West Point; others, like Zemke, were aviation cadets.

Somewhat to Zemke's surprise, given his basic lack of interest in airplanes, he loved flying, although he was not a natural pilot. He flew biplanes that were only moderately more advanced than those Rickenbacker had flown, including the Consolidated PT-3, Douglas BT-2, and Boeing P-12. He most enjoyed the P-12, a favorite of everyone who flew it, and learned formation flying and rudimentary World War I tactics.

Radios were still to come, and on one flight, his formation leader suddenly began a steep letdown, landing his P-12 in a tiny field. Assuming that it was part of the instruction process, Zemke and five others in the formation followed him down, landing behind him and almost piling up in a ball. The instructor was furious with them. He had experienced an engine failure and landed in the only field available. It was so small that none of the planes could take off, and all had to be disassembled and trucked back to Kelly Field.

Given Hub's somewhat truculent independent nature, he was even more surprised that he enjoyed the purely military side of flying school, demonstrating such excellent qualities as an officer candidate that he was promoted to cadet squadron commander. It was an important achievement, for in a climate where the washout rate was a wasteful 50 percent, it meant that he was identified as a comer. As a result, he was able to select a career in fighter aviation and was earmarked for a highly prized regular commission, which he received in 1939. Curiously, this achievement made no impression on Zemke's atrophied ego.

He was assigned to Langley Field, Virginia, then the site of General Headquarters, a semiautonomous command and the first step toward an independent air force. There he would meet many future air force leaders, including William Kepner, Curtis LeMay, and Carl Spaatz.

Unlike many of his brother officers, Zemke did not take advantage of the "flying club" lifestyle. Still somewhat reticent and uncomfortable in the company of young women, he assiduously pursued his flying even in his leisure time, often visiting other bases for the chance to fly different kinds of airplanes. Checking out in a new aircraft was an informal procedure in those days, because if you had wings on your chest, you were presumed capable of flying anything in the inventory. A checkout usually meant getting in the cockpit while someone pointed out any unusual features and going through the starting procedure, after which you were on your own. The natural result was many accidents, often fatal.

At Langley, Hub started out in the beautiful but dangerous Curtiss P-6E biplanes, which were generally similar in performance to the P-12 but which were beset with structural and engine problems that gave them a high accident rate. The advanced-appearing Consolidated PB-2 two-place fighter followed in 1937. It was a very clean low-wing monoplane with retractable landing gear and a supercharged engine. The Air Corps had purchased thirty of them, for there was a small, vocal section within headquarters that advocated the two-seat fighter. Unfortunately, the G forces of any maneuver, particularly at the high altitudes for which the PB-2 was designed, rendered the rearguard helpless. The additional weight of the gunner and his equipment made the aircraft so heavy that it was not maneuverable enough to use the fighter tactics of the time.

Three airplanes, all from the Curtiss company, would arrive in the next three years. They would shape Zemke's career and prepare him for a combat command. The first of these was the P-36. The second was the YP-37, a derivation of the P-36 equipped with an Allison in-line engine and a cockpit set far to the rear of the fuselage to balance the weight of the power plant. Only one XP-37 and thirteen YP-37s were procured, and while fast, they were very difficult to land, for the nose and the wing blanked out the pilot's view. The third aircraft was another P-36 hybrid, the P-40.

The first XP-40 was actually the tenth production P-36 mated to a 1,160-horsepower supercharged Allison V-1710 in-line engine, and first flown on October 10, 1938. After evaluation in May 1939, 540 were ordered, a staggering number for the budget-tight era, and one that established Curtiss as the premier builder of fighter planes in America. Great Britain also placed orders for the aircraft, calling it the Tomahawk. The airplane would eventually be used in every theater of war. In almost every engagement, it had to fight against more advanced aircraft, but it was strongly built, and when used with the correct tactics, could give a good account of itself.

The XP-40 was not yet a serious warplane, but production aircraft were successively modified with armor, self-sealing tanks, heavier armament, and all the other equipment necessary for modern warfare. The airplane's performance deteriorated with the additional weight, but it had the great advantage of being available, and was thus pressed into service everywhere.

Zemke already followed the practices that would make him successful as an ace and a commander. He immersed himself in the details of the new airplane, working on the line with the mechanics, just as Rickenbacker had done. It was not enough for him to become expert in flying the P-40—he wanted to see and understand its maintenance as well.

As a result, Zemke was selected to conduct an accelerated service test of the aircraft at Wright Field that led to the solution of some engine main-bearing longevity problems. His expertise came to the attention of Lieutenant Colonel Ira Eaker, who would win fame as commander of the Eighth Air Force in Great Britain. Eaker sent Zemke to Detroit to demonstrate the P-40 to the top engineers of the Ford Motor Company and to Henry Ford himself, with the object of getting Ford interested in converting the famed River Rouge plant to building airplanes. The ploy succeeded, and Ford eventually agreed to build Consolidated B-24 bombers.

Still ill at ease with those he considered his social or military superiors, Zemke was nonplussed by the personal attention he was receiving. He simply did not understand how much his outstanding work was appreciated. This lack of understanding may have compounded a natural truculence that manifested itself in being too outspoken. Often, where silence would have served him well, Zemke would speak his mind, and over the years, this tendency would cost him. Even when he received a plum assignment in February 1941, he still did not realize that it was clear evidence that he was regarded as a comer.

ENGLAND DURING THE BLITZ

Two old friends, Lieutenants Hubert Zemke and John Alison, were picked for the best job in the Air Corps, being sent to assist the Royal Air Force with the 1,180 Curtiss Tomahawks Great Britain had purchased. Because the United States was still neutral, it was necessary for the two men to go as "observers," although their mission was to instruct on the assembly and operation of the fighters.

After an introduction by the Germans to the Blitz on the night of their arrival, Zemke and Alison were sent to RAF Station Old Sarum, near Salisbury, the traditional Royal Air Force training area. While getting used to British customs such as having a personal batman, taking tea at regular intervals, and engaging in riotous barroom brawls in the Officers' Club, Zemke threw himself into the work of introducing the P-40 to the RAF.

In the process, he was shocked with the realization of just how far the warring powers had advanced and how totally unprepared the Air Corps was for combat. The RAF had been drubbed by the Luftwaffe during the Norwegian and French campaigns and had only begun to assert itself during the Battle of Britain. In the hard school of war, it had established a radar and ground-observer system for air defense that had tipped the balance against the Luftwaffe. In addition, it had established an efficient air-sea rescue service and a comprehensive flying control system that identified and tracked the flights of all British aircraft. An emergency homing system was also in use, one that permitted lost aircraft to be vectored to the best available base. The United States had nothing like any of these systems, and, in their role as observers, both Zemke and Alison made comprehensive reports through the Air Attaché.

Zemke got to fly many different British aircraft, and after a brief flight in a Spitfire he understood why the P-40 had been relegated to British Army Cooperation duties. The Spitfire climbed better, was faster, was more maneuverable, and had a much heavier armament. The British thought so little of the P-40 that they were happy to turn over 200 of them to the Soviet Union, an act of largesse that sent Zemke and Alison on a new and dazzling assignment.

MOY TOVARISCH

Told only that their new job was going to be top secret, Zemke and Alison were amazed to be ushered into the American embassy in London. There they were met by the Ambassador, John Wyant, and President Roosevelt's personal representative, Harry Hopkins. Also present were the head of the American Lend-Lease program and future ambassador to the Soviet Union, W. Averell Harriman, and Brigadier General Joseph McNarney. McNarney, who would go on to four-star rank, was one of the toughest, most capable officers in the newly reorganized United States Army Air Forces.

Zemke and Alison were stunned to find that they had been selected to go to the Soviet Union to help assemble the 200 P-40s supplied by Great Britain and train the Soviet pilots to fly them. The importance of the mission to future Allied relations was so great that they were being personally evaluated by some of the most powerful men in the government. Alison was to accompany Harriman and Hopkins by plane, while Zemke was to follow by ship.

The stark privations and primitive lifestyle of the Soviet Union were a revelation to both men. Zemke worked at Arkhangelsk with the same zeal he had displayed in England, and ignoring the cold, bedbugs, rough food, and enforced vodka toasting, proceeded to get an assembly plant for the P-40s into operation. There was virtually no equipment, and most of the heavy work was done through sheer manpower. The runway had been built by sinking a forest of pilings into the tundra's swamp, then laying huge smoothed timbers over them to create a smooth wooden platform for takeoff and landing.

Zemke admired the Soviet pilots for their skill and their pugnacious attitude, so similar to his own. They had little trouble transitioning into the P-40, and while they recognized that it was no match for the Messerschmitt, they did not care—they were just glad to have something to take into combat.

By December 1941 the German Army had advanced almost to Moscow, and Zemke and Alison were ordered to the capital to help evacuate embassy records. They were in Kuybyshev, more than 500 miles from Moscow, on December 7, 1941, when the Japanese struck Pearl Harbor. Both men immediately sought a combat assignment, and orders came through for Zemke to report to the brand-new 56th Fighter Group. Alison was to remain behind for the time being, but after a turbulent series of happenstance assignments he eventually went to the 75th Fighter Squadron in China, where he became an ace.

Zemke believed that he had been released first because he was married while Alison was single. The irony was that Zemke's marriage was not working out. He had dated very little up until the time he met a nineteen-year-old woman of Italian lineage on a quick trip to Florida. They were married in five days, but soon found out, in Zemke's words, that they were "incompatible." He attempted to have the marriage annulled, but could not. They were later divorced.

SWIFT PROMOTIONS

It took almost four months for Zemke to get to his new assignment because of the difficulties of wartime travel. To his distress, he found a desk job waiting when he arrived.

The 56th Fighter Group was one of many new organizations being formed by the rapidly expanding Army Air Forces. Unlike the Germans, who had a systematic way of forming cadres from parent units, the United States Army simply activated new units by decree, threw a handful of personnel at them, and then let nature take it course.

Even though the 56th was virtually a shadow organization, with only a few P-40s and Bell P-39 fighters on its strength, the three squadrons of the 56th were charged with the air defense of New York. Fortunately, the threat was nonexistent, as no Japanese carriers had appeared in the Atlantic, and the Germans had quite enough to do invading the Soviet Union.

Zemke protested his desk job and was rewarded with a promotion to captain and assignment as Operations Officer of the 56th. Besides running the Combat Operations center, with its map of New York and its plotters to show the movement of any enemy aircraft that might show up, one of his "additional duties" was training Chinese students to fly the P-36. The first job was pretty boring, but the second was filled with thrills, as all communication had to be accomplished through a translator. It was difficult enough on the ground, but downright hairraising when the Chinese pilot was in the air and experiencing difficulties.

Change and promotions came rapidly in wartime. After having been a lieutenant for five years, Zemke was promoted from captain to major to lieutenant colonel in just six months. Commands followed in a similar rapid progression. His first command was as the CO of the new 89th Fighter Squadron. Two weeks later he was given the command of the 56th Fighter Group. He would take it from a ragtag collection of individualists without operational experience to become the most successful fighter unit of the Eighth Air Force, scoring more total victories than any other outfit in the theater. In the process, he not only would become an ace, but also would devise the essential tactics that would enable many others to reach that august status.

FORMING UP THE 56TH

During World War II, one of the most demanding and rewarding tasks in the Army Air Forces was the command of a fighter group. The commander had to assemble a group of brand-new flight school graduates, all eager to become the Rickenbacker of World War II, and train them to fly in a disciplined but aggressive manner. On the one hand, the CO had to keep them from killing themselves in stupid accidents from flying under bridges, doing slow rolls on takeoff, or buzzing their hometowns, while on the other hand encouraging them to push the airplane to the maximum. During the training, and later in combat, the commander had to assess their performance under stress, to determine who was capable of command, and who had to be sent back to fly a less-demanding airplane. All through the process, he had to watch young men kill themselves with reckless abandon.

Besides all the problems in creating a new fighter unit from scratch, Zemke was faced with a unique task. He was also charged with the operational test and evaluation of a brand-new and quite radical fighter plane, the Republic P-47 Thunderbolt. No one had ever had such an assignment before, but Zemke would carry it out with the same drive and tenacious determination that made him a great middleweight champion and a great commanding officer. He took on the assignment with some apprehension, because while he felt the P-47 was better than the P-40, he was worried that its relatively slow rate of climb and acceleration would make it ineffective in its intended role as an interceptor.

The Thunderbolt, fondly called the Jug by its pilots, was the biggest, heaviest single-engine fighter to see combat in World War II. It was, in fact, the heaviest single-piston-engine fighter ever to enter production, because it ultimately reached a maximum operating weight of 21,200 pounds. Its rotund appearance and sheer mass contrasted sharply with the petite lines of the Spitfire or the Mustang, and many pilots automatically rejected it as a fighter on first sight. Those who flew it came to love it.

The origins of the P-47 lay with the Seversky P-35, an aircraft with pleasing lines and mediocre performance. The Seversky company had committed some grievous management errors, which led to its takeover in early 1939 by the Republic Aviation Corporation. Seversky's chief designer, Alexander Kartveli, was retained and given the task of meeting a new specification from Wright Field calling for a fighter of extremely high performance, fully equipped to the modern European standards of warfare.

Kartveli knew that to meet the performance goals, he needed the 2,000 horse-power provided by the new turbosupercharged Pratt & Whitney R-2800 radial engine. The Russian-born engineer literally designed the aircraft from the inside out, first laying out an efficient engine and turbosupercharger arrangement.

Aircraft engines were built to run at maximum power at sea level. Power was lost as the aircraft climbed into less dense air. Superchargers were used to restore rated power at altitude. Most foreign countries used internal mechanical super-chargers of one or two stages, sometimes fitted with an intercooling device. The United States, using pioneering work conducted by Sanford Moss at General Electric, tended to favor the turbosupercharger. In the turbosupercharger, an exhaust turbine drove a centrifugal compressor that increased the fuel-air mixture supplied to the engine.

The engine-turbosupercharger combination of the P-47 dictated its relative size and weight. The general outline of the aircraft followed that of the P-35, and it retained the capacious and graceful elliptically shaped wings. The Army approved of the design in September 1940, and a series of orders followed that saw the aircraft continually improved. Some 15,683 Thunderbolts were produced and about 10,000 reached overseas stations. Of these, 3,499 were lost in combat and another 1,723 were lost in accidents. Over time, the aircraft assumed many roles Kartveli had never contemplated, including reconnaissance, dive-bombing, level bombing, and long-range escort.

Zemke had the good fortune to be able to select three excellent captains to be his squadron commanders; they would be critical in molding the 56th. Loreen McCollum was an old friend and received the 61st Fighter Squadron. Dave Schilling, flamboyant but brilliant, was selected to head the 62d. Philip Tukey was very sharp and headed the 63d. All three would distinguish themselves in combat, but they first had to address the challenge of solving the P-47's teething problems. To do so, they used the unbridled talent of brand-new graduates of flight school, each one intoxicated with the prospect of flying such a hot fighter. The teething problems were eventually solved, but almost a score of bright new pilots died in the process.

Zemke faced exactly the same problems with the new pilots as had Ricken-backer. Young, delighted to be flying, and imbued with a collegiate spirit, they grossly overestimated their capabilities and were totally unaware of the harsh reality of air combat. They flew with the conviction that they and their planes were the best, and that they would prevail as an all-American team should prevail. Zemke had seen the same misplaced enthusiasm in some squadrons during his tour in England. He knew how many casualties they suffered and how quickly those casualties reversed the morale and dampened the fighting spirit. He also knew that words would not do the trick; that his young pilots would have to learn the hard way, in battle.

Some of the P-47's difficulties were typical of those of any new aircraft. The ignition harness gave problems, and the radios were almost impossible to use because of interference. The fabric surfaces of the rudder and elevator could be ripped off in a dive. The fabric was replaced by aluminum, and the problem was solved. The standard radio mast, made of wood, could not withstand the high diving speeds, and a metal fixture was substituted. One problem was new, encountered previously only on the equally radical Lockheed P-38.

In a terminal velocity dive, that is, at the greatest speed it could achieve, the P-47 would encounter compressibility. As it reached speeds near 500 mph, it reached a Mach number sufficiently near the speed of sound to cause the controls to be locked into position by the force of built-up air pressure. If power was reduced, it was sometimes possible to pull the aircraft out of the dive when it reached the higher density of lower altitudes. In too many instances, however, the end result of the dive was a smoking hole in the ground. It was a new phenomenon, one for which there was no easy fix, and one that was very likely to occur at the worst possible time—in combat.

On Thanksgiving Day, 1942, the 56th Fighter Group was alerted for transfer to Great Britain to enter combat. Zemke received the orders with a mixture of relief and apprehension. He wanted to get into combat, but he was very much aware that the 56th had had very little gunnery or formation flying practice, and no experience at all in bad-weather operations. Zemke ached with the knowledge of just how much the 56th had to learn. He hoped to live long enough to teach them—and to kill a few of the enemy in the process.

★ FIVE ★
ZEMKE BEATS THE SYSTEM

The course of the fighter air war in Europe had been reversed in just one year. In January 1941 Germany was attacking Great Britain, its fighters and bombers wreaking havoc on their long and hazardous round-trip flights across the English Channel. The Luftwaffe had shifted to night operations in large measure, but it still conducted some daytime bombing, especially "tip and run" raids by fighter bombers. In these, small formations of Messerschmitt Bf 109s or Focke Wulf Fw 190s, each carrying a single 250-kilogram bomb, would race across the Channel, drop their bombs, and race back. These raids had at most a nuisance value, and probably were of more value to the English as a training device than they cost in damage or casualties. Their importance to the Germans lay in providing the propaganda machine with something to say about the war against England.

By January 1942 Germany was locked in a death struggle with the Soviet Union, its armies frozen by the Russian winter. The Luftwaffe was fully occupied in this struggle, and only two fighter units were positioned on the coast of occupied Europe to defend against daylight incursions by the Royal Air Force.

These were the elite *Jagdgeschwader 26* ("Schlageter") and *Jagdgeschwader 2* ("Richthofen"). JG 2 derived its name from the famous eighty-victory ace of World War I, but JG 26's namesake was more obscure. Also a World War I veteran, Albert Leo Schlageter became a German hero by being shot by a firing squad for resisting the French occupation of the Ruhr. (JG 1 was stationed in northwest Germany and would not be heavily engaged until the U.S. Eighth Air Force daylight raids began to build up.)

The authorized strength of each of these units was about 120 single-engine Messerschmitts or Focke Wulf fighters. Actual strength varied, sometimes declining to 50 percent of the authorized strength. There were also about twenty Fw 190 fighter bombers used for the "tip-and-run" raids. Air Marshal Sholto Douglas now commanded RAF Fighter Command, and he, in Trenchard style, decreed that the Royal Air Force fighters had to earn their keep by raids on German-occupied territory. Fighter sweeps were called "Rhubarbs," while bomber missions with fighter escort were called "Circuses." Once again, as in World War I, Germany was letting "the customers come to the shop."

It was sensible Luftwaffe policy not to oppose the Rhubarbs and to attack only the Circuses that seemed to threaten their vital interests. Germany now had all the advantages that the RAF had exploited in the Battle of Britain. The incoming British aircraft were tracked by radio intelligence and by radar almost from takeoff. The Luftwaffe could choose when and where to fight, and usually with an altitude advantage. If a British pilot was forced to bail out, he became a prisoner, while German pilots were immediately returned to their units. And, not least, when the battle was over, the German planes had many airfields to land on, while the short-ranged Spitfires had to make the long flight back across the chill Channel, fuel warning lights winking red.

In terms of equipment, the Messerschmitts had a performance equal to the Spitfire V, while the new Focke Wulfs were clearly superior. Even though outnumbered seven to one, the Luftwaffe's tactics and planes enabled it to achieve a four-to-one victory ratio over the RAF. The biggest Luftwaffe success had come during the famous August 19, 1942, raid on Dieppe, where 106 RAF aircraft were lost, while only 48 German aircraft were shot down.

This was the milieu into which Zemke was to introduce his new wing of untried pilots and unproven airplanes. He was aware that the 56th had experienced rivals already in place, veterans of the famous Eagle Squadrons.

THE AMERICAN BUILDUP

Just as France had welcomed the Lafayette Escadrille, so had Great Britain welcomed the American Eagle Squadrons, and for much the same reasons. The additional strength in the air was appreciated, but the propaganda and morale value of having an American unit fighting the Germans was paramount.

Young Americans embraced the idea of volunteering to fly and fight for Great Britain, and no fewer than 49,000 applied to join what was originally just the

Eagle Squadron. Of these, 6,700 were accepted, but only a fraction of this number made it through the subsequent examination and training process.

The first unit, No. 71 (Eagle) Squadron, RAF, was formed on September 19, 1940, and went into action in the spring of 1941. The second Eagle Squadron, No. 121, was formed in May 1941 and entered combat in August. The last squadron, No. 133, was formed in August and went into battle in October. The Eagle Squadrons scored seventy-three victories in their air battles over Great Britain, France, North Africa, and Malta.

On September 12, 1942, the three Eagle Squadrons were assigned to the Eighth Air Force, becoming the nucleus of the 4th Fighter Group as the 334th, 335th, and 336th Fighter Squadrons. The 4th retained the Spitfire Mark Vs that it had flown with the RAF until April 1943, when, amidst cries of horror, they were replaced by P-47Cs. Led initially by veteran Eagle pilot Colonel Chesley Peterson, the 4th would go on to fly 447 combat missions, claiming 582½ aerial victories and the destruction of 469 aircraft on the ground. In the process, the 4th would lose 241 planes.

The 78th Fighter Group was the second American unit assigned to the Eighth Air Force, arriving on November 29, 1942, equipped with the much-sought-after Lockheed P-38 Lightning. After initially being used as a source of replacement planes and pilots for the war in North Africa, the 78th also converted to P-47s and went on to an illustrious career, flying 450 missions and claiming 338½ aircraft destroyed in the air and 358½ on the ground. It lost 167 aircraft in action.

THE LONG DRY BUILDUP

Zemke and the men of the 56th had endured the long workup period in the United States with patience, because they knew that they would soon be in England, and—they thought—in the thick of battle.

They found themselves instead in the thick of mud, fog, and bureaucratic delays. After a crowded but not unpleasant trip on the *Queen Elizabeth*, they disembarked at Gourock, Scotland, and proceeded to Kings Cliffe in the East Midlands. The aircraft began to arrive on January 24 and the next weeks were spent in bringing them to operational condition. As the airplanes came together, Zemke immersed the men of the 56th in learning the local geography, the RAF's methods of flight control, the British system for retrieving lost aircraft by radio direction, and other necessary if sometimes mundane matters. As they learned, they endured the piercing English winter and the wretched English food (beans on toast for breakfast never became a great favorite). Their difficulties were made easier to accept by the friendly reception of the British pub keepers and the welcome smiles of the British girls that led to the most famous British joke of the period, that the Americans were "overpaid, oversexed, and over here."

There is no little irony in the fact that many of the qualities that allowed Zemke to excel as a leader of men would work against him in his relations with officers of equal or superior rank. Like Rickenbacker, Zemke had an inferiority complex originating in his humble origins. Zemke's basic flaw was a lack of confidence that manifested itself almost immediately when faced with a person he considered to be of higher rank or greater refinement. Unlike Rickenbacker, who had learned to use charm and a big smile to overcome this sense of inferiority and win his point, Zemke's gut response was to argue, often in a blustering manner that cost him the friendship of the very people he needed most to help him. Where Rickenbacker sought and used mentors like Frayer or Lufbery with great profit, Zemke not only failed to seek them, he failed to recognize them when they offered to help. A secondary aspect of this personality quirk was a resentment amounting to suspicion of officers under him who were more outgoing and socially adept. This handicapped his judgment and caused him to hold back some officers, such as future ace Dave Schilling, when advancing them might have helped the 56th. On balance, these were minor deficiencies, but it was many years before Zemke recognized them.

His first problem occurred almost immediately. Colonel Lawrence Brower was commander of the 33d Service Group, which was responsible for the 56th's engineering and maintenance requirements. The 33d was an inexperienced unit, and Brower operated it on a peacetime, eight-hour-a-day basis. This was totally unsatisfactory for Zemke, who would always be a 24-7 man, and he had a long series of arguments with Brower, who was senior to him in age and rank. The twenty-eight-year-old Zemke privately regarded Brower as more sensitive and refined than he was himself, and was initially reluctant to bring about his replacement.

Zemke exacerbated the problem by storming into Ajax, as Bushey Hall, the headquarters for VIII Fighter Command, was called, and raising hell about Brower and other problems with the staff and the commander, Brigadier General Frank O. D. "Monk" Hunter. Zemke had little respect for staff officers, and while he admired Hunter's record as an ace in World War I, he was not convinced of his qualifications for command.

Hunter was the prototype of the dashing fighter ace, with a flowing mustache, piercing eyes, beautiful uniforms, and a reputation for being something of a ladies' man. Despite the glamorous appearance, he was not an outstanding combat commander and would in time be replaced.

Zemke's opening remark to the effect that Hunter had the lousiest staff he had ever seen was hardly the way to initiate the relationship. It was as stupid as it was unjustified, for the staff personnel were as much beginners in the business of the air war as Zemke, and they were the people who would decide many questions affecting him and his unit. They would learn, as he was learning, and eventually would do a first-rate job.

Hunter's response to Zemke was militarily correct. Zemke was to tell Brower, in writing, exactly what was expected of him. If Brower did not comply, he could then be replaced. In a single meeting, Zemke had thus set the tone for his relations with headquarters for the future, and probably sowed the seeds of discord that ultimately prevented him from becoming a general officer.

Fortunately, the personal traits that hurt him politically were offset by many other positive characteristics. These would enable him to become a leading ace and to fashion the 56th into the most outstanding group in the Eighth Air Force.

THE COMPETITION BEGINS

The first three American fighter groups—4th, 78th, and 56th—immediately fell into a competition with one another to score the most kills. The competition was so fierce that it sometimes seemed to be more important than the air war against Germany. There had been rivalries in World War I among the squadrons of the 1st Pursuit Group, but they never reached the perfervid intensity of their World War II counterparts.

The 4th had a great advantage in experience and equipment. Its pilots and mechanics were seasoned veterans, well experienced in the Spitfire. The missions assigned to it were within the aircraft's capability, and despite their groans, they were able to transition into the P-47 easily when the time came. The 78th was less fortunate. It was almost immediately apparent that although the relatively long-ranged Lockheed P-38 had excellent firepower and a good turn of speed, its Allison engines were not suitable for the humidity and temperatures of European skies.

As previously noted, the 78th was also hampered because its pilots (other than the flight leaders) and its planes were selected to replace the severe losses being incurred in North Africa. The acquisition of P-47s, while resisted at first, was soon recognized as a blessing in disguise. The 78th would illustrate the tremendous value of a good Group leader. Under Colonel Armand Peterson, the 78th became a premier fighting unit. When Peterson was shot down on July 1, 1943, the group went into a long decline.

The 56th was well trained, well equipped, and well led, yet despite Zemke's innate aggressiveness, it had difficulty in coming to grips with the Luftwaffe. Zemke had worked intensively with his RAF colleagues and had the benefit of the insight provided by Colonel Cass Hough, one of the unsung heroes of World War II. Hough ran an experimental unit at Bovingdon airfield, where he analyzed the results of comparison tests between the P-47 and captured German fighters. He would also be the prime instrument in the vital task of stretching the range of USAAF fighters as the war progressed.

Hough found that up to an altitude of 15,000 feet, either the Messerschmitt Bf 109 or the Focke Wulf Fw 190 was superior to the P-47C, especially in regard to the rate of climb. Above 15,000 feet, the P-47C could turn with both the 109 and the 190, if the airspeed was maintained above 200 mph. The German planes could outdive the P-47C initially but were soon overtaken. Thanks to Kartveli's masterful use of the turbosupercharger system, the P-47C became superior to both fighters between 25,000 and 30,000 feet, except in rate of climb and acceleration.

Zemke interpreted Hough's results and decreed that the P-47s were to avoid combat at low altitudes and speeds and were never to try to climb away, except after they had acquired the energy imparted by a long dive at high speed. The first victory for a Thunderbolt came on April 15, 1943. To Zemke's chagrin, it did not fall to him or even to the 56th, but to Major Don Blakeslee of the 4th, who destroyed an Fw 190 over Ostend. (When complimented about the superior diving abilities of the P-47, Blakeslee, a Spitfire advocate, replied, "By God it ought to dive, for it certainly won't climb.")

The failure to engage the Luftwaffe was not for lack of effort, because Zemke had his men in the air on every possible occasion. The Luftwaffe chose not to fight, because it did not wish to waste fuel and suffer losses in fighter-versus-fighter conflict. Within months, this would be seen to be a grave mistake by the Germans. Had the Luftwaffe attacked the fledgling American units with all the strength it could have mustered, it would have scored a great victory, because it was superior in experience and tactics. As events played out, the Luftwaffe essentially trained the American units over an extended period until their numbers and their skills became overwhelming.

During this initial period of drought, Zemke was viewed by his men with mixed emotions. He could be warm and receptive to ideas at one moment, then turn rigid and dogmatic the next. There lurked within him an atavistic desire to settle things with his fists, once expressed by his entering an enlisted men's boxing tournament under an assumed name. He fought as Corporal Billy Mills, the name he had used as a professional in the United States. "Mills" won his three-round match, and promptly received a rocket from General Hunter, who told him in no uncertain terms that officers did not enter enlisted men's boxing matches.

In marked contrast, Zemke's air leadership was impeccable. He saw to it that his squadron commanders rotated with him in flying as group leader, and he also made sure that he flew with each of the squadrons in turn to ensure that there was no preferential treatment.

Hard luck dogged him. Equipment problems caused him to abort two missions he was leading, and he became concerned that both his men and his headquarters would assume that he was fainthearted about combat. By early May, more than ninety days after the P-47s had begun arriving, the 56th's record was abysmal. It had shot down two aircraft—both Spitfires, unfortunately—and lost two P-47s. Hunter called him on the carpet to explain. Zemke was distraught, certain that he would be replaced as commander of the 56th. Then, in the mysterious ways of the armed services, he received a message on May 9, promoting him to the rank of Colonel and giving him a new lease on life.

The 56th did not get its first confirmed kill until June 11, when Captain Walter Cook shot down an Fw 190. The jinx was broken. On the following day, the 56th made a fighter sweep that resulted in the following report, which sums up in classic Zemke style the problems and the possibilities of combat in the P-47.

As a flying wing commander of the 56th Fighter Group on this mission, I had decided that I would lead the 61st Fighter Squadron as bouncing squadron. The 62nd Fighter Squadron was to be close escort at the same altitude and slightly to the rear. The 63rd Fighter Squadron was to be high cover for the other two squadrons with a superiority of 1,000–2,000 feet more or less to the inside of the course and slightly ahead where I could direct their direction and disposition.

[Zemke's iron hand is revealed in this paragraph; he wanted to lead the bouncing squadron, because it would be in the thick of the fighting.]

Take-off and climb of the squadrons was normal in that nothing of importance can be mentioned. The squadrons positioned themselves on the climb so that the 63rd was to the left and the 62nd was on the right. From Felixstowe to

Gravelines the course was 174 degrees through a thin layer of about 6/10 Cirrus clouds. This gave me considerable anxiety as the 56th Group was to give high support to the 4th Fighter Group. The layer being at 26,000 feet. At this time, which was about 09:30 plus hours, contrails were reported ahead going into France and were believed the 4th Fighter Group. Shortly thereafter, the Ground Operations reported bandits in the vicinity of Ostend heading west along the coast. Since the group had not reached France and were trying to give support to the 4th Group, who were only in visual contact by their occasional condensation trails ahead, it was decided to continue on plan.

[Contrails were the long white clouds caused by the condensation of vapor generated by the water content of the engine exhaust under certain atmospheric conditions.]

At about 09:35 hours, while still over water, the Ground Operations reported that twenty-plus bandits were in the Lille area, heading to the northwest (in our direction) altitude unknown.

When the coast was reached at 09:37 hours, a slight turn left was made placing the 63rd slightly ahead and well to the left, they having gained 2,000 feet of altitude over remainder of the group. Again Ground Operations gave me instructions that twenty-plus bandits were flying north-west at 20,000 feet in the vicinity of Ypres, this being due ahead of us on course.

["Bandits" was the radio expression for enemy aircraft. Zemke's keen situational awareness is apparent here. Long after the fight, after the mission debriefing, he can recall the events of the battle in intervals as small as two minutes.]

A split second later I looked ahead at 11 o'clock and down slightly toward a very large hole in the cirrus clouds and saw fifteen or twenty spots climbing in our direction. Some of these spots were leaving distinct vapor trails. They must have been fifteen or twenty miles away at the time. They, as well as us, never altered course but closed at a very rapid rate.

[Zemke's vision, like that of most aces, was exceptional, and he was effective in picking out the smallest moving dot at the greatest distance. When he speaks of closing speeds, the P-47s were probably operating at about 300 mph True Air Speed, while the Germans were climbing at perhaps half that speed. The closing speed would then be about 450 mph, and the interval of twenty miles would be covered in less than three minutes.]

When a distance of two or three miles between forces had been reached, I saw that they were flying in three groups of approximately six each in what would be called a company front formation. They were then below some three or four thousand feet and well to my left. The altitude of my squadron was 27,000 at that time.

[The use of the expression "company front" is interesting, for it was a tactic introduced by Captains Egon Mayer and Georg-Peder Eder of JG 2 in November 1942 to combat the firepower of the B-17 formations. It involved the German fighters following the B-17 formation, then passing it. They would then turn in on a head-on pass. It was effective and led to the installation of chin turrets on the B-17G.]

The squadrons were told that I was taking the first section of eight of the 61st Fighter Squadron in a left diving attack. It may be noted that I forgot to touch my throttle and it remained at 31 inches Hg manifold pressure and 2,550 rpm for the entire combat.

[Two things about Zemke are immediately obvious here. First, he is aggressive, going in to attack. Second, he is brutally honest, acknowledging that his nervousness made him forget to alter power as required. He could easily have "forgotten" this, and no one would have known. It was the first of several mistakes he would admit in the report.]

At first I dove to attack the lower lead unit but changed my mind and continued down to attack a group who were slightly to the rear and above the lead unit. As the attacking dive commenced the lead E/A group began turning to the right and the remainder to do likewise. This fact plus the fact that they never flew more than two or three lengths apart, leads me to believe that I was never seen but that all eyes were on the 63rd Fighter Squadron which was well to my left and directly over the hole in the overcast.

[The German leader apparently lacked Zemke's vision. In this paragraph, Zemke gently calls attention to the success of his tactical dispositions before the battle.]

As I approached the last of four enemy aircraft, directly astern, I noticed that the tail end aircraft had white stripes around the horizontal stabilizer and elevators. This made me hesitate for I thought these aircraft might have been P-47s coming out of France. Perhaps this hesitation helped me, for I closed to 150 to 200 yards before firing. There was no doubt in my mind then. To destroy this aircraft was a mere matter of putting the dot on the fuselage, and pulling the trigger. A split second after firing, the fuselage burst into flames and pieces of the right wing came off. I immediately went down to the right leaving the number three plane of the four aircraft string just ahead.

[Zemke's honesty surfaces again. He could well have condensed his report to ignore his concern about identifying the aircraft, and simply stated that he closed to 150 yards to fire. That he did not reflects his desire to use the report as a learning experience for others. In the past he had often berated himself for underestimating the distance to the enemy when he fired. "Putting the dot on the fuselage" refers to the illuminated spot of his gun sight, used to target the enemy aircraft. Firing for only a split second saved the machine gun barrels and saved ammunition for another attack.]

This plane must for some reason have been weaving so that I had to give it some deflection. The deflection proved to be a bit excessive and I noticed strikes out on the right wingtip. The plane being in a right bank went down placing me directly in back of the number two plane of the string, which sat in the gun sight as one would imagine for the ideal shot. Again, when the trigger was pulled this aircraft exploded with a long sheet of flame and smoke.

Unfortunately the number one man of the flight of FW 190s must have become aware of the unhealthy situation and left the scene of battle in a dive so I didn't see him go.

Each gun fired an average of fifty rounds in the three bursts mentioned above.

["Deflection" is the computed lead necessary to hit a moving target. Deflection shooting is difficult and the mark of the ace. His comments reflect the power of the eight .50-caliber guns of the P-47 and Zemke's austere use of them. A less experienced pilot might have fired off the 450 rounds available to each gun in such an attack. Zemke had a light finger on the trigger.]

Recovery was thereafter made due ahead to 26,000 feet where a slight turn to the left revealed that Dunkirk was directly down to the left. On looking over the sky again, everything was well broken up and miles away. Only two other P-47s were with me out of the sixteen first taken out. Combats were noted at great distances away so I ordered an assembly over Dunkirk. This was exceedingly difficult as the R/T was as nearly jammed with pilots reporting each other as E/A as can be imagined.

[The sixteen first taken out refers to the sixteen aircraft in the 61st Fighter Squadron that he led. R/T stands for radio transmitter and E/A for enemy aircraft. His reference is to the excited pilots who would call for their friends to break because of an enemy aircraft that was in fact another P-47. American radio discipline was generally good, far better than the Luftwaffe's, which was often described by German pilots as chaotic.]

The assembly point was moved out over the sea from Dunkirk as quite heavy anti-aircraft fire was put up over the area. The squadrons were then ordered home, since the E/A had gone to the deck and it was believed all organizations were disorganized. In reality the 62nd and 63rd Fighter Squadrons never entered battle. I had failed to call them down until too late.

The group continued to home base with the two above mentioned squadrons giving support and picking up my stragglers. I claim two FW 190s destroyed and one FW 190 damaged.

[Zemke is again being honest, although his failure to call the two squadrons down would undoubtedly have been revealed in the debriefing process. "Picking up my stragglers" refers to the 61st Fighter Squadron aircraft that got separated from him following his dive.]

Zemke was not the only member of the 56th to score, a fact that gave him some immediate problems. Lieutenant Robert Johnson, who had disobeyed instructions before, violated the most important rule in the fighter business when, as a wingman, he left his formation to attack a German fighter. He shot the Focke Wulf down, which undoubtedly tempered the chewing out that Zemke administered. Johnson would go on to become the first American pilot in the European theater to exceed Rickenbacker's twenty-six victory total and end the war with twenty-seven kills.

Zemke was a very tough disciplinarian, but he also had a sense of humor. He appreciated pilots who were aggressive and desired to mix it up with the enemy, and he was willing to give the benefit of the doubt to first mistakes. The young and promising Walker "Bud" Mahurin tried to fly too close to a B-24 and collided with it. Mahurin had to bail out, and the bomber barely made it back to its base. Zemke was furious and offered Mahurin the choice of a court-martial or a fine of $500. Mahurin gladly took the fine. It was a good call on Zemke's part, for Mahurin went on to become one of the top aces, scoring twenty victories before being shot down.

Zemke could be tolerant even when he was personally affected. On one mission, his new wingman left the formation and bolted back to England when the flight came under attack. Zemke's first instinct was to court-martial the culprit, but he allowed his squadron commanders to talk him out of it and gave the man a second chance—but Zemke never flew with the man as his wingman again.

It should be noted that the leader-wingman relationship was a special one. The leader did the shooting and the wingman was supposed to protect him from attack. The standard grisly instruction of a leader to a wingman was "If I fly into a mountain, there better be a hole right next to me where you hit."

AIR FORCES IN TRANSITION

The 56th's first victories signaled a transition point in the air war, one that gathered momentum as the days passed. The American air force would be continually reinforced with new and improved aircraft and provided with an unending stream of pilots who had from 375 to 450 hours flying time, and as many as 100 hours in the fighter they would use in combat.

In contrast, the Luftwaffe was in the beginning of a meltdown that would accelerate over the coming months as the strain of fighting on many fronts would bankrupt Germany's dwindling ability to train effective pilots. There was no shortage of planes, for Albert Speer, Germany's Minister of Armaments, had used Germany's immense industrial overcapacity to achieve a startling increase in German fighter production. The old standby Messerschmitt and Focke Wulf fighters were modified and improved over time, but the quality of their manufacture was in a steady decline.

The critical deficiency was in pilots. The Luftwaffe had no "fifty-mission" tour of duty; its pilots fought on until they were killed. The veterans, well trained and aggressive, melted away in the continual combat, until there were just a few "old stagers" on hand to carry on the brunt of the fighting. German flight training was repeatedly interrupted by the withdrawal of instructor pilots for combat missions, a reflection of *Reichsmarschall* Herman Goering's sophomoric "just do it" mentality. The training was handicapped by the poor weather that dogged Germany for much of the year, but the crucial element was the shortage of fuel that prevented students from receiving an adequate number of flight hours. German pilots began reporting to operational squadrons after only 130 hours or less of flying time. Later in the war, even this amount was reduced.

The operational units tried to mitigate the problem, but the demands of the war were so great that there was little time to train the novices in fundamental tactics. It was soon evident to Zemke and others that the Luftwaffe, when it appeared, had difficulty in forming up to attack the bombers and that it was becoming totally inept in the tactics necessary to win a one-on-one fighter engagement.

There was thus an ever-increasing margin of victory for American units as the Luftwaffe was ground down. In time, American aircraft roamed the skis over Germany with almost complete freedom, as if they were on training flights, while Luftwaffe units had to scuttle from base to base, attacking in secrecy, and continually fleeing from superior numbers. It should be noted that however severe the odds, the Luftwaffe never asked for quarter and fought as hard as it could with its limited means until the last day of the war. It is also worth noting that within its dwindling ranks there still dwelled the most expert, highest-scoring fighter pilots in history, and no American pilot could be sure when he would meet one of these superaces in combat.

THE LEARNING CURVE IMPROVES

Zemke began to introduce new tactics early in the campaign. Where in the past he had followed standard RAF practice in sending the 56th out in flights using the close "finger-four" formation, Zemke ordered that the two-plane elements be staggered 200 yards apart and the flights separated by 500 yards, in very loose formation. The squadrons flew 1,500 yards apart. The new arrangement was easier to fly, used less fuel, because it required fewer throttle adjustments, and provided better visibility and more flexibility in the event of an attack. The change was just a small step, but it caused immediate comment. When it proved to be useful, Zemke's stock went up. His increase in confidence also enabled him at last to fire his 33d Support Group commander, Brower.

There was still much to learn. On June 30, 1943, the 56th flew a bomber support mission led by its Flying Executive Officer, Captain Loren MacCollum. The Luftwaffe attacked from above and shot down four aircraft flown by some of the unit's most experienced pilots. Four other pilots barely made it home, their aircraft completely shot up. Two German aircraft were claimed destroyed, but it was a bitter day.

The only bright spot of the debacle was a long-running battle that proved just how tough the P-47 was. The future ace Robert Johnson had been hit by the Focke Wulfs in their first pass, 20-mm cannon shells tearing great chunks out of the Thunderbolt, stunning Johnson and setting the plane on fire. Johnson attempted to bail out and found that the shells had jammed his canopy; it could not be opened no matter how he struggled.

After spinning down several thousand feet, the barely conscious Johnson finally got the P-47 under control and began limping for the coast at 170 mph, hoping to be able to crash-land in England, where a rescue crew could pry him out before the airplane burned.

As he was about to cross the French coast, another Fw 190 pulled in close behind him and began firing. Johnson was a sitting duck, unable to maneuver. He could feel the shells thumping into the fuselage and into the armor plate behind his back. Somehow, the Thunderbolt kept flying, and the German pilot pulled up and flew formation with Johnson, staring across the ten yards that separated them, then saluting. For a brief moment, Johnson thought that the German was being chivalrous. Instead he pulled back behind the P-47 and began firing again at point-blank range, with Johnson trying to squeeze himself into the smallest possible ball behind the armor plate.

The German returned to fly formation with him, shaking his head at the damaged P-47, amazed that it could stay in the air. He then circled back to fire the last of his ammunition. When his guns ran dry, he pulled in formation with Johnson for the last time, saluted once more, and left.

Johnson managed to get the airplane to his home field and make a safe landing. The aircraft never flew again, but it showed once and for all just how rugged the Thunderbolt was.

THE 56TH TURNS INTO ZEMKE'S WOLFPACK

As his confidence grew, Zemke introduced still more new tactics. He now ordered that the 56th fly 5,000 feet above the bomber formations they were escorting. This contradicted the standing instructions from VIIIth Fighter Command that the escort fighters stay close to the bombers. And instead of the standard tactics of peeling off individual flights to attack incoming German planes, Zemke now decided that the entire squadron, forty-eight aircraft, should attack en masse.

There were no immediate returns on his new tactics. The 56th still trailed the 4th and 78th Fighter Groups in victories, and this ate at Zemke's fighting soul. Like Rickenbacker, he was born with a desire to succeed. Determined to have a disciplined unit in the air and on the ground, Zemke insisted on continuous training, and it cost him popularity within his own Group and at Headquarters. His pilots objected to the Zemke demands for perfection and Headquarters criticized him for using too much fuel on training flights. He did not care; he knew he was right and he persisted.

His first big break came on a bad day for the Eighth Air Force. On August 17, 1943, a two-pronged attack by Eighth Air Force bombers was made on the ball bearing factories at Schweinfurt and the Messerschmitt factory at Regensburg. Both targets were well beyond the range of escort fighters, and the Luftwaffe was up in strength. Of the total of 168 bombers that got over the target at Schweinfurt, 36 were lost and 118 were damaged. Of the 127 bombers that made it to Regensburg, 24 were lost and 50 were damaged. It was one of the worst defeats in Eighth Air Force history, as the Germans established air superiority over their territory. The damage to the Germans was substantial, with ball bearing production reduced from 140 tons in July to 50 tons in September, but the Germans compensated by purchasing ball bearings from Sweden and using other types of bearings in less critical applications.

Yet for the 56th, it was a field day. The P-47s were equipped with a bulky 200-gallon, bathtub-shaped auxiliary tank that gave them an extra thirty minutes over enemy territory. On the afternoon of August 17, the mission of the 56th was to provide escort for returning Schweinfurt bombers at the Dutch border. Zemke led his group into Germany, where he surprised a swarm of German fighters attacking the B-17s. The Germans did not expect a fighter escort so far inland, and had massed the slow and vulnerable twin-engine Messerschmitt Bf 110 fighters in the attack.

The 110s had originally been intended to be long-range escort fighters, but were inadequate for the role. Their mission was changed to night fighting, and in this they proved to be excellent. Flown by highly experienced pilots and radar operators, the 110s were too valuable an asset to be used in daytime operations, for which they were unsuited. Once again the Luftwaffe leadership tried to show its zeal by equipping the 110s with air-to-air rockets and throwing them into battle in the daytime, where they could not hope to survive in air combat. The 56th helped prove the point.

Zemke's Thunderbolts fell on the unsuspecting Messerschmitts like wolves on a flock of sheep. All three squadrons engaged the enemy and knocked down seventeen in the space of a few minutes. Zemke scored his third victory, while the previous week's bad boy, Mahurin, got two. (Headquarters staffers were nonplussed when the paperwork for Mahurin's fine was followed by paperwork recommending him for a Distinguished Flying Cross.) Another future ace—and future Lieutenant General—Captain Gerald W. Johnson shot down three of the enemy. The 56th had suffered three losses. (Johnson proved to be a good name for an Army Air Forces ace. The 56th's own Robert S. Johnson scored twenty-seven victories; Gerald R. Johnson got twenty-two victories in the Southwest Pacific theater; and four other Johnsons, Arthur, Clarence, Donald, and Evan, each scored five or more victories.)

The jinx had been broken. Two days later the Group was again engaged, and this time nine Germans were brought down. Gerry Johnson scored his fifth victory, making him the first ace in the 56th. Zemke's emotions were mixed; he had wanted to be the 56th's first ace, but he was happy for Johnson and happier still that all of his efforts were now obviously paying off.

Zemke was running his organization at a double level of risk. The first was that of air combat. The second was the possibility of court-martial for failing to carry out orders exactly as written. Every directive from VIII Fighter Command called for the fighters to stay close to the bombers. Under General Hunter's leadership, the official mission of VIII Fighter Command was to bring the bombers home. This was interpreted as flying so close to the bombers that enemy aircraft would have to attack the fighters first.

This sounded all right in the headquarters briefing rooms, but it was wrong in the air. Hermann Goering had made exactly the same mistake during the Battle of Britain. When the fighters were tied to the bombers' coattails they had to fly slower and weave to stay with them. This used up fuel faster and handicapped them when the enemy fighters attacked. Further, it was always possible for the opposing fighters to position themselves so that they could attack the bombers and ignore the protective fighters.

Zemke knew this and rebelled. He began taking his unit farther and farther away from the bombers, trying to catch the Germans as they were assembling for an attack. As long as he got results—and as long as bombers were not shot down in his absence—he was safe. But if, as could easily happen, he missed the German fighters and they caused heavy casualties to the bombers he was supposed to be protecting, he would be fired on the spot.

Despite his reputation as an authoritarian commander, Zemke demonstrated that he trusted his squadron commanders, delegating responsibility to them in the air and giving them authority to conduct aggressive operations as they saw fit. The pilots were unaware of it, but this gnawed at Zemke's controlling soul. He liked to run everything, and delegating authority in the air was difficult for him. On a personal level, it also denied him many opportunities to score, and in effect, kept him from being an ace for a protracted period. This was a true sacrifice on his part, done in the knowledge that it was good for the unit.

Zemke's escort tactics grew more flexible as events proved them to be correct. Typically, he would position one squadron on each side of the bomber formation. These squadrons would separate into two units, each one with two flights of four aircraft. The two units on each side of the bomber formation would fly at different altitudes, providing better coverage and a much better chance to detect the enemy. The third squadron was designated as a "freelance" unit to fly a few miles ahead of the group. The freelance unit was also a mobile reserve, ready to reinforce either of the flanking squadrons. Zemke preferred to fly with the freelance unit, for it had the best chance to score, but he religiously rotated this duty with his Flying Executive Officer and the various squadron commanders. He knew they wanted to become aces as much as he did. It was the mark of a great commander—few Group leaders were as careful to share the opportunities to score as Zemke was.

Nor were many as modest as he was. Most pilots named their personal aircraft, and when Zemke was asked by his crew chief, Sergeant Joe Froncek, what name he wanted on the P-47, Hub chose *"Moy Tovarish,"* Russian for "My Comrade." Later, however, he decided that the name and his victory markings were too showy for a group commander, and he had them painted out.

ZEMKE BECOMES AN ACE

In later life, Zemke described himself as an indifferent pilot and a poor shot. He was neither of course, but in his mind's eye he was comparing himself to the best he knew in both categories, a habit of his. Yet he was in truth not a meteoric success as an ace. Zemke was far more important as a Group Leader than he was as an individual killing machine and was recognized as such by VIII Fighter Command Headquarters. In September 1943 General Hunter had been replaced by Major General Ira Kepner, whom Zemke had known at Langley Field before the war.

Kepner and his staff saw Zemke as "force multiplier," recognizing that his presence and leadership multiplied the effectiveness of his group to a far greater degree than would have been the case if he had just sought victories for himself. Ironically, he was unable to sense the esteem in which he was held, perhaps because of his frequent arguments with Headquarters. They accepted this as an idiosyncrasy, just as they took his arguments as one of the characteristics of a good commander, one who was willing to go to bat for his unit with anyone.

The Luftwaffe was still tough and aggressive and on September 2, Zemke was almost shot down by an unseen German assailant who had used his own tactics. The German fighter had stalked Zemke and then had made a quick dive out of the sun, pumping his P-47 with shell fire. Before Zemke could react, the German was gone, disappearing in the mists below.

The attack had blown a huge hole in his wing that forced him to apply strong aileron control to counteract it. The roar of the huge Pratt & Whitney engine stopped, replaced by a virtual silence, the sound of the wind over the canopy mixing with the crackle of the radio. Zemke established a glide, hoping that the German would not return to finish him off. He went through the standard drill to restart his engine, checking the fuel, but there was no response. He got ready to bail out, checking his parachute harness, making sure he had no documents with military information and disgusted with the prospect of becoming a prisoner of war. Without any warning, the propeller suddenly began ticking over and the engine regained power. Zemke realized the enemy attack must have knocked out his turbosupercharger. When he had glided to a low enough altitude, the engine was able to run again and carry him back to England.

Like a thrown rider getting back on a horse, Zemke was determined to fly the next day. High over Romilly, France, he saw a group of Focke Wulfs forming up to attack the B-17s the 56th was escorting. Calling for his flight to follow him, Zemke arced over in a dive that placed him between the sun and the still-unsuspecting German fighters. He fired at 400 yards, then drove on in to fire again. The Fw 190 in his sights caught fire, and the rest of the enemy formation dove for the deck. It was his fourth kill, and the taste to be an ace was hot in his mouth. It would be almost a month before he succeeded.

PERSONAL PERSONNEL PROBLEMS

In the meantime, one of Zemke's biggest problems was the penchant of VIII Fighter Command Headquarters to siphon off the people he had trained—and now depended on—for promotion to head other units. He resented what he considered an invasion of his authority, instead of seeing the situation in its positive light. Headquarters obviously liked what he was doing and wanted people he had trained to lead other units. His 56th had become a "repot-depot" in the term of the time, a source of qualified replacements for the many new units being formed in the Eighth and Ninth Air Forces. Had Zemke a modicum of introspective confidence, he would have accepted this as a sign that he was admired and his work was appreciated by the very staff with which he had so many fights.

All of his misgivings were submerged in the joy of the October 2, 1943, sortie on which the 56th escorted B-17s to Emden, a 250-mile journey to the limit of the P-47's range. The mission was uneventful until the return, when Zemke spotted a lone Focke Wulf trying to attack a crippled B-17. His first shots, fired from a longer distance than usual, apparently killed the pilot, for the Fw 190 flew on in a straight line. Zemke closed the range and fired until the enemy plane rolled into a vertical dive.

It was his fifth victory. He was formally an ace, the second in the 56th, and he savored the triumph. It was more than vainglory. Leading a fighter unit was hard work, and being an ace made it easier. He knew now that he could demand even more from his men, and they would respond without any gripes. In a very meaningful way, the title of ace was the hard currency of the air war. If you possessed it, your credentials were established.

To his great credit, he put out of his mind the question of becoming the Rickenbacker of World War II, the American Ace of Aces. In his position as Group Commander, he could have arranged his schedule to take the missions that were likely to be most productive. As air commander, he could have positioned himself to have the greatest chance to score. But he did not, placing the morale and the achievement of the group above his own very real desires. A lesser man might not have.

He was also brutally honest with himself. Zemke knew that the combination of his duties and the raw talent of men such as Mahurin; of the two Johnsons, Robert and Gerry; or of the likeable Francis "Gabby" Gabreski made it unlikely that he would win an individual scoring contest. Instead, he determined that the 56th would become the top-scoring group in the Eighth, and he bent every effort to that effect. To his immense chagrin, he would find himself taken out of the contest at its height. In his absence, a decision was made for the 56th that would be almost fatal to his hopes. In the process, he would blight his postwar career with a typical Zemke "head for the sound of the guns" action.

UNWANTED VACATION AND CRUCIAL CAREER DECISION

Major General Ira Eaker, the Commander of the Eighth Air Force, selected a small group of officers to return to the United States under the leadership of a rising star, Brigadier General Curtis LeMay. Their task was to tell the story of the achievements of the Eighth Air Force, which had come under considerable criticism within the United States Army Air Forces. The Commanding General, Henry H. "Hap" Arnold, was an old friend and writing collaborator of Eaker, but he was not satisfied that the Eighth Air Force was getting the maximum effectiveness from its resources.

Eaker was in a difficult position. The Eighth had been continually drained of its resources to supply other theaters and was only just beginning to gather the strength necessary to have an impact in the war. No one had realized the effect that adverse weather would have on an air campaign, nor just how amateurish the preparations for the conflict had been. Eaker knew that the Eighth, with its limited strength, had begun to wear down the Luftwaffe and that it was becoming more proficient every day. Thus the trip to the United States was an immensely important assignment in Eaker's eyes.

For all of his hard-boiled, two-fisted demeanor, in some respects Zemke was a naïf. Zemke saw his invitation from Eaker as merely another attempt to take a leader away from the 56th. When his protests were rebuffed, he extracted a promise that at the end of the visit he could return to command the 56th.

Zemke was sometimes too human. He wanted to return to the 56th so much that he was reluctant to recommend the most qualified man for the job, his Flying Executive Officer Major Dave Schilling, to succeed him in his absence. He rationalized that Schilling, although an ace, was too impulsive, and the 56th would be better off with a steadier, if less talented, leader. His reasoning was disingenuous; he really did not wish to leave Schilling in command because he might do too well and jeopardize Zemke's return. Instead, Zemke recommended Colonel Robert Landry for the job, based on his administrative ability, and Kepner accepted the recommendation. Landry had little experience with combat or the P-47, and Schilling was going to have to lead the air war—but as second in command.

It was an insulting decision, one that naturally galled Schilling. Hub let his past resentment of Schilling's good-natured exuberance and his sometimes excessive drinking play too large a role in the decision. It was not the first time that Zemke had been less than fair to Schilling—he had initially passed him over for the position of Flying Executive Officer—and it would not be the last.

While waiting in London to depart to the United States, Zemke found that the 56th had a mission scheduled on November 5, which Schilling would, of course, lead. Hub bolted from London, arriving at the 56th just as Schilling was about to conduct the mission briefing. With total insensitivity, he grounded Schilling for the day and reassumed command of the group. The mission went off well, and the 56th scored six victories, one of the Focke Wulfs falling to Zemke's guns. The day's total brought the 56th score to 101 victories, by far the largest in the VIII Fighter Command. It was a triumph that should, by all rights, have gone to Dave Schilling.

To his great credit, Schilling accepted the situation with as good a grace as could be mustered and went on to perform well for Landry, leading the 56th in the air if not in title.

The tour in the United States went very well, and Zemke at last understood the importance of his selection. At the conclusion of the tour, he found to his abject horror that his orders had been changed. Instead of going back to command the 56th, he was assigned to the 1st Air Force at Mitchel Field in New York, working for his newly promoted old boss, Major General Monk Hunter!

Zemke attempted to fight the orders, eventually calling Hunter himself and asking that they be changed. Hunter, probably with some sense of revenge, refused, saying that he had personally arranged it with General Arnold himself.

Zemke had not as yet received written orders for the new assignment. Clutching his old orders in his hands, he secured a ride in a C-54 back to Scotland, then took a train to VIII Fighter Command Headquarters. They were surprised to see him, for word of his transfer to Hunter's staff had already reached them. Zemke was absent without leave. He had deserted his post in wartime and was a prime candidate for a court-martial.

He was allowed to present his case to General Kepner, who knew a hot potato when he saw one. Kepner ordered Zemke to get out of sight, and Zemke spent seven days on leave in Edinburgh, his present career hanging in the balance and his future irreparably damaged.

Kepner knew that few commanders could resist the story of a soldier who wanted to fight and managed to smooth the situation over. Zemke (to Schilling's undoubted dismay) was reassigned to command the 56th. He would lead it to its greatest moments of glory, inventing new tactics and scoring eleven more victories. And he would do it all without ever realizing that his failure to obey orders had scuttled his chances to become a general officer. Had he known at the time, he would not have cared; later in life, it would mean much to him.

A POOR DECISION

Ironically, in selecting Landry as his replacement commander, Zemke had outfoxed himself. The remarkable North American P-51 Mustang was now being produced in great numbers, and Zemke knew that this airplane, with its great range and other outstanding characteristics, would become the premier air-superiority fighter. He wanted it for the 56th, so that his group could range ever deeper into Germany and do most of the air-to-air fighting.

The Mustang was one of those rare happy hybrids. Originally powered by a twelve-cylinder Allison engine, the P-51 was fast but lacked high-altitude performance. A decision was made to mate the airframe with the superb Packard-built Rolls Royce Merlin engine, and the result was the most outstanding piston-engine fighter of World War II. With its laminar flow wing and its very advanced low-drag radiator system, the Mustang had a greater range than all other U.S. fighters. It could fly 700 miles into combat with external tanks that were soon supplemented by an additional eighty-five-gallon internal fuselage tank. With

external tanks, it could fly anywhere in Germany and when engaged still be superior to the German fighters. Hermann Goering was supposed to have remarked
that when he saw the Mustangs over Berlin, he knew the war was lost.

Its disadvantages were few when compared to the P-47. With only six .50-
caliber machine guns, it had slightly less firepower, and its liquid-cooled engine
and radiator system were more vulnerable than the big radial engine of the Thunderbolt. It was much more susceptible to damage in ground strafing, because a
single bullet through the coolant system would cause the engine to seize within
minutes. Zemke knew these disadvantages and considered them minor compared
to the Mustang's greatest advantage: its ability to get out in front and force the
Luftwaffe to fight.

Yet, while Zemke was in the United States, Landry, probably influenced by
Schilling, declined the offer of transitioning the 56th to the Mustang, preferring
to stay with the "tried and true" P-47. The Mustang did indeed take over most of
the air-to-air combat as the war progressed, while the P-47 was relegated to the
ever more dangerous role of ground support.

As the German fighter force was ground down, the Luftwaffe vastly increased
the number of its antiaircraft artillery batteries. (In a fit of pique at the Luftwaffe's
failure to stop the bombing raids, Hitler at one point demanded that Albert Speer
stop the production of all aircraft and produce antiaircraft weapons exclusively
for the defense of German airspace. Speer pointed out that you could not shift the
light metals of aircraft making to the heavy steel of the antiaircraft industry.)
Some airfields, particularly those from which the new German jet fighters operated, had so many flak emplacements that the guns could cordon off the glide path
for landing aircraft, putting up a sheer wall of fire to fend off Allied intruders.

Of all the aircraft in the USAAF's inventory, the Thunderbolt's rugged structure and great load-carrying capability made it the best for the ground-attack
task. For Zemke, however, the glory lay in shooting down enemy fighters, not
strafing their airfields. To his great credit, he was able to keep the 56th in the
lead of victories scored in the air while at the same time evolving new and more
effective tactics for the ground-attack work.

Part of Zemke's success resulted from improvements made to the P-47. It was
modified to have a water injection system for increased power for limited periods.
A brand-new "paddle-blade" propeller was installed. The wide blades could absorb
more of the engine's power and gave the airplane a much better rate of climb.

Zemke continued to fight for the escort role; when he received it, he com-
plained to Ajax that the 56th was being relegated to areas where the German

fighters were less likely to be found. Fortunately for his hopes, Major General James Doolittle had succeeded Ira Eaker as Commander of the Eighth Air Force and revised the mission of the fighters from bringing the bombers home to destroying the enemy fighter force wherever it could be found, in the air or on the ground.

This was a far more effective strategy, and it validated Zemke's clandestine tactics of ranging far out in front of the bomber force. It also permitted the fighters to operate at lower altitudes where the Luftwaffe had previously not been aggressively pursued. The change enabled Zemke personally to begin scoring more rapidly in the air and on the ground even as it allowed him to lead his unit to greater victories.

The 56th now boasted a stable of high-scoring aces. Bud Mahurin, who had a choir boy's face and a total lack of ego, had scored fifteen victories. The difficult-to-discipline Bob Johnson had fourteen, and Francis "Gabby" Gabreski had eleven. Schilling had nine victories, while Zemke was less than content with his total of six. More satisfactory to Zemke was the fact that by January 30, 1944, the 56th had scored 200 air-to-air victories, while its nearest rival, the 4th, had scored just over 100.

The month of February marked the beginning of the end for the Luftwaffe, as Doolittle's fighters and bombers set out to destroy it. The removal of the Luftwaffe as a fighting force was essential for the coming invasion, and every unit was taxed to the utmost. The Luftwaffe's only recourse was to fight selectively. It would stand down, husbanding its waning strength, and attack only when weather, fuel, and circumstances permitted.

ZEMKE: SCORING IN THE AIR AND ON THE GROUND

February was a watershed both for the Luftwaffe and for Zemke. He now accepted that the P-47s were going to be assigned the less desirable missions and that it was up to him as leader of the 56th to maximize the performance of the aircraft in that role. To do so, Zemke devised tactics to exploit every new technological advance. He recognized that given the reduced state of Luftwaffe effectiveness, he could now cruise into battle at reduced throttle and turbosupercharger settings. This, with the improved 108-gallon drop tanks (see appendix 4), raised the Thunderbolt's endurance to three hours, more than double its original capability. As soon as the necessary shackles and fittings were ready, he saw to it that there was a 108-gallon tank strapped under each wing. He enabled the group to fly protective cover for the bombers with the tanks still attached and still have the fuel available to make low-level attacks on the return trip home.

P-47s were pouring into England, along with the pilots to fly them, and the 56th's strength was increased from 75 to 108 aircraft. This permitted two formations (A and B), consisting of three squadrons of three four-plane flights each, to be sent out on each mission. The new tactics were essentially a net that Zemke cast wide, trying to catch the declining numbers of Luftwaffe fighters in the air.

The 56th's catch was good on January 30, when the Germans appeared in force only to lose seventeen aircraft. Mahurin's single victory brought his total to fifteen, while Bob Johnson hammered two to raise his total to twelve. Gabby Gabreski, whom Zemke had taken after he had been rejected by two other groups because of his seniority, also got two and raised his total to ten. Quiet and unobtrusive, Gabby was a rising star who ultimately would be the top scorer in the European Theater of Operations.

The phenomenon of the rarity of aces was now clearly demonstrated. While a very few were running up double-digit scores, the majority of the other fighter pilots in the 56th (as in all units) not only did not score, they rarely engaged, and some never even saw a German plane. Many of these zero-score pilots were dedicated warriors but were flying as wingman. Their job was not to shoot, but to protect. Some were simply unlucky—they never happened to be in the right place at the right time. Others may have lacked the blood lust—or conversely, had a shade too much "common sense"—to become involved in a life-or-death battle.

There was one unequivocally clear sign that differentiated the aggressive pilots from those less so. The nominal combat tour was 200 hours. Upon request, the tour could be extended once for fifty hours, and then again for another twenty-five hours. The aggressive pilots extended their tours; their less aggressive colleagues did not.

Zemke soon found an outlet for his own aggression in ground strafing German airfields. He made his first attempt on February 11 and destroyed a Bf 109 sitting in the open. Zemke quickly realized that ground strafing was far too hazardous to do on an ad hoc basis and determined to develop tactics that would minimize the danger as much as possible. He knew there was no way to eliminate it.

Knowing the layout of the German fields was essential to determine where the flak batteries were, if there were any high-tension wires or other obstacles, and where terrain could be used to mask both the attack route in and the even more dangerous escape route out. German airfields were photographed by reconnaissance planes on a regular basis, but there was a long delay in getting the results out to the squadrons. The German system of moving units from airfield to airfield often rendered the photographs obsolete. Zemke took matters into his own hands and had a K-25 aerial camera bolted at right angles to the armor plate behind the seat of his new P-47-D-25 "Superbolt." This latest version of his favorite fighter had a clear "bubble" cockpit canopy and an extra sixty-five gallons of internal fuel. To use the camera, Hub would descend over the area he wanted to reconnoiter and fly over it in knife-edge flight, his wing pointed straight at the ground. Pressing a button on his control stick took the pictures, which were developed as soon as he landed. This was pure Zemke: see a task that needed to be done and figure a way to do it, ignoring red tape and the bureaucracy.

These "homemade" photos of German airfields were studied intently, and the routes in and out were carefully planned. Usually, the first man in had the benefit of surprise, while the later flights caught the most hell from the antiaircraft guns. Even with these precautions, it was extremely hazardous work. Casualties were heavy, and the 56th would lose some of its top people in attacks on airfields.

The weather over Europe improved during the third week in February, and on the February 20 the 56th initiated what became known as "Big Week," with a seventy-two-plane effort. Using new oval cross-section 150-gallon belly tanks, the 56th penetrated to Hanover, over 350 miles from its home base at Halesworth.

Zemke had positioned Gabby Gabreski and the 61st squadron ranging out in front, and they dove down to surprise twenty of the hapless Messerschmitt Bf 110s assembling for an attack. The 61st claimed eight shot down and ten damaged, but postwar reports revealed that all eighteen had been lost. The other planes of the 56th scored six additional victories.

It is worth noting that while the claims of the gunners on USAAF bombers were wildly exaggerated, sometimes by as much as a factor of ten, the fighter claims were usually fairly accurate. The gunners' claims were high because in the wild melee of battle, as many as a dozen gunners might be shooting at a single German fighter; if it went down—or looked like it might go down—each of the twelve claimed it with complete honesty and confidence. In contrast, most fighter pilots had to validate their claims by means of gun camera evidence or else by very credible witnesses.

The odds had shifted so heavily in the favor of the VIII Fighter Command that central Germany was now called the Happy Hunting Ground. By the end of Big Week, the 56th claimed seventy-two victories for the loss of two aircraft, an incredible 36-to-1 victory ratio. Ironically, most of the comparatively small damage inflicted on the 56th's aircraft came from their running into the debris of exploding German planes.

The press picked up on the 56th's exploits and began writing glowing stories about "Zemke's Wolfpack." Although he professed to deplore the publicity, Zemke knew that it was good for morale back home and that it provided an incentive for the people who were working so hard for him.

He was more than a little disappointed in his own score that had stood at seven since November 5. Things improved on March 6, 1944, the day the Americans made their first full raid on Berlin. Zemke was leading the A group of the 56th near Dummer Lake, a large body of water that was used by both Allied and German forces as an unmistakable geographic landmark. By now the German sky and landscape were as familiar to Zemke as his Montana home, and he knew where the German aircraft would be prowling.

Constantly scanning the sky, Zemke picked out the fleeting shape of an Fw 190 moving into position to attack a returning Fortress formation. Zemke signaled the attack and peeled off, the elliptical wings of the P-47s glinting in the sun. He hurtled down, letting the Thunderbolt's speed and weight accelerate and coming so close to the enemy that he could get off only fifty rounds into a Focke Wulf Fw 190 before pulling up to avoid a collision. The fifty were enough, for the 190 rolled over into a dive, headed for the ground.

Within minutes, he spotted a Messerschmitt and promptly dispatched it with the same tactics. Moments later, he was positioning himself for an attack on another Bf 109 when it suddenly burst into flames and went spinning to the ground. Zemke had not fired a shot at it, and there was no one else in the area. He could only presume that it had been fleeing from another engagement and finally caught fire. He did not claim it.

When the Luftwaffe stayed on the ground, the Eighth Air Force fighters would drop down to brave the incredible flak ringing the airfields to shoot up aircraft parked in revetments or in hangars. On the way back to England, the fighters would strafe anything vaguely resembling a military target, including factories, locomotives, canal barges, barracks, staff cars, and couriers on bicycles.

The results were phenomenal. No one had predicted that the fighter attacks would be the last nail in the Nazi industrial coffin. The tremendous bombing of German manufacturing centers by the Eighth Air Force during the day and by the Royal Air Force at night had forced the Germans to disperse their industry into hundreds of smaller factories making standardized components. The components were then moved to centers where they would be assembled into completed aircraft, trucks, and other complex weapons. Despite the additional transportation required, the system actually raised production of almost every weapon, including fighter aircraft, to a peak in 1944.

It was only when the fighter-bombers systematically destroyed the road, rail, and canal transport of the component parts that German industry at last lurched to a halt. Zemke indulged his own pugnacious nature by specializing in railroad trains. His gun camera revealed the destruction of more than sixty locomotives and innumerable freight cars, trucks, barges, and other means of transport. They also revealed the hail of antiaircraft artillery fire and the wild explosions of ammunition and fuel through which he routinely flew.

THE 56TH ASCENDANT

Zemke had now molded the 56th into a disciplined killing machine that was joined by other VIII Fighter Command units to destroy the Luftwaffe. Zemke scored only intermittently, destroying three in May and June, two in September, and getting one half credit for a victory in October. Yet it was during this period that he made his greatest tactical contribution, with the introduction of the "Zemke Fan."

The Luftwaffe had continued to consolidate, moving its active airfields into Germany, giving it a home-field advantage, especially in regard to radar warning of incoming aircraft. The 56th was now flying far beyond the range of Allied radar, and Hub knew that the enemy radar picked up his units and relayed their positions to Luftwaffe formations. Zemke believed that he could confuse the enemy radar and increase the possibility of finding German formations by breaking up the group into individual flights.

He ordered that the 56th would fly as a group to an easily recognized geographic point, from which the unit would fan out in flights of four to cover a 180-degree arc. One section would stay over the designated point, acting as a mobile reserve.

He put the plan into action on May 12, and soon found that it was not foolproof, for breaking up the group into smaller flights gave the usually outnumbered Germans a chance to attack. Zemke himself was twice surprised and almost shot down. He evaded each time, and scored one victory. Hub landed at his home base, shaken by his personal experiences during the four-hour mission, but pleased with the results of the Zemke Fan. The 56th scored eighteen victories, while losing three aircraft.

Ten days later, the Zemke Fan was put into action again; there was less opposition this time, but twelve victories were scored against two losses. The losses hurt Zemke, who had to write the customary letters home to the parents. He tried to harden his feelings by keeping an emotional distance between himself and his men, but it was difficult. Losing the oldtimers was particularly painful, and in the game of ground strafing, they were as vulnerable as the newest novice. It gave him some solace to know that Headquarters had noted and approved of the Zemke Fan as a tactic, and that using it would hasten the Luftwaffe's demise.

As time passed, Zemke proved the versatility of the P-47 by devising both level bombing and dive-bombing tactics for it. He borrowed a specially modified "droop-snoot" P-38 from another unit, complete with a bombardier and one of the supersecret Norden bombsights. (The droop-snoot P-38 was specially modified with an extended nacelle into which a bombardier and a bombsight could be crammed.) Zemke flew the P-38, with twenty-four P-47s, each carrying a 1,000-pound bomb, tucked in tight formation with him. The P-47s dropped on Zemke's command, taking out three spans of a railroad bridge near Chantilly.

The 56th did its duty during the invasion of France, fighting the Luftwaffe whenever it appeared. By July 5, the 56th had scored its 500th aerial victory, and Gabby Gabreski had become the American Ace of Aces, with twenty-eight victories. Twelve days later, the indestructible Gabby took off on what was supposed to be his last mission before his rotation home. Attacking a German airfield near Koblenz, he broke a cardinal rule by electing to make a second firing pass. The decision was not characteristic of him and probably reflected his combat fatigue. On the second run, his propeller bounced into the ground, and Gabby had to force land. He was captured and spent the rest of the war in a German prison camp, joining among others, Gerry Johnson, who had been shot down in March. It would be six years and another war before Gabby would get into battle again. When he did, he would score six and a half victories over North Korean MiG-15s.

A TOUGH CHOICE

Hub would not have admitted it, but he was now freely recognized as the most expert fighter group commander in the European theater. The 56th had the highest total of victories and was the most expert in attacking airfields, the most hazardous mission of all.

Almost daily, Zemke expected to receive orders sending him home, for he was long overdue for rotation, having accumulated close to 300 combat hours. Hub knew that he was not indispensable, because he believed he had the best squadron commanders and the best pilots in the VIII Fighter Command working for him. Accordingly, he was not surprised on August 11, 1944, when he received a call from Headquarters, asking him to release Dave Schilling so that he could command the 479th Fighter Group.

To his surprise, Schilling refused the transfer, because the 479th was flying P-38s. Hub told him that they would soon be reequipped with Mustangs, but Schilling still refused. It dawned on Zemke that this was a golden opportunity. He would give Schilling the 56th—at last—and take over the 479th himself. In that way, he would finally get to fly the Mustang in combat and he would not be ordered home.

Once again, he had outfoxed himself.

THE 479TH AND A REUNION WITH GABBY

Zemke was an excellent choice to lead the 479th, for it was suffering a morale crisis. After almost three months in combat, it had scored only ten victories, but lost thirty-five of its own pilots. Part of the problem was the P-38, which was still suffering its engine problems in the moist cold climate of Europe. Another part of the problem was a lack of leadership, which Hub was eager to provide.

Hub immediately let the men of the 479th know who was in charge. A sign with his name on it had been placed on his office door. Below it he added another, saying "I AM A SON-OF-A-BITCH TOO, LET'S SEE YOU SALUTE." Just as in the 56th, the uniform had to be worn correctly, shoes had to be shined, and full military courtesies rendered. But Zemke had other things to teach, as well, including the best way to attack an airfield.

He put this into practice on August 11, when he led fifty planes on an escort mission. Hub detached one squadron and made an attack on an airfield in eastern France, where about seventy aircraft were sitting in dispersal areas. Zemke's tactics took out the antiaircraft batteries with the first few passes. The 479th then beat up the field for almost thirty minutes, destroying forty-three aircraft and damaging twenty-eight more. It was a shot in the arm for the group, restoring its confidence.

Instilling discipline and confidence was made easier when the P-51s began arriving in late September. On September 26, Zemke led a mixed group of thirty-one P-38s and twelve P-51s in an attack deep in Germany. They encountered strong resistance from an aggressive Luftwaffe unit and were soon engaged in a series of tumbling dogfights. When the 479th pilots got back to their base at Wattisham, they found they had broken their airborne jinx. Twenty-nine enemy aircraft had been destroyed, for the loss of one P-38. Zemke himself had scored twice, shooting down two Messerschmitts.

The 479th was suddenly transformed, and the pilots looked on Zemke as a demigod who had brought them sure and sudden success. Hub was willing to be their totem if they needed one, but he knew that the success was caused by two things: new technology and luck. The technology came in the form of their new P-51s, which were equipped with the spectacularly successful K-14 gunsight. The K-14 made deflection shooting easy, permitting relatively inexperienced pilots to make kills that they would otherwise have missed. Luck came in the form of just finding the Luftwaffe in the air and bringing it to battle.

Zemke continued to fly mission after mission, once encountering the latest in German technology, the Messerschmitt Me 262, the world's first operational jet fighter. Powered by twin jet engines suspended in nacelles beneath the wings, and carrying an armament package of four 30-mm cannon, the Me 262 was by any measure the greatest advance in aviation technology of the war. It was clearly the wave of the future and would influence both U.S. and Soviet fighter designs in jet aircraft. Many of the members of the 56th would fly and fight in jet fighters just a few years later. Fortunately for the Allies, there were far too few Me 262s, and they were introduced far too late to make any difference. They were spectacular to see and difficult to engage except when landing or taking off.

Hub's experience paid off in his first fight with a Me 262, because he came up with exactly the right tactics. Unable to contest its 120 mph speed advantage, Zemke turned into it each time as it made four separate firing passes. With the rate of closure approaching 800 mph, neither plane had much of a chance at a kill, and the fight was a draw.

In this fight, Zemke demonstrated the very essence of an ace. To turn, unblinking, into a stream of 30-mm cannon shells erupting from the German jet's four Mk 108 cannons required an instinctive pugnacious tenacity that was Zemke, through and through.

By the end of October, Hub had flown 154 combat missions and logged more than 450 combat hours. He was ordered to give up his command and report as Chief of Staff to the 65th Fighter Wing. Zemke tried to fight the order, but knew that it was futile. His flying days were over, but, like Gabreski, he insisted on flying "one last mission." The 479th was to escort bombers to northern Germany. On the way in, Zemke encountered a violent thunderstorm that literally tore his

Mustang apart, battering the right side of his body and throwing him, seat and all, into the heart of the storm.

Badly injured by the airplane's breakup, he was just able to pull the parachute ripcord. Hub landed hard in a marshy area and spent a miserable day evading capture. He was ultimately picked up and put through an arduous process of interrogation, being shuttled from one prison to another. In the process, he had an opportunity to see how badly Germany was being destroyed by the bombing. Ironically, he had another experience with his own specialty—train strafing—but this time he was on the receiving end in a German train.

Eventually, he was sent to Stalag Luft 1, where he became the Senior Allied Officer for 9,000 prisoners. Zemke's career as a prisoner of war was as brilliant as his career as a Fighter Group Commander had been, for he used his sterling qualities of leadership to inspire the same type of team spirit that he had in combat. His command of German and his indomitable spirit gained him a respect from his captors that did much to alleviate the hard living conditions.

Like Rickenbacker, Zemke was a self-made ace. Far more important for the USAAF, he was a self-made leader, one who found the right way to run a fighter group, even though it proved to be the wrong way to run a career.

Despite his disclaimer about being only an ordinary pilot and an average shot, Hub eventually wound up with an official tally of seventeen and three-quarters destroyed in the air and eight and a half destroyed on the ground. He never claimed to be an ordinary leader, however, and recognized that it was far more important for his pride and joy, the 56th Fighter Group, to score well. It did, ending the war with no fewer than 674½ claims in the air and 311 on the ground.

To Zemke's credit, both he and the 56th achieved their great successes while using an airplane that was not as well suited to its task as it might have been. Zemke offset this by creating tactics that maximized the Thunderbolt's potential and offset its shortcomings. He took advantage of every element of new technology that was introduced to improve the P-47's capability to perform its mission. His leadership really stands out in this regard, for some of the developments (e.g., carrying two large external tanks) reduced the P-47's speed, altitude, and maneuvering capability in exchange for providing extra range. Zemke gladly accepted the trade-off, for it enabled him to come to grips with the enemy.

Zemke's leadership style might have failed in a noncombat situation. It succeeded because he not only applied it to combat, but also led his unit in the air while doing so. His pilots could see that Zemke's methods paid off in the air and were therefore acceptable on the ground. Hub was able to achieve the combat

leader's most difficult task in leadership, eliciting all-out aggressiveness in combat while at the same time insisting on the most rigorous rules on safety in noncombat situations. He did it with fines and with threats, but most of all he did it
with his steely eye of command, which could make the most ebullient Second
Lieutenant behave.

Unfortunately, while Headquarters personnel appreciated Zemke's combat
results, they did not appreciate his manner. The military bureaucracy is no different than other bureaucracies, and just as Rickenbacker had a reputation of not
being "officer material," so did Zemke gain a reputation of not being "general
officer material."

Hub's decision to disobey orders and return to combat set the stage for his
career to plateau as a Colonel. He reinforced this view in some other dealings after
the war, when his on-the-spot judgment in dealing with removing valuable industrial equipment from seizure by the Soviet Union was second-guessed at higher
headquarters.

The result was that Hub Zemke, the premier Fighter Group Commander of
World War II, served out his career in a series of important positions but was
never promoted to flag rank. Further, he was not allowed to fight in Korea, as so
many of the men (Gabreski, Johnson, Mahurin, and others) he had led in combat
were able to do. Another of his protégés, Robin Olds, would carry the Zemke tradition on to the Vietnam War.

To his eternal credit, Zemke kept any bitterness to himself and carried out his
duties with the same zeal he had shown since he had been an aviation cadet. Later
in life, if caught in a philosophic mood, he would express some nostalgic regret
that his career had turned out as it did. But there was never a time when one
would get the impression that, if given the chance, Zemke would have changed
one thing that he had done. He was, after all, Hub Zemke, ace and leader, and he
did things his way.

Zemke died in 1994 at the age of eighty, much beloved by those who knew
him. He felt pride in what he had done, but was even more pleased by the men
who followed in his footsteps.

★ S I X ★
BLESSE'S LITTLE PRAYER
TO THE LORD

September 4, 1952, was like the great majority of days in MiG Alley: crystal clear, cold, and empty of the enemy. The Yalu River trickled in a thin line that divided the sanctuary of Manchuria from the triangle of North Korean territory over which the battle for air superiority was fought daily.

Major Frederick "Boots" Blesse, on his 104th combat mission in his North American F-86 Sabre understood the situation. He'd learned a lot in his previous 103 trips up and down the Korean peninsula. The Communists flew and fought their chunky little MiGs only when it suited them. He knew that you saw a MiG only about once in eight sorties and that you engaged a MiG in battle only about twice in five sightings. This meant you flew an average of twenty missions before you could hope to bring a MiG to battle. Shooting it down was another matter.

By his ninety-fifth mission, Blesse had four victories to his credit, about one every twenty-three missions. He'd had a choice: go home after five more missions, or extend his tour for twenty-five more missions and have a chance to become an ace. It was an easy decision then. Nine missions later, he wasn't so sure. He and his wingman, twenty-four-year-old Second Lieutenant Earl "Brownie" Brown (later a Lieutenant General), were making their third pass through MiG Alley in their Sabres, once again with no contact.

Fuel was beginning to run low when he saw two MiG-15s glinting in the sun, above him at the eleven o'clock position. Blesse transmitted a single word to Brown: "Padlock." It meant that Blesse had the enemy in sight and Brown was to "check six," that is, cover their rear.

Simultaneously, the two men jettisoned their drop tanks, sending the four silver cylinders tumbling down, destined to be salvaged by some frugal North Korean peasant and turned into troughs or water tanks. They banked sharply to cut off the MiGs. Blesse was wondering if this time the enemy would stay to fight when the lead MiG brought his cannons to bear in a sudden steep diving turn. The fight was on!

Innately aggressive, Blesse pulled up and over the plunging enemy fighter, Brownie hugging his wing. The MiG's wingman, obviously a beginner, was thrown to the outside of the turn; he hesitated, then dove back toward safety on the other side of the Yalu River.

Blesse's maneuver had put him behind the MiG, the glowing orange pipper of his gun sight tracking the intersection of the enemy fighter's wing and fuselage. He closed, firing his six .50-caliber machine guns in a long barrel-burning burst. In quick succession, the MiG blew its canopy and the pilot ejected, his seat flashing up from the cockpit like a cork from a champagne bottle. MiG Alley was empty of the enemy once more.

Brown moved out a little now that combat was over and Boots, breath coming hard from the excitement of the life-or-death engagement, headed back toward the base. Suddenly it dawned on Blesse—he had just achieved his life-long ambition—he was an ace. He mumbled a prayer: "Lord, if you have to take me while I'm over here, don't do it today. Let me get back and tell someone I finally got number five."

THE GREAT ADVANCES

World War II had seen many advances in technology, particularly in Germany. Curiously, few of the great German advances in aeronautics were absolutely brand-new; most had been seen in experimental form in many countries before the war. The great difference was that the Germans had succeeded in bringing them to operational, or near operational, use. The practical demonstrations made it virtually mandatory for every postwar air force to follow suit.

The respect accorded the world's first operational jet fighter, the German Messerschmitt Me 262, led most air forces to place the swept-wing jet fighter at the top of their requirement list. (Oddly enough, the original design of the Me 262 had called for a conventional straight wing. Engine development problems led to center of gravity problems whose solution required sweeping the wings. This ad hoc engineering response turned out to validate theoretical and wind-tunnel studies on the advantage of swept wings, which, just incidentally, used a National Advisory Committee for Aeronautics wing section.) The compressibility problems encountered by the Republic P-47 and Lockheed P-38 in a dive now loomed on the horizon for jet-powered aircraft in level flight. Sweeping the wings delayed the onset of compressibility, thus permitting higher speeds without loss of control.

The Soviets had been aware of the potential of swept wings since 1935 and initiated work on a modern jet fighter with swept wings in March 1946. The prototype of the MiG-15 first flew on December 30, 1947, and the aircraft would become the mainstay of Soviet bloc forces, with more than 5,000 being built. The Soviets made no attempt to keep the plane secret; it was flown at the 1948 Tushino air show, and it was generally well known that the production rate had already reached 200 a month.

Designed as a high-altitude interceptor able to operate from the rough fields found in the Soviet bloc, the MiG-15 was both an engineering and a production triumph for the Soviet Union. The design incorporated all of the many advances provided by Lend-Lease aircraft (including gun sights) but also included Soviet innovations, such as the wing fences to conform the airflow over the swept wing. The pressurized cockpit was air conditioned, a luxury found in few other venues in the Soviet Union at the time, but both the pressurization and the temperature controls were primitive by American standards. In contrast, the instrumentation was extraordinarily advanced, for it included an instrument landing system (the first for a Soviet fighter), an automatic direction finder, and a radio altimeter. Its armament package was particularly ingenious, for it incorporated one 37-mm and two 23-mm cannons in a tray that operated like a dumbwaiter for quick servicing. Perhaps most important, like the German Fokker D VII of World War I, the highly maneuverable MiG-15 could be flown well (within the limits of its performance envelope) by pilots of only average ability.

The inherent soundness of the MiG design was reflected in its longevity and in the many variants that were built over its many years of service. It led directly to the MiG-17 and -19 aircraft that would prove extremely effective during the Vietnam War, long after they were considered obsolete.

If the MiG had a major defect, it was in aesthetics; its short fuselage and squared-off wings presented a chunky appearance accentuated by the gaping mouth of its air intake. When compared to its arch opponent, the beautiful North American Sabre, the MiG could only be called "homely."

Originally envisioned as a straight-wing aircraft, the North American XP-86 Sabre was redesigned to incorporate swept wing and tail surfaces, making its first flight on October 1, 1947. (Many have claimed that the XP-86 actually exceeded the speed of sound in a dive shortly thereafter, thus preceding the official October 14, 1947, date for the first Mach 1.0 flight, set by then Captain Charles "Chuck" Yeager in the Bell X-1. There is only apocryphal evidence for the XP-86 claim, but it has many strong adherents nonetheless.)

The great engineer Robert T. Jones had advanced his own concept of swept wings to the National Advisory Committee for Aeronautics (NACA) in 1945, only to be rebuffed. He was among the American scientists who visited Germany at the end of the war, and there he found his ideas confirmed. The German data led to 35-degree sweep wings not only on the Sabre, but also on the Boeing XB-47 jet bomber.

The basic Sabre design was excellent, and more than 8,300 examples were built in the United States, Canada, Australia, Japan, and Italy. There were many variants, and the design led to the first USAF supersonic production aircraft, the North American F-100 Supre Sabre.

THE ADVERSARIES COMPARED

The basic size, design, and equipment of the two aircraft reflected their respective missions and affected how they could be used in combat. The MiG-15 was smaller and lighter than the F-86 (Air Force designations changed from P for Pursuit to F for Fighter in 1948), and as a result was slightly faster and possessed a better rate of climb and a higher ceiling.

The reduction in weight and gain in performance came at some sacrifice. The MiG-15 was less well provided with armor and bulletproof glass and lacked a radar-ranging gun sight and hydraulically operated flight controls. In contrast, the F-86 was a more stable gun platform and had redundant operating systems that made it less vulnerable to damage.

While the swept wings were apparent on both aircraft, other important developments were less obvious. As noted, both fighters had pressurized cockpits, used only on reconnaissance versions of fighters in the past, and both had ejection seats. The American Sabre pilots were equipped with modern "brain buckets" (protective helmets), and efficient G suits to offset the effects of prolonged tight turns. The Soviet pilots had less advanced versions of each of these items of personal equipment. (MiGs were flown almost entirely by Soviet pilots during the first two years of the war, although neither side admitted this to be the case. In the third year of the air war, some Chinese and North Korean pilots flew the MiG in combat.)

American equipment was generally better built and more efficient, particularly instruments and radios. Opinion was divided on the armament packages. The MiG-15's cannons packed a powerful punch, while the F-86's had six .50-caliber machine guns mounted in the nose, the same firepower the Mustang had employed. The final production version of the Sabre, the F-86H, had four 20-mm cannons installed in place of the machine guns, a tip of the hat to the MiG armament.

In September of 1952, an improved Sabre, the F-86F, was introduced into Korea. A more powerful engine substantially improved its performance. The F-86F climb rate now reached almost 10,000 feet per minute, and the MiG could no longer use "dive and zoom" tactics with impunity.

As will be shown later, the most important difference in the two aircraft was the manner in which their respective air forces operated them and the skill and training of the pilots who flew them.

DEMOBILIZATION AND THE KOREAN WAR

The seeds of the Korean and the Cold Wars were sown in the months immediately after the end of World War II. While the United States plunged into a frenzy of demobilization, the Soviet Union maintained its armed forces on a war footing and systematically extended its influence throughout Eastern Europe.

When, with Joseph Stalin's approval, Marshal Kim Il Sung sent highly trained North Korean forces to invade South Korea on June 25, 1950, the newly independent United States Air Force had not yet recovered from the devastating demobilization after World War II. The powerful Army Air Forces plunged from a 1944 peak of 2,253,000 military and 318,514 civilian personnel to a low of 303,600 military and 110,000 civilians in May 1947. The force of more than 100,000 aircraft dropped to fewer than 25,000, of which less than 20 percent were fit for combat. The best and most serviceable aircraft were those found in the United States, where the original manufacturers were available to provide support. The more distant the location, the lower the in-commission rate. At many overseas outposts, more aircraft were out of commission than were ready for flight. Besides the material shortages, there were insufficient pilots and ground crewmen to create combat-ready units.

Jet fighters were still relatively short ranged, and overseas deployments were just beginning to be experimented with. More important, the Air Force was properly concerned with what the Soviet Union *could* do if it decided to launch a one-way atomic strike with its Tupelov Tu-4 bombers. The Tu-4 was a reverse-engineered Boeing B-29, obsolete by U.S. standards, but still capable of delivering a devastating nuclear attack on a dozen or more American cities. As a result, the most modern aircraft, particularly the new Sabres, were retained in the United States, leaving overseas stations largely equipped with World War II types.

When President Harry Truman made his decision to defend South Korea, he had at his immediate disposal only the Far East Air Forces, consisting of 365 Lockheed F-80s, 32 North American F-82s, 26 Douglas B-26s, and 22 Boeing B-29s. These proved to be sufficient to slow down and then halt the North Korean invaders, buying the time necessary to build up additional forces. The initial buildup would be made from North American F-51s in storage in the Far East, followed by more F-51s from U.S.-based National Guard outfits. In an amazingly regressive move, the USAF was forced to convert six F-80A squadrons to the piston-engine-powered Mustangs.

The Mustangs could operate from the primitive fields available in South Korea, while the more sophisticated F-80s initially had to fly from bases in Japan. With the inevitable irony of service life, it would be the utility of the Mustangs that would first gain the piloting services of the man who was to be the first double ace to survive the Korean War, Boots Blesse. (Major George A. Davis Jr. was the first American to down ten aircraft in Korea. Davis had seven victories in World War II and scored fourteen more in Korea before being killed in combat.)

EARLY DAYS

Eddie Rickenbacker and Hub Zemke had both experienced rough spots as children, although Zemke had a slightly easier time of it. In comparison, Frederick C. "Boots" Blesse had a protected youth, despite the tragic loss of his mother when he was only nine. His father, a physician and a rising star within the Army, saw that his three children were raised in the Spartan comfort and complete security of Army bases. Military bases were oases of gentility during the hard days of the depression. Even though service budgets were cut to the bone, the bases were still able to provide swimming pools, golf courses, horseback riding, and other sports for their happily insular communities. It was a perfect milieu for a natural athlete, as the future ace would prove to be.

Blesse was born in the Panama Canal Zone on August 22, 1921, and the nickname "Boots" was given to him early in life. Blesse adored his father, and when he had just learned to walk, he would don his dad's shoes and shuffle around the house in them. The shoes looked like boots on his short legs, and his parents would comment, "Here come the boots again." The term soon became a nickname that was somehow so "right" that it has stuck through the years.

At Fort Leavenworth, the young Blesse played baseball and competed in track and swimming. His natural forte was golf, perhaps because his father had made a lasting impression by making a hole-in-one on the very first day they played on a regulation golf course.

Doctor Blesse remarried in 1936, the same year he took the family to his next assignment in the Philippine Islands. Boots and his siblings went to school at Fort McKinley, which, because of the heat, was held from 7:00 A.M. to noon. By one o'clock, Boots was out on the links, and by the time he was sixteen, he was a scratch golfer, winning the Junior Philippine Department Championships in 1937, 1938, and 1939. In doing so, he demonstrated some of the qualities that would later make him an air ace: persistence, practice, and the establishment of a set of religiously followed rules for himself, rules that worked to improve his game every time he played.

In 1938 he had a significant experience, being selected to play golf with the great Gene Sarazen. Sarazen shot a 65 to set a course record on their round, while Blesse shot a 67. After the match, he summoned up the courage to ask Sarazen if he should give up his ambition to go to West Point, and instead become a professional golfer. Sarazen gave the matter some thought, then advised him that he would be better off going to West Point and using golf as a social skill. It was not that he didn't have the skill to become a winning professional—it was just that there were so many good golfers, and the prize monies were so slight that it was hard to make a living. (Golf prizes have changed considerably!)

Boots was already using his golf as a social skill, both with the local girls and with the pilots at Nichols Field. He struck up a strong friendship with a Lieutenant Calhoun, and the two would fly around the island in an observation plane, stopping at various points to play a round of golf. The trips affected Boots in two important ways. It improved his golf game, and it gave him a devouring ambition to become a pilot. This was whetted by the pulp heroes of the day, including G-8 and His Battle Aces, Tailspin Tommy, and other fictional aviators who served as inspiration to thousands of young lads who subsequently became flyers themselves.

The Blesses' stay in the Philippines was an idyllic paradise for the family—for most of the tour. Boots had especially enjoyed the golf and the flying and, precociously, the favors of the wife of a young Lieutenant on the base. When Doctor Blesse became aware of the affair, he intervened. As it happened, their tour of duty was over, and it proved to be a good time to leave the Philippines. Doctor Blesse was relieved to get his family back to the United States without any further difficulties.

Golfing—and the Lieutenant's wife—had matured Boots, and he realized it was time to buckle down and do sufficient studying to pass his exams for West Point. To his amazement, he had no trouble with the competitive exams, but he failed the physical, disqualified because of a spot seen on the X-ray of his lungs. It was a shattering experience, the first time in his life that his expectations were thwarted. All his dreams of West Point and flying were dashed, and his ebullient nature was depressed. Boots enrolled in the University of Denver in 1940.

His father was in a position to note any change in the rules for West Point qualification. In the summer of 1941, he found that the entrance requirements had been relaxed, and Boots's problem was no longer disqualifying. Even before Boots had secured an appointment to the Academy, he entered Millard's Preparatory School in Washington, D.C., in August 1941. So serious that he gave up his Saturday golf games, Boots instead pounded around the halls of Congress, trying to find a congressman who would be willing to give him an appointment. Appointments to service academies were a valuable congressional perquisite, and were usually doled out to the families that had a political connection.

Congressman John B. Sullivan of Missouri had been disappointed by the failure of those he had selected in the past to qualify at West Point and had just adopted a new policy of giving competitive exams. Boots took the exam and was waiting for the results when the Japanese attacked Pearl Harbor on December 7, 1941. His first inclination was to enlist, but his father advised him to wait and see what happened with his appointment. On December 18 he learned that he was to report to the U.S. Military Academy at West Point on July 1, 1942.

There was some irony in the fact that like many warriors Boots was not an outstanding student, for he would later write *No Guts, No Glory*, a manual on fighter tactics that was officially adopted by the Air Force. Oswald Boelcke had gained lasting fame with the "Boelcke Dicta," his short set of rules for air combat. *No Guts, No Glory* was a far more comprehensive work, entailing a detailed analysis of air combat in both offensive and defensive situations.

Blesse found himself at the Point at a time when the already-tough academic program was being accelerated to graduate officers ever faster to meet the demands of the expanding Army and Air Force. Two years after he entered, and carrying just over the minimum 2.0 average (on a 3.0 basis), he was finally selected to go to flying school.

PENGRA OF PINE BLUFF

Boots took to flying as he had taken to golf. Much of a pilot's future success stems from his interaction with his flight instructor, and Blesse still reveres his association with Floyd V. Pengra, who gave him his first instruction. After spending six hours in a Fairchild PT-19, a little low-wing, open-cockpit training plane, Pengra got out, saying, as most instructors say when it comes time to solo a student, "This is too dangerous for me. You go fly by yourself, and be careful."

Just as he had been a natural athlete, Boots was a natural pilot. He went through basic and advanced training with no difficulty. He won his wings and received his commission on June 5, 1945. In just three years, West Point had changed him from an indifferent student into an officer, a gentleman, and a pilot. He was ready to go to war and become an ace.

FIRST FIGHTERS

Boots's graduation came at a time when the war was clearly grinding down. Germany had surrendered the month before, and the pipeline of pilots to fly against Japan was completely filled. When the war ended with Japan's surrender on September 2, 1945, he felt superfluous. He knew that the USAAF was going to be reduced, and that meant that thousands of pilots would be discharged.

His worries were groundless, for his status as a West Point graduate would ensure that he would eventually be given a good assignment. In the meantime, he was happy to be able to fly the aging Curtiss P-40s at Napier Field, in Dothan, Alabama. The P-40s, worn as they were, were a considerable step up from the North American AT-6s he'd flown as a cadet, and he began the systematic exploration of his skills, flying "combat" against anyone he met in the Alabama skies. To Blesse, winning these impromptu dogfights was a deadly serious business, and he often pressed past the limits of his airplane and his own skills. More than once he realized that he had been saved only by pure luck, and more than once he felt that he was being saved for some—higher—reason.

In the helter-skelter atmosphere of demobilization, service life and flying were, to say the least, relaxed. Blesse had bounced from station to station, getting conflicting assignments and being scheduled for one school after another. He didn't mind, for there were always airplanes to fly. At Hunter Field, Georgia, he was serving as Airdrome Officer one day when a young officer landed in a bright shiny new North American P-51. Blesse, jesting, asked if he could borrow the airplane. The Lieutenant agreed, and when Blesse confessed that he had never been checked out in the Mustang, he was told, "No problem. The flight manual is in the cockpit."

As eager as ever, Blesse checked himself out, logging five hours over the weekend and having the airplane fully serviced when the Lieutenant returned. Those few hours would dictate the course of his career; five years later, to his amazement, he would be flying the P-51 in combat.

Blesse's self-checkout in the P-51 was par for the course; the general feeling was that if you were wearing wings, you should be able to fly any airplane without any special training. Nothing could have been further from the truth, and both the Army Air Forces' and the U.S. Air Force's accident rates in the postwar years were scandalously high. The fact was that you could kill yourself swiftly even in an airplane with which you were completely familiar. On the first flight in a strange, complex aircraft, you were totally dependent on the luck of the draw. If nothing went wrong, the chances were that you could get it around the pattern and land safely. But if there was a malfunction, even a slight one, the odds were that you would crash and be killed. Far too many were. The war had ended, life was cheap, and no one thought to halt the ceaseless flow of accidents.

OVERSEAS ASSIGNMENT

The American method of demobilization had been based on a point system, with so many points being awarded for length of service, time overseas, and so on. When your number came up, you were sent home, regardless of the impact your departure might have on the operational readiness of your unit.

The direct result of the system was that the American military machine, particularly units serving on foreign soil, was quickly reduced to a hopeless state of inefficiency. The Army Air Forces were in September 1945 the most powerful assembly of aerial might ever seen. No combination of nations could begin to resist its tremendous power. But by March 1946, when Blesse reached the 413th Fighter Group on Okinawa, the Army Air Forces were in a major state of disarray. (The Army and the Navy were experiencing the same difficulties, for the same reason.)

Only nine months before, Okinawa had been wrested from the Japanese in one of the bloodiest battles of the war. There were still Japanese on the island who had not surrendered, and the place was studded with booby traps, unexploded ordnance, and probably the most complex and most ill-maintained aircraft in the USAAF.

After flying the P-40 and the P-51, Blesse now found himself assigned to Republic P-47Ns, the last and most sophisticated of the Thunderbolts to reach production status. In appearance similar to the P-47D "Superbolt" flown by Hub Zemke late in the war, the P-47N had been specifically redesigned for operation in the Pacific theater. It featured the fuselage and wings of the P-47M (which had been intended to combat the German buzz bombs), combined with a new, larger wing that contained two new fuel tanks. With external tanks and ordnance, the maximum gross weight of the P-47N was 20,700 pounds. It had a range of 2,350 miles, and top speed of 470 mph at 30,000 feet. When well maintained, as it was when used for escort fighter duty with the B-29s during World War II, it was an excellent aircraft.

The key words here are "well maintained," because there were far too few mechanics on Okinawa to maintain the P-47s at all, much less maintain them well. The aircraft suffered badly from salt air corrosion. A P-47 had to be perfectly maintained to be safe, and even small hazards—bad hoses, dirty fuel lines, and so on—could cause a fatal crash.

And just as maintenance was lacking, there were few flying hours available and little training. Procedures and safety were of little concern. Within three months after Blesse's arrival, the shortage of mechanics was so acute that pilots were ordered to perform the maintenance on their aircraft. This was the rough equivalent of tasking hospital orderlies to do brain surgery, but there was no alternative. The pilots stumbled through the work as best they could, calling on the few remaining mechanics for help when necessary, and for approval when the job was done.

The quality of the work might have been reflected in the bail-out statistics. During the two years Boots was on the island, there was a total of nineteen pilots in his squadron. Of these, fifteen had bailed out once, several had jumped twice, and one unlucky pilot had to take to his parachute three times. Boots himself experienced a wider variety of misfortunes. On one of his very first flights in the P-47—which he had never flown before—the engine quit and he had to make a forced landing. A few days later, he rolled his Thunderbolt and was drenched in 100-octane gasoline. When he rolled level he could see the fuel sloshing about on the floor, and knew that one spark would be enough to blow himself out of the sky. He landed very carefully, shut the engine down on the runway and ran to the sidelines, waiting for it to blow. For some reason, it did not.

Boots had accumulated ten hours in the aircraft before going to the gunnery range on the island of Tonaki Shima, west of Okinawa. In company with another pilot, he flew standard bombing and strafing runs on rusting Japanese barges still marooned there. On his last pass, his engine quit, and he was able to zoom only to 2,500 feet before deciding he had to bail out. After rolling his canopy back, he tried to dive out of the cockpit, only to be restrained by his oxygen hose. By the time he got loose he was only a few hundred feet above the water. He pulled the ripcord, the parachute opened, and his feet hit the water just as his airplane crashed nearby. After thrashing around in shark-infested waters, he finally managed to get his Mae West inflated, but his rubber raft refused to inflate. He was picked up by a local fisherman, who was amazed to find him alive. It was not the first time he had had a close shave with death; it would not be the last. By now he was convinced that he was being saved for some special purpose.

Many of his comrades had similar experiences with the P-47 and were not so lucky. Losses were heavy in the 413th, as they were in most operational units. There were two, mutually contradictory responses to the situation. At units around the world, the gross amount of flying was reduced, and the simulation of wartime conditions faded away. Night and instrument flying in the P-47 was virtually eliminated; the smaller, less demanding North American AT-6 trainer was used instead. P-47 flights were conducted within sight of the home base, and missions that strained the equipment—flights at high altitudes or with heavy loads—were eliminated. The result was a decline in the loss rate, but also an absolute decline in mission capability.

The dollar and the human costs were horrendous. In 1947, the first year for which reliable USAF statistics can be found, the major accident rate was 44 per 100,000 flying hours. No fewer than 536 aircraft were destroyed and 257 pilots killed. And while the accident rate showed a steady decline, primarily because of an increase in the number of flying hours, the total number of accidents and fatalities climbed, reaching a peak of 2,274 accidents in 1952, when 421 deaths were recorded.

The USAF began a long and intense safety campaign. Even though aircraft became more complex, and missions more dangerous, the emphasis on safety and training steadily reduced accidents. By 1998 the accident rate was 1.14 per 100,000 flying hours. Twenty aircraft were destroyed, but only eight pilots lost their lives. Put another away, major accidents decreased from 1,555 in 1947 to 24 in 1998.

These statistics revealed that flying was inherently dangerous and flying fighters even more so. You had to be both good and lucky to survive, and Boots was both.

SOME CRITICAL DECISIONS

Blesse never met an airplane he didn't like, nor did he ever turn down a chance to fly a new one. His tour on Okinawa had not been without its hardships—the food was bad, and there were no golf courses and few women available. He'd enjoyed the P-47 somewhat warily, given its predisposition to maintenance problems, and like others in the 413th, he had his eye on the date when he would be sent back to the United States.

A few of the new Lockheed P-80s had now arrived, and everyone wanted to fly the first U.S. operational jet fighter. The P-80 was not without its hazards. It was slow to accelerate and burned fuel at an alarming rate. In the early models, there was a single engine-driven fuel pump. When it failed, the engine quit, and some top pilots, including Lockheed test pilot Milo Burcham, were killed before a backup electric fuel pump was installed. (The American Ace of Aces of World War II, Dick Bong, was killed in a P-80 that had been modified with an extra fuel pump—he had forgotten to turn it on.)

But the P-80 was new, fast, and compared to the P-47, relatively easy to maintain. Colonel Homer Boushey, CO of the 413th, made a rational decision. There were only a few P-80s to go around, and he decided he would train only those pilots who had at least five months to go on their tour of duty. Boots had only two, but he wanted in the program.

Boushey made an offer: if anyone wanted to extend so that he would be there for the required five months, he'd approve the application. Blesse immediately applied, and in the next two months got thirty hours in the P-80. When his two months were up, Boushey told him to pack his bags and go home—he did not have to stay for the extra three months. The CO was using an old commander's ploy: find out who is really eager to fly by making it difficult to do so. Blesse, predictably, was eager to fly. He always would be.

Upon his return to the United States, Boots was, to his delight, assigned to the 56th Fighter Group, Zemke's old Wolfpack, stationed at Selfridge Field, Michigan.

Selfridge was named for Lieutenant Thomas Selfridge, the first person to be killed in powered flight. It had always been one of the premier fighter bases, and Zemke's protégé Colonel Francis "Gabby" Gabreski was its commander. For Boots, it was a graduate school of aces, and he was a bit unsettled. All of the famous names— Gabreski, with twenty-eight victories, Bill Whisner with fifteen and a half (six of them scored on one mission), Dave Schilling, with twenty-two and a half victories—were just about his age and they were combat-proven veterans. Here he was, in a group of aces, and he had never even seen combat. It gave him something he had never had before: an inferiority complex. To offset it, he flew harder than ever, flying cross country almost every weekend to build up time and soaking every tip he could from the more experienced pilots. (One of the by-products of his cross-country flights was very positive: he courted and married Dorothy Kent.) Another by-product was a buildup of his flying time. By his fifth year as a pilot, he had about 2,300 hours, far more than average. Twelve hundred of these were in the "hot" P-80 and 120 in the even hotter F-86.

The 56th had just converted to the new and still trouble-prone F-86 when the Korean War erupted on June 25, 1950. The next month, a requirement came down to the 56th for an experienced Mustang pilot to go to Korea. Since his bootlegged flights in a borrowed Mustang at Hunter, Blesse had logged only another two or three hours in F-51s, but he still volunteered for the job.

Gabreski thought he was crazy, trading the first-line F-86 for a World War II relic. He also thought that there might easily be a major war with the Soviet Union and that the important fighting would be going on in Europe.

Blesse was adamant. He told Gabreski, "Sir, if I had your combat time and had shot down as many airplanes as you have, I could afford to wait. I'm a career officer, and I really need some combat time." In short, it wasn't much of a war, but it was the only war Blesse had.

OPERATIONAL DEBUT IN KOREAN MUSTANGS

There is an ironclad rule in every armed service of every nation, and that is "never volunteer." Blesse had violated the rule, and found himself first at Nellis Air Force Base, Nevada, training not in F-51s but F-80s. When he reached Japan, in October 1950, he found himself once again at the tail end of a pipeline of pilots. There were so many F-80 pilots on hand that he was told he could expect a two- to three-month wait before being assigned to a combat unit.

By that time it seemed likely that General of the Armies Douglas MacArthur would achieve another smashing victory. The North Korean enemy was in full retreat, and it appeared to be more than probable that the war would be over before Blesse got into combat.

Once again he made a critical, apparently retrograde decision: he volunteered for the 18th Fighter Bomber Group, which had two squadrons of Mustangs and was operating out of Pusan, Korea.

Blesse arrived in Pusan on November 10; at three o'clock in the morning on the following day he was awakened for his first combat mission. It was a typical Korean November day, with a ceiling of 400 feet and sheets of rain falling from the lowering sky. The heavily laden Mustangs taxied out in the pitch-black morning over the undulating PSP (pierced-steel planking) that was the only thing that kept them from being swallowed up by the mud. Blesse began to wonder if he'd made the right decision in opting for Mustangs.

As he taxied out, slipping and sliding on the PSP, he realized that he had never flown a propeller-driven fighter at night. Flying a jet at night was relatively easy. The jet exhaust was at the end of the airplane and did not interfere with night vision. With the Mustang, the flames crackling from the exhausts were blinding, robbing him both of his night vision and the misty horizon. He'd have to depend on his instruments—turn and bank, altimeter, attitude indicator—immediately after takeoff, and then hope he could fly formation on the flight leader, Captain Joe Lane.

He also realized that he had never flown a Mustang loaded down with napalm, a full load of .50-caliber ammunition, and rockets. In just a few minutes, he would learn that the extra weight and drag turned a thoroughbred racehorse into junk wagon's nag. Top speed went down, stall speed went up, and handling became far more difficult.

When the radioed launch command came through the headsets, Lane advanced the throttle on his Mustang. The flames from its barking exhaust stacks illuminated the enveloping beads of mist, blanking out the wings and fuselage with an incandescent glow. Blesse rolled beside the glow, lifted off, and flew for forty-five minutes in clouds before breaking out on top. Drenched with sweat and exhausted, he knew that the hard part of the mission—air-to-ground combat—was still to come. It began to dawn on him. This was no way to become an ace.

The four F-51s checked in with their Forward Air Controller, a World War II innovation that had become a permanent part of air-to-ground warfare. Lane's flight worked the target over, the Mustang feeling better to Blesse each time a store was dropped. When they'd finished dropping their napalm, a call came through advising them that the home field was closed and that they should divert to the 3,900-foot strip at Pyongyang East, where the ceiling was still about 500 feet, but dropping fast.

Pyongyang East was only a few minutes away, but it was obscured by the time they arrived, and they had to circle. On the ground, mechanics lit oil fires in two fifty-five-gallon drums, one on each side of the runway. The thick black smoke curled up into the clouds, dissipating quickly, but forming a smoky arch over where the edge of the runway should be.

Lane pitched out and Blesse followed, lagging back far enough to let Lane be well down the runway before his own touchdown. Blesse saw Lane touch down and begin his rollout, then touched down himself, a three pointer that would keep his own landing roll down. As he peered over the long nose of the Mustang, at a speed too fast to ground loop and too slow to go around, he saw an Army truck start across the runway. He tried to turn, but the left wing of his Mustang caught the truck, cart-wheeling him down the runway, spewing the rockets he hadn't fired from the wings. The battered F-51 slowed then reared up and fell over on its back, trapping Blesse, unhurt, inside the cockpit.

He had shut off his magneto switch and battery immediately before the collision, but he could smell gasoline and knew that he was dead if a fire started. Two brave men of the ground crew raced to the airplane and dug down to free him. As soon as the hole was big enough, he wriggled out and sprinted away from the airplane. Like his P-47, the Mustang didn't burn.

Forty minutes later he was strapped into another F-51 and sent on another mission. It was a hell of a way to start a combat tour, and Blesse was worried about the effect his crash might have on his efficiency report.

As it turned out, nothing was said. His crash had only been one of seven that took place at Pyongyang East within thirty-five minutes. The Air Force was tasked to support the Army, and was ready to take the inevitable casualties of combat to do so.

THE FOUNDATIONS OF AN ACE

Boots flew often in the F-51, always hoping that he'd run into some enemy aircraft. Unfortunately, most of the North Korean Air Force had been destroyed in the first days of the war, and he saw no enemy aircraft. Instead, he flew seventy ground-attack missions in the Mustang, shooting up troops, trucks, trains, and anything else to which the FACs directed him. Like everyone else, he was stunned in November 1950 to learn that the North Koreans were now employing swept-wing MiG-15s, because he knew that the Air Force had nothing in Asia that could compete with them. In the first jet-versus-jet battle in history on November 7, 1950, Lieutenant Russell Brown, flying an F-80, shot down an attacking MiG-15. The fight presaged two facts that would be demonstrated again and again in the coming months: despite its loss, the MiG was far superior in performance to the F-80, but American pilots were far better trained than their counterparts.

Blesse had learned of the MiG's debut with a feeling of frustration. Every step he had taken in the Air Force seemed to have led him away from the one thing he wanted most: victories in air-to-air combat. A chance meeting with an old friend from Selfridge, Colonel John Murphy, let him move one step closer. The training situation had shifted, and there were now more F-51 pilots than F-80 pilots. Murphy offered him the opportunity to come to the 49th Fighter Group at Taegu and return to jets.

Blesse jumped at the chance. The F-80 Shooting Star did not exactly shoot off the muddy PSP runways of Korea, but once airborne, it was a safer and more reliable ground-attack aircraft than the Mustang. Boots flew thirty-five more air-to-ground missions, all without seeing an enemy aircraft. When his tour was up, he returned to the United States, convinced that it would take another war and another airplane before he could be an ace. He was wrong; it would just take another tour in the same war, and another airplane.

★ S E V E N ★
LOTS OF GUTS AND GLORY

Boots had not expected to shoot down any MiGs while flying his F-51 in Korea, but he had always hoped that he would encounter one of the enemy's piston-engine fighters, or even one of their twin-engine bombers. There were not very many of them, and they rarely ventured into the areas where he flew his Mustang. Nonetheless, he would have been ready for them, for he had intuitively been laying the foundation for becoming an ace, doing all the right things. Now all he needed was another chance at combat.

As a veteran pilot, with a lot of time in first-line airplanes, his excellent performance in Korea had gained him a choice of assignments. He selected flying F-86 fighters at George Air Force Base, California. George AFB was the home of the 94th Fighter Interceptor Squadron, which still proudly carried Eddie Rickenbacker's Hat in the Ring insignia. The 94th was part of the 1st Fighter Interceptor Group, which was soon to be commanded by the legendary Colonel Walker "Bud" Mahurin.

Mahurin, a veteran and one-time leading ace of Zemke's 56th Fighter Group, had scored twenty and a half victories in Europe before the tail gunner on his last kill, a Dornier Do 217, managed to shoot him down. He survived the crash, evaded capture, and somehow even managed to put on weight while waiting for the French resistance to spirit him back to England.

Like all who evaded or escaped from occupied countries, Mahurin was not allowed to return to combat in the European theater. Instead, he transferred to the Pacific, where he scored one victory and was shot down again, this time by ground fire. He would go on to score three and a half victories in Korea before being shot down and captured. His record was unique. Besides his cumulative high score of twenty-five kills, he was the only ace to score victories in Europe, the Pacific theater, and Korea, and the only person to be shot down in all three theaters of war.

A natural pilot, Mahurin found himself at George in the uncomfortable position of commanding a unit made up of men who had fought in Korea, were proficient in the Sabre, or both. He was determined to catch up, and Boots Blesse was assigned the task of checking him out.

Blesse had mixed emotions. He was in awe of Mahurin because of his war record, but wanted to be sure to demonstrate that he was a professional who followed all of the regulations concerning a checkout. The prescribed checkout called for a very gradual introduction into formation and mock combat, and for the first two flights, Blesse followed the rule book. At the end of the second flight, Mahurin ended the debriefing with a question: "When are we going to do some real flying?" Blesse's response was that he was going to follow the prescribed curriculum, unless Mahurin asked to be an exception to the general rule.

Mahurin did, and the next day Blesse began to put him through his paces. The two flew in close trail formation as Blesse went through maneuver after maneuver, trying to evaluate Mahurin's level of proficiency. He then tightened up the turns, going from 3 Gs to 4, and making sharp reversals of direction. On one flight, they had reversed, then counterreversed, and wound up in a spiraling dive, canopy to canopy, noses pointed straight down. They spun down, looking across at each other, unable to gain an advantage, until the approaching ground made it mandatory to break off and fly back to base. As it developed, even though Boots had several hundred hours in the F-86 against Mahurin's twenty, Bud could match anything Blesse could do. As he said later, "Mahurin looked like a decal on my mirror; no matter what I did, he never moved out of position." Blesse's tutelage won Mahurin's confidence, and this would stand him in good stead a few months later, when they were back in combat.

Under Mahurin's leadership, the 1st Fighter Group began to operate their Sabres as if they were going into combat tomorrow. Day after day, the pilots would rat race across the desert floor, then mix it up in realistic dogfights that lacked only the chatter of machine gun fire.

It was dangerous work, for the F-86 was brand-new and had a very high accident rate. The potential for accidents was greatly increased in the tough mock combat that Mahurin and Blesse advocated, and the inevitable losses were accepted as the price paid for combat proficiency. In using these rigorous tactics, the two men were a generation ahead of themselves. Later, the Air Force turned from realistic combat practice to safer practices. When it got to Vietnam, the Air Force found that the safety-minded training was terribly deficient. The result was the institution, after the Vietnam War, of Red Flag operations where training once more was rigorous, dangerous—and effective for combat.

Blesse, now a flight leader, flew as often as he could, competing against everyone in the unit, pushing himself and his aircraft to the limits as he prepared for a second tour in Korea. One tactic that he practiced as often as he could was mock combat against the propeller-driven fighters—Mustangs from a local P-51 Group—that he encountered. This was not generally popular, for despite the Sabre's much greater speed, it was a difficult task. A good Mustang pilot would slow down almost to the stall and keep making tighter and more abrupt turns, forcing the Sabre to overshoot. It took many hours of practice, but Blesse created the tactics to use the advanced technology of the F-86 against the antiquated—but maneuverable—F-51. Not many other pilots bothered, but Blesse never overlooked a chance to perfect his skills.

Boots loved his family, but he was totally consumed by his desire to become an ace. His wife, Dorothy, was five months pregnant when he told her that he had volunteered to return to Korea. She was not very happy about his decision, and the incident was a harbinger of future problems.

BACK INTO BATTLE

Major Blesse had eight years of active service and almost 2,500 hours flying time when he returned to Kimpo Air Base, Korea, in March 1952. His entire career had been spent in single-minded preparation to become an ace. As a member of the 334th Fighter Squadron, 4th Fighter Wing, he would be flying the very best the USAF had to offer, the North American F-86. He knew that all he needed to achieve his dream was a chance to mix it up with the enemy.

Bud Mahurin, who had used all his considerable charm and wit to wangle his way overseas, was now Commander of the 4th. There were no vacancies in any of his three squadrons in Operations, so he gave Blesse an assignment as Squadron Maintenance Officer, which he promised would be temporary.

GUNS VERSUS AIRSPEED

Blesse did not relish the job, but he attacked it with his usual ferocious intensity. As he labored to get the 334th's maintenance procedures in line, he was struck by the poor tactics being employed by the unit. There were many fine pilots in the squadron, some veterans of dozens of missions, but there was no tactical doctrine and no manual to prescribe guidelines for the only reason they were there: shooting down the enemy. He was totally unaware of it, but the basic seed for *No Guts, No Glory* had been planted in his subconscious.

MiG sightings were relatively far and few between, and victories even fewer. Mahurin was unhappy with the performance of the 334th, and quietly alerted Blesse to stand by—some changes were going to be made.

In preparation for the changes, Mahurin reversed their roles at George and selected Boots to fly on his wing for his introduction to aerial combat in MiG Alley. Blesse's first fight came on their second mission together, and it was not one that Blesse likes to remember.

Mahurin had spotted the two enemy fighters and turned to attack them. They saw the Sabres, and, refusing to engage, darted toward their sanctuary beyond the Yalu River. The F-86s gained very slowly as the MiGs edged ever closer to the border. Boots clamored for permission to open fire, but Mahurin told him to hold off.

The mercurial Blesse could not wait. Calling "Colonel, I'm going to get me a MiG," he fired. What Mahurin knew and Blesse did not was that the F-86 slowed down by three or more knots when its six .50-caliber machine guns were fired. He missed the MiGs, which rapidly increased the distance and disappeared into Manchuria.

When they got back, Mahurin gave Blesse a straightforward critique on pilots who fire from too far out, and particularly pilots who fire when their lead tells them not to. It was a classic dressing down, one that did not take into consideration their previous friendship or Blesse's tutelage. When it was over, Mahurin, in his typical fashion, broke into a grin, and took a subdued Boots to the club for a beer.

Blesse's next forty-five combat missions in the F-86 can only be called fascinating agony, for as interesting as each one was in its own right, on none of them did he see a MiG.

LURING THE MIGS TO BATTLE

The total number of F-86s in operational units in Korea never exceeded about 250 aircraft. Of this number, as many as 50 percent could be out of commission at any one time. The Soviet Union had built its strength up to about 900 MiG-15s in the theater, and these were all located at airfields in Manchuria, where they could engage in battle over MiG Alley. More than 5,000 personnel were sent to back up the Soviet effort. The Soviets attempted to conceal their participation by flying MiGs carrying Chinese markings, learning rudimentary Chinese phrases, and wearing Chinese-style clothing in the cockpit. Under the stress of combat, however, they lapsed into Russian and eventually gave up the ruse.

Initially, the Soviets committed entire units made up of World War II veterans to the battle. Then, just as they had done during the Spanish Civil War, they began to use the Korean War as an advanced training school. Younger pilots would be rotated through the theater to learn from the more experienced pilots and then pass their knowledge on when they returned to their home squadrons.

The Soviets had in effect conceded air superiority to the Americans, for they made only periodic forays south of the Yalu and made few attempts to conduct the close-air support operations for which they had been famous in World War II.

In the training process, the Soviets took full advantage of their favorable tactical situation. Their airfields were beyond the Yalu River and thus off-limits to American fighter-bombers. The MiGs would take off in formation, climb to altitude, and patrol on their side of the Yalu, going into combat only when it seemed advantageous to do so. At the end of their mission, they could return to base within a few minutes. They had much more time to patrol, for they could literally run out of fuel, if necessary, and make an engine-out landing back at their home base.

The Soviets had installed an intricate system of radar sets, and their pilots conducted their flights under strict control from the ground. This strange system, inevitable perhaps under Communist rule, greatly inhibited the Soviet pilots, stifling their aggressiveness and giving the initiative to the Americans. There were some excellent Soviet pilots, however, and some of them ran up larger scores than their American counterparts would do. Captain Nikolay Sutiagin scored twenty-one victories against the United Nations' forces, including fifteen F-86s. Colonel Evgenyi Pepelyaev had twenty kills, including twelve F-86s. These two top aces led a list of forty-four Soviet aces who were credited with a combined total of 391 victories.

In sharp contrast to the Communist forces, the Sabres had to take off from airfields as much as 200 miles from MiG Alley. The 400-mile round-trip limited their combat time to about twenty minutes, about the same amount of time Messerschmitts had over London during the Battle of Britain.

The Sabres would take off in four-plane formations and climb as quickly as possible to about 43,000 feet and establish a cruise speed of Mach .90 if possible. They knew that the MiGs would be above them and equally fast, but the high cruise speed permitted swifter closure when the enemy was sighted—or swift escape if the enemy somehow surprised them.

Once in the air, the USAF forces were completely independent of ground control, free to seize the initiative, as long as they remained within the fairly simple rules of engagements. The Sabres were strictly forbidden to cross the Yalu, unless they were in hot pursuit of a fleeing MiG. The restriction was broken more than once, however, when USAF pilots, frustrated by the refusal of the MiGs to fight, would take matters into their own hands and dart across the Yalu to attack. More than one pilot had to have his mechanic destroy his gun camera film because it registered too clearly that the action was on the wrong side of the river.

MIG ALLEY

The tiny, irregularly shaped rectangle of land called "MiG Alley" stretched from the northeast end of the Yellow Sea for about 150 miles along the Yalu River past Sinuiju to Changju. It then ran about 90 miles southeast to Huichon, and from there 120 miles back to the Yellow Sea. A huge air base at Antung, directly across the river from Sinuiju, usually housed seventy-five MiGs, but at times would have twice that number. Another 75 to 150 MiGs could be found within a short distance of Antung.

The terrain in MiG Alley (called "the Sosiska area" by the Soviets) was so mountainous that it appeared to be like a sea in a heavy gale even at the altitudes at which the battles were fought. When the fight spun down to the ground, as it often did, the craggy mountains loomed as harsh and inhospitable as the native population was to downed flyers. The combination of the terrain and the usually foul weather inhibited any attempts at evasion, and the few helicopters available lacked the range to operate very far behind the front lines. The best hope for a Sabre pilot in trouble was to head for the ocean to bail out where a Grumman SA-16 Albatross amphibian could be vectored in for a pickup from its orbit station north of Cho-do. When a pilot bailed out, the rest of his flight would provide rescue combat air patrol until the Albatross arrived.

The Soviet pilots used exactly the opposite tactics for survival. They would elect to bail out over North Korean territory, confident that they would quickly be returned to base, but they would not conduct operations even one mile offshore.

The United Nations' navy controlled the seas, and they knew if they bailed out into the Sea of Japan to the west, or the Yellow Sea to the east, they would be captured.

In Korea, bailouts over water in summer were not too difficult. In the winter the freezing waters made survival times short. The SA-16s had difficulty landing in seas over five feet high and were susceptible to icing. But because the MiGs never operated over the water, the SA-16s, and later, the helicopters, could operate with impunity from Cho-do, an island only fifteen miles off the coast of North Korea.

Sabre tactics evolved during the war, but the principal task of the F-86 units was always to form a barrier to intrusive MiGs during those hours when United Nations' bomber and fighter-bomber operations were being conducted. When the MiGs could summon the will to intrude, the F-86s were more than happy to mix it up and shoot them down.

The American tactics called for flights of four F-86s to be dispatched at intervals and assigned to orbit various well-known landmarks in MiG Alley. Thirty-six to forty-eight F-86s would spread out in flights of four, hoping to tempt their opposite numbers into the air. They received radioed warnings of MiG action from two radar stations, one at Kimpo Airfield and one at Cho-do Island, where the rescue equipment was stationed.

The first flight usually flew to Sinuiju to watch the MiGs at the big Antung airfield and, if possible, to lure them into a fight. The Sabres would cruise at high speed, and the flights, flying in the standard "fluid four" formation, would be staggered to get the maximum coverage. The great planning difficulty was with the average twenty-minute patrol time. If weather conditions were good and landing at the home base would not be a problem, the time could be extended by reducing fuel reserves. In many ways, it was like a relay race, with relief flights sent to pick up the combat baton at carefully timed intervals to maintain continuous coverage.

If more MiGs came up than could be handled by the individual flight, they called for assistance, and the other flights on alert would scramble.

Under ideal conditions, the Sabres would find some unsuspecting MiGs and bounce them, but this was relatively rare because of the ground control system under which the MiGs operated. Combat usually took place only when the position and estimated fuel remaining on the Sabres was favorable to a quick slicing attack by the MiGs.

BREAKING THE ICE

The performance of combat squadrons is always directly related to the quality of their leadership. When the 334th Squadron had been led by Major George A. Davis, it had been a premier outfit. Davis had scored seven victories in 266 combat missions in the South Pacific during World War II. In Korea, he had scored fourteen additional victories, eleven of them over MiG-15s, and was the American Ace of Aces at the time of his death. On his last mission, he led his flight of four F-86s down in an attack on twelve MiG-15s. Davis had destroyed two MiGs and was lined up on a third when he was shot down by the Soviet Lieutenant Mikhail Averin of the 147th Fighter Regiment.

Davis was awarded the Medal of Honor posthumously, but his loss seemed to take the heart out of the 334th. In the three months before he was killed, the 334th had scored twenty-two victories. In the three months after his death, it had scored only four.

In early May 1952 Mahurin cleaned house, appointing Major Dick Ayersman as Commanding Officer of the 334th, and making Blesse the Operations Officer. Ayersman tasked Blesse with developing—in twenty-four hours—a plan to get the 334th back to its earlier standards. Blesse replied by pulling a report out of his briefcase: he had already prepared a plan, but it depended on Mahurin going along with the unprecedented request it contained.

In Blesse's analysis of the 334th, he had noted that the squadron flew in a loose defensive formation, ideal to repel attacks, but counterproductive if the goal was to force the MiGs to flight. He asked for permission to stand the squadron down for one week from combat. In that week, Blesse promised to train the flight leaders in the kind of aggressive, hell-for-leather flying that he knew was essential to win victories.

Mahurin balked at first. Asking to stand a squadron down from combat was unheard of, especially when F-86s were in such short supply. But Mahurin respected Blesse and agreed, however, with a warning that he had to produce results—or else. Blesse knew what that meant. He either delivered, or he would be on his way to a staff job, far away from combat.

As he knew it would, the 334th resented Blesse's request, and initially resisted his training, which consisted of taking each flight commander out and flying with him as he had flown with Mahurin back at George. Blesse would start them out flying on his wing in accordance with current procedures. This put the wingman too far out, where a turn would quickly throw him out of position. He then moved the wingman in closer, gradually increasing Gs and turning tighter. This made it clear that the wingman had to be in close to maintain his position in a fight.

His motives were simple. If you flew a jet fighter in combat, the wingman had to stay close in, on the leader's wing, or they were both going to get shot down.

Day by day, sortie after sortie, he worked his way through the flight commanders. As each flight commander learned from Blesse, he was tasked to pass the instructions on to other members of his flight. By midweek, the entire outfit was flying tucked in a tight formation, not so good for defense, but perfect for knocking down MiGs.

At midweek Boots also introduced some personnel changes. He called in two of the flight commanders and told them, "You've been here for sixty-five missions and haven't had a fight with a MiG. You are either unlucky or don't want to fight. Either way, I cannot afford you." The two were packed off to staff jobs and replaced by younger, more aggressive pilots.

Boots went public with the slogan he'd long lived by and for which he would become famous in air forces all around the world: No Guts, No Glory. In four words, it told the men of the 334th that he was going to lead them into the heart of MiG Alley, and they were going to get some MiGs.

Now all he had to do was get one himself.

FIRST KILL

Blesse was a ferocious competitor—on the golf course, at the Ping-Pong table, or in the air. But he was not foolish. The lessons he taught his squadron, which eventually became the basis for his book on combat tactics, were based first on intelligent survival, then on brutal, sharklike aggressiveness. He ordered that if a lead and a wingman got separated, they were to go home, immediately. The corollary to the order, though, was that any wingman who lost contact with his leader in combat was grounded for a week.

And as much as he liked to control things, Blesse took the unprecedented step of allowing his flight commanders to choose those pilots they wanted to fly in their flight. There was one rule for all, however: every pilot had to engage in at least three dogfights per week. If they couldn't find any MiGs, they had to break off early and return to the base, where they could hassle with each other to keep their skills honed to a fine edge.

By this time, Blesse was on thin ice. He had imposed his will on the squadron, had stood it down from combat and trained it as he wanted it trained. The squadron had responded, but he himself still did not have a single kill.

Mahurin's warning still rang in his ears, even though Mahurin had been shot down and captured on May 13. He had been hit by ground fire as he violated one of his own rules—making a second pass at a target, this time a North Korean truck. His loss hurt Blesse and the 4th Fighter Interceptor Group badly. It would be the start of sixteen months of solitary confinement for Mahurin, during which he was continuously starved and subjected to brutal beatings.

On May 25, 1952, when he was leading his flight well inside MiG Alley, Blesse's thoughts had wandered to Mahurin, wondering how he was doing. A moment later, however, everything came into sharp focus as he saw two MiG-15s flying above them. Blesse, flying as Red Lead, led his wingman into a turn, just as the Communist ground control system alerted the MiGs to his presence. The two MiGs, silver-gray against the sun, turned and began to dive, upping their speed to perhaps 600 mph. Blesse banked and climbed into them at 400 mph, closing at a combined speed of 1,000 mph.

Either a cocky expert or a beginner, the MiG leader tried to turn behind Blesse's flight, overshooting as he turned. Realizing his mistake, the Soviet pilot tried to reverse, but all of Blesse's training paid off as he slid behind him, firing and scoring hits.

To Blesse's astonishment, nothing happened. Nothing flew off the MiG and there was no fire and smoke; the chunky little fighter just accelerated away toward the Yalu. Boots watched in disbelief, then saw a thin trail of smoke started from his enemy's engine. He edged toward the MiG cautiously, worried about running out of fuel, yet unwilling to let this fish get away.

The MiG seemed certain to cross the Yalu, and Blesse gave up, starting a turn that would take them home. As his bank increased, his wingman called, "There he goes, Red Lead, he's punched out." Astonished, Blesse turned to see the MiG spiraling toward the green Korean hills, the pilot safely descending beneath the white canopy of his parachute.

All of the weeks of training, all of the jawboning, all of the notes he had pinned to the squadron bulletin board were now validated. Blesse's methods paid off, and the 334th took on a new life.

He used the momentum from his kill to begin fleshing out his ideas of air combat. At first he had put them in the form of a single pithy statement, typed out on a single sheet of legal-size paper and pinned to the squadron bulletin board. They were serious advisories, sometimes masked with a sprinkling of humor. More than anything else, they were utterly practical. Often they were one-liners, easy to understand and easy for a brand-new fighter pilot to remember. "Guts will do for skill, but not consistently. Know your job in combat or someone else will be flying in your place." "When in doubt—Attack." "During a dog fight, the wingman should 'Check Six' every ten or fifteen seconds, then call the leader and tell him he's clear. If he's not clear, then the call is to tell him to break."

The reactions to his little list of maxims were positive, primarily because of the dedication with which he taught his new people. Each flight with Blesse was a learning experience for the new men. Before the flight, he would conduct the briefing, studding it with tidbits of information on tactics and flying that could not be obtained anywhere else. After the mission, he would do the debriefing, giving constructive comments on everything that had gone well, and analyzing everything that had gone wrong. His manner made the young new arrivals feel that they were part of the first team—and they were.

One of those new arrivals was William Earl Brown. Then a Second Lieutenant, he is now a retired Lieutenant General and one of the most proficient ski instructors in Pennsylvania. In 1952 he was twenty-four years old, fresh out of flying school, and well aware that more would be expected of him, simply because he was black. Black officers were rare in 1952, black pilots even rarer, and black F-86 pilots the rarest of all.

He recalls that "Boots was clearly the best pilot in our squadron, and probably the best in the 4th Fighter Interceptor Wing. He could not only fly and fight in the Sabre, he could tell others how to do it. He was the natural leader of the squadron. I had the impression that if we were all on a desert island, with no military rank, Boots would still be the leader."

Brown would become Blesse's wingman, a tough assignment for a new pilot, but one where he would learn more in six months than he might have in six years elsewhere.

SCORING AND TEACHING

Boots's next kill was not a MiG, but it was welcome anyway, and it compensated for the time he had spent at George, hassling with F-51s. The Soviets would periodically attempt to begin close-air support operations, using Ilyushin Il-10s or the piston-engine fighters like the Lavochkin La-9.

The La-9 was the aircraft with which the Soviet aviation industry had "caught up" with the West. Introduced in the spring of 1945, the La-9 was an all-metal fighter with a performance similar to that of the F-51, particularly at lower altitudes. It was highly maneuverable and capable of a top speed of 428 mph at sea level.

Blesse happened on to an encounter between no fewer than sixteen F-86s and two La-9s. The Sabres would dive, rip off a burst of machine gun fire, then zoom back up to altitude. The La-9s had slowed down and were using their superior maneuverability to turn just before the F-86s fired.

Boots watched the engagement for an opening. He dove down and behind the La-9, coming up on him with speed brake out and throttle back. The La-9 pilot began his turn into Boots just as he had done with the other pilots. He made a sharp 90-degree turn and rolled out, assuming that Boots had climbed for altitude after his pass, as all the other pilots had done. Instead, Boots turned with him, sliding up and to the rear as he had done with the Mustangs back at George AFB. He dropped behind the La-9 and began to fire at a range of about 500 feet, closing fast. A two-second burst blew the La-9 up, covering Blesse's plane with oil.

Boots had done what Jimmy Doolittle was famous for doing, taking a calculated risk. If his gunnery had been bad, he could have slid in front of the La-9, speed brakes out and throttle back, and would have been an easy target. But he didn't miss, and the calculated risk paid off.

The victory gave him confidence that he transmitted to his squadron in the form of expanded concepts on air combat. These took into consideration the advantages and disadvantages of the aircraft they were flying, for as much as Boots wanted his pilots to kill MiGs, he didn't want them killed in the process.

The lessons Blesse taught showed just how technologically advanced air combat had become. It was not longer possible to fight intuitively. The demanding nature of the aircraft and the physics of aerial combat at high subsonic speeds and altitudes over 40,000 feet had changed all the equations. Boots's rules started with very basic instructions, including making certain that you relieved yourself immediately before takeoff. They covered the basic positions of offensive and defensive formations, from climb out, through cruise, combat, and return. He worked out the basic strategy for situations in which two aircraft were attacking two enemies, or four enemies, and the reverse situations as well.

Through all his instructions, Boots demonstrated his intimate knowledge of the exact performance of which the Sabre and the MiG were capable. His instructions to his pilots on what they were to do if they found a MiG on their tail are classic for their succinct sophistication. The following excerpt is a modified version, expanded slightly for clarity, and with my comments in parentheses.

1. If a MiG is on your tail, get your aircraft into a 5- or 6-G turn as soon as possible.
2. As your airspeed drops off, lower your nose so that you can continue to pull high Gs.
3. Losing 5,000 or 10,000 feet of altitude at this speed will lose an enemy pilot who is unsure of himself. If he is a good, aggressive pilot, though, the fight has just begun. (Blesse always considered the psychological factors affecting the enemy.)
4. At about 15,000 feet, you are going to have to make a "do or die" effort to shake him. Increase your G forces to 6 or 7 Gs, if you can, and slowly reduce the throttle to idle. (Reducing the throttle would be contrary to a new pilot's instincts.)
5. When you reach idle, throw out speed brakes and reverse your direction of turn without easing up on G forces. You can do this easily merely by pulling the nose up and over in a high-G barrel roll opposite your original direction of turn. (A technique that newer pilots might not yet have used.)
6. After about thirty degrees of this turn, reverse your turn again.
7. As he sees your speed brakes out, he will instinctively throw his out, but he has not yet noticed your decreased throttle setting. Even a good pilot will usually not recognize the initial decrease in throttle, because the increase in G forces keeps the two aircraft about the same distance apart. (This is the great differentiator, the kind of thinking that elevated Blesse's concepts beyond those of Boelcke and others. It takes into consideration the new phenomena found in jet air-to-air combat.) By doing this, you have created the one thing always sought by the defender in any dogfight—lateral separation.

Item 7 says it all. Blesse pours his years of sophistication into just a few lines, showing how you can maneuver a 600 mph jet fighter as a matador moves his cape. After the war, when he compiled all his notes and comments into *No Guts, No Glory*, he provided the entire USAF fighter force with the tactical manual they had needed to master the jet aircraft.

Not a few were amazed by Boots's book. He was recognized as an aggressive fighter pilot and as an athlete. Yet the book was a stunning intellectual achievement, an amazing synthesis of experience and the knowledge of the complex physics of air combat when two jet aircraft are being maneuvered by two pilots trying to kill each other through a vast range of speeds and altitudes.

Boots was now thirty years old. He was in first-rate physical condition and as fiercely competitive as ever, whether it was Ping-Pong, softball, or shooting down MiGs. The squadron Operations Room had a Ping-Pong table, and the junior officers kept it pretty busy. When Boots came in, he would grab a paddle and challenge anyone to a game. If he won, he would leave to attend to business. But on the rare occasions he lost, he would stay and play until he did win. It was gut instinct, but it also had a purpose. He wanted only winners in his unit, and he wanted to show that you had to do whatever was necessary to win. It was a physical corollary to his written aphorisms.

Earl Brown attributed some of Blesse's success as a pilot and a leader to his proficiency in golf. The skills he had learned in observing the effect of even a tiny change in the angle of the club head or the velocity of the swing translated directly to understanding the delicate flying characteristics of the Sabre when it was at the very edge of its flying envelope. Most of the pilots in his squadron were proficient in flying the Sabre within its normal operating limits. Boots was able to teach them how to fly it at the very limits of the Sabre's capability, when they were close to the stall at high altitudes, or were pulling lots of Gs at high speed at low altitudes. When the Sabre was operating at its maximum altitude, an ounce of excess pressure on the stick could send the aircraft into a shuddering high-speed stall, with a consequent loss of thousands of feet of altitude and many miles of airspeed. The same mistake, close to the ground, could result in a quick spin and a crash. Flying at the limits of the Sabre's envelope could kill you if you were not proficient—but it would enable you to kill MiGs if you were.

The combined effects of Boots's teaching and scoring became obvious in August 1952. He scored on August 6 and 20, bringing his total to four, but even more important to him was that his squadron got eleven kills. He had broken their slump, and they were functioning as the hot, aggressive unit that he wanted.

Sometimes Blesse's pugnacious nature paid off without firing a shot—or gaining a score. Earlier, during the spring of 1952, a large number of fighter-bomber raids were scheduled, and the Sabres were assigned the task of keeping the MiGs suppressed. They were to fly within sight of the principal air bases in Manchuria and to attack any MiGs that took off. Blesse drew Fencheng, an airbase he was familiar with because he had frequently broken the rules of engagement and crossed over into Manchuria to scout out what the Chinese were up to.

Arriving over Fencheng about twenty minutes before the American fighter-bombers were scheduled to hit their targets, he was dismayed to see about fifty MiGs taxiing out for takeoff.

He knew that his flight could never stop that many MiGs once they got airborne—and he also knew that the rules of engagement forbade his strafing them on the ground. Boots watched the MiGs until the first pair started their takeoff roll. With a signal to his wingman, he peeled off and dove down as if he were coming in on a strafing run. The MiGs were ordered by their ground control to stop. As Blesse pulled up—not having fired his guns—he could see blue streams of smoke from the brakes of the two aircraft in the lead flight as they tried frantically to stop.

He made a hard turn to the left, and as he came around, he saw the MiGs had plowed off the end of the strip, sheared off their nose gear, and were sitting, tail up, 100 yards off the runway. The rest of the MiGs were docilely taxiing back to their hard stands. With one pass, he had destroyed two MiGs and stopped the rest from taking off. It was almost as satisfying as a kill in the air.

THE SCORE BEGINS TO MOUNT

As noted in the previous chapter, Blesse's decision to extend for another twenty-five missions had enabled him to achieve his ambition and become an ace. It also provided him time to capitalize on all he had learned in the previous 100 missions, and to teach his squadron what he had learned. At the time of his first victory, he had been so excited that he was unable to relate any of the details to the intelligence officer. Now after a flight, he could recall with cold precision each and every thing that had happened to him—and everything that had happened to everyone in the rest of the squadron. His situational awareness was phenomenal; he could sense where everybody was and where they were going to be during the fight, then in the debriefing paint a three-dimensional portrait of the battle as it had unfolded.

The 334th scored seventeen victories in September, five of them falling to Blesse. Earl Brown recalls the mission on September 8, when the two of them jumped twelve MiG-15s near Sinuiju, almost at the Yalu. It did not occur to Brownie, as Blesse called him, that 6 to 1 were not good odds—he was flying with the best. Brown remembers that Blesse called to him just before they dove, "If these guys have read chapter 2, we're not going to be here very long," meaning that if it looked like the enemy pilots were veterans, they would break off the attack after the first pass.

Blesse was a smooth, predictable leader to fly wing on, and Brown had no difficulty staying with him. The two 86s closed on the rear flight of MiGs, which broke away and kept on going. Blesse pressed on to the next flight, and it broke away as well. They hadn't shot anyone down, but they had reduced the odds by half.

Blesse engaged the next flight, and after some sharp maneuvers, shot the leader down. Then, as Brown recalls it, "Boots latched on to the remaining MiG. The enemy pilot maneuvered vigorously until Boots got some good strikes in his fuselage. Then the MiG leveled out and slowed abruptly, making me think he had lost his engine. Boots put out his speed brakes and slowed with the MiG, staying behind him and continuing to get strikes on him. I was hypnotized by the scene and was late extending my speed brakes and pulling my throttle to idle. My plane drifted past Boots and I pulled off to the left to try and stay in the proper position, behind and to one side. Instead, I slid right up besides the MiG. I looked over to my right and I could see the pilot sitting upright, staring straight ahead. Suddenly he turned and looked directly at me. Then he faced front again and ejected. I guess he thought, 'If that guy can shoot me and fly formation with me at the same time, I'm getting out of here.'"

Missions like this brought the decorations in; Boots got the Silver Star and Brown a Distinguished Flying Cross. The two victories had raised his total to seven, making Blesse the leading ace of the Korean War.

Blesse got two more MiGs, on September 15 and 17, his eighth and ninth victories. Up to this point in the war, Boots had never lost a wingman, and he was as proud of that as he was of his MiG kills. On September 17, Blesse was chasing a MiG that was doing a series of tight turns. Boots followed it closely, cracking the whip for his wingman, who had to cross over from outside to inside at each turn.

On one of the turns, Blesse fired, and big chunks came off the MiG—directly into the jet intake of his wingman, Lieutenant Norman Smith. It demolished the Sabre's engine, and Smith had to head for the ocean, where he ejected safely and was rescued. It was the only time Boots came to base without his wingman.

The Communists monitored USAF air activity closely, and Blesse was getting famous as a leading ace. "Pyongyang Sally," the North Korean version of "Tokyo

Rose," announced that the North Koreans planned to hang him from the Han River Bridge if they captured him. The threat was good for a laugh—until a few days later.

On October 2, 1952, Boots followed a practice he had recently introduced, bringing a new wingman (whose name Blesse does not recall) along for the experience. The 334th had learned that if a new man saw some real action during his first missions, he was likely to develop into an aggressive combat pilot.

The mission started out as a four-plane flight, but one aircraft had to abort and was escorted home by his wingman. Boots and his wingman continued their patrol, but saw nothing. On their trip home, they saw four MiGs, but lacking the fuel to fight, Boots continued on his way.

The MiGs were obviously flown by veterans who were well aware of the Sabres' probable fuel situation. The lead MiG tracked them, and at far too great a distance began firing his cannons. The MiG's two 23-mm cannon didn't make much of an impression, but the 37-mm fired shells that looked like Roman candles, huge blobs of flame. Blesse recognized that the MiG pilot was shooting for effect, and that the cannon shells were falling far behind. His wingman did not; in a typical beginner's move, he broke left, away from Blesse—just where the Soviet pilots in the two MiGs wanted him to go.

The MiGs curved in behind the fleeing F-86, gaining every second. Blesse knew that his fuel state was too low to fight and get back, but he called out to his wingman to follow last-ditch procedures, putting the F-86 into a curving, high-G spiral. Blesse fell in on the tail of the two MiGs, and two more MiGs followed him—it was F-86, two MiGs, F-86, two MiGs in a deadly daisy chain.

Blesse scored hits on the MiG flying as wingman; parts broke off and the pilot dove away. As soon as he did, the lead MiG, unwilling to fly without a wingman, followed him. As he left, the MiG trailing Blesse fired. Blesse turned into him, glancing at his fuel gauge, and realized that he was not going to get back. He called his own wingman and told him to fly out over the water and head for home.

Blesse rolled inverted, looking for the two MiGs that had been shooting at him—they were gone, but he was down to 8,000 feet and his last 1,100 pounds of fuel. There probably was not enough JP-4 to get him back to his base, but he could get out to sea and bail out there. As he climbed, he saw yet another MiG diving down from ten o'clock, his left front quarter.

The MiG pilot must have had his mind on other things, for he did not see Blesse's F-86, which was low and to his right.

The situation was clear-cut. Blesse was at low altitude, low on fuel, well behind enemy lines, and not certain where the two MiGs were that he had been fighting. Naturally, he attacked, rolling his Sabre into a 4-G turn, closing to two hundred yards and firing. The MiG exploded, with the pilot ejecting. It was victory number ten—but Blesse knew he would never get his gun camera—or his airplane—back to base to prove it.

Fortunately, the fight's progress had been monitored at Kimpo Air Field, and a flight of four F-86s, led by Captain Robinson Risner, was scrambled. "Robbie" would score victories over eight MiGs in Korea, then go on to fight in the Vietnam War, where he spent seven years as a prisoner of war.

Risner was on the scene with his flight when the MiG blew up, and he was able to confirm it for Blesse. Boots in the meantime had some other problems. He tried to make it back to Kimpo, climbing to 32,000 feet in altitude, then shutting off his engine and gliding at the F-86's best glide speed, 180 knots. By the time he had used most of his altitude, he realized he was not going to make it. With his last drops of fuel, he restarted his engine, climbed back up to 13,000 feet and headed for the coastline.

His engine flamed out when he was well within North Korean borders, but he coaxed the little Sabre to glide, passing over the coastline at 3,000 feet. At 1,200 feet, he ejected, about a half mile off the coast. An Air Force Grumman SA-16 Albatross—a "Dumbo" in air-sea rescue parlance—swooped in and picked him up, taking fire from the North Korean coastal batteries as it did so.

(Boots talks about his ejection almost casually, as if it were like ducking out on a fire escape. Ejection was in fact extremely hazardous. The sudden G forces, applied directly to your body, could cause spinal damage, particularly if you were not sitting up straight. During the ejection process, any part of your body that was not tightly controlled could flop out and be severed by the windscreen canopy or the cockpit walls. Once out of the cockpit, the opening of the parachute snapped your body again, and any damage done during the ejection was reinforced. Despite all the hazards, however, pilots loved the idea of having an ejection seat, for it provided one last chance at survival when all else had failed.)

The entire fight and subsequent rescue operation had been monitored by the 334th, back in squadron operations at Kimpo, and a roaring celebration was already in progress when Blesse arrived, still dripping wet, but happy. Something else had also arrived: his orders back to the United States. The Air Force had lost one leading ace when Davis was killed. They were not going to allow another leading jet ace to be shot down. Blesse still had two sorties to go on his 125-mission commitment, but he was the leading ace in Korea, and the brass was sending him home.

His next combat sorties would come in 1967 and 1968 in Vietnam, leading the "Da Nang Gunfighters."

THE LEADING ACE IN KOREA

Blesse knew that he would not be the leading ace for very long, for the USAF was becoming more and more accomplished in its combat tactics, thanks in no small measure to him. After he left, the race to become Korea's leading ace was disputed among three men: Captain Joseph C. McConnell, Major James Jabara, and a protégé of Blesse's, Captain Manuel J. Fernandez. At the end of the war, their scores were sixteen, fifteen, and fourteen and a half, respectively.

McConnell had flown as a navigator in Consolidated B-24s during World War II and became a pilot in 1948. On his 106th combat mission in Korea with the 39th Fighter Interceptor Squadron, he shot down three MiGs to raise his total to sixteen. He was immediately ordered to return to the United States and was stationed at Edwards Air Force Base. He was killed flying an advanced Sabre, the F-86H.

Jabara had scored one and a half victories as a P-51 pilot in Europe during World War II, and six victories in F-86s on his first tour in Korea, which ended in 1951. He returned in 1952 to score another nine victories. He had reached the rank of colonel when he was killed in an automobile accident in 1966.

"Pete" Fernandez was a member of the 334th Fighter Squadron, and had been mentored by Blesse. He ran a neck-and-neck race with Jabara and McConnell for the leading ace title. Pete had won his wings in 1944 but had not seen combat during World War II. His life was perhaps the saddest of all three men. Very much against his will, he had been ordered home with McConnell, which meant, of course, that McConnell was going to be the leading ace. He attributed being sent home to the Air Force desire that a non-Hispanic person be the leading ace. In his Air Force career, he continued to feel that he was discriminated against. He retired from the service as a major in 1963 and was later killed in an aircraft accident.

Fernandez's suppositions may or may not have been true, but the great irony is that in the 1990s, his Hispanic heritage would have been welcomed as an illustration of the diversity within the Air Force.

BETWEEN TWO WARS

Major Blesse returned to the United States and was immediately returned to his regular rank of Captain—his promotion to major had been a "spot" promotion, reflecting his responsibilities in conflict. There followed a series of assignments that recognized his administrative and leadership ability and that saw him gain early promotion to the rank of Lieutenant Colonel. His leadership style was matched by his flying ability, because as an "old man" of thirty-four, he won all six individual trophies in the annual worldwide air force gunnery meet at Nellis Air Force Base in 1955. His feat has never been equaled and was roughly comparable to winning six gold medals in the Olympics. It established him as a man to watch in a peacetime Air Force.

Unlike Zemke, Blesse had the political skills to survive even when he ran into bosses whose methods were far different than his own. By applying *No Guts, No Glory* precepts to the command of a squadron, he brought the 32d Fighter Interceptor Squadron at Soesterberg Air Base in Germany to the peak of performance. He pioneered the introduction of the "century series" of fighters in Europe, using both the North American F-100 and the Convair F-102.

History repeated itself, however, in an unfortunate manner. As a youth in the Philippines, he had courted trouble in the form of a Lieutenant's wife. As a Lieutenant Colonel in Germany, he made the same mistake. While the cultural mores of the time were less severe than they are today, the indiscretion had an adverse impact on his career. His old wingman, Earl Brown, says unequivocally that Blesse would have become a four-star general, and probably Chief of Staff, if the incident had not occurred.

BACK IN THE SADDLE

Combat beckoned again when the United States became involved in the Vietnam War. Blesse checked out in the McDonnell F-4 Phantom II, the hottest fighter in the inventory, and in 1967 was sent to the 366th Tactical Fighter Wing, at Da Nang Air Base, South Vietnam. There, as Director of Operations, Blesse pioneered new tactics, including the installation of gun pods on the F-4 for air-to-air combat. He renamed the unit "The Gunfighters," and, although he did not get a MiG himself in the course of 108 missions over North Vietnam and a further 46 over South Vietnam and Laos, the Gunfighters registered the first gun kills of MiGs of the war. Before the war ended, a total of seventeen MiGs had fallen to the guns of the F-4s.

World War I German ace Max Immelmann, proudly wearing his Blue Max around his neck. Such photos appeared on postcards, sheet music, cigar boxes, and other commercial items, all serving to glorify the German fighter pilot. PETER KILDUFF

Oberleutnant Immelmann
an seinem Fokker-Flugzeug

Censorship rears its ugly head in 1915. Immelmann is shown with his Fokker Eindecker, but the censor has erased both the rotary engine and the forward-firing machine gun, revolutionary innovations that made the airplane famous. PETER KILDUFF

The Fokker scourge in flight.
Note the single machine gun on this
Eindecker directly in front of the pilot.
PETER KILDUFF

Many considered German ace Oswald Boelcke to be the finest aerial tactician of World War I. He was also a consummate teacher and leader. PETER KILDUFF

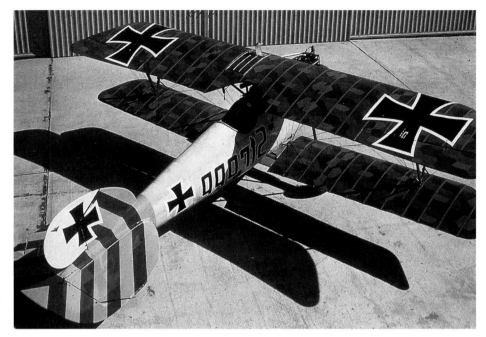

The Albatros D Va, as restored by the artisans of the National Air & Space Museum's Garber facility. AUTHOR'S COLLECTION

Perhaps the best fighter of World War I, and certainly a harbinger of future fighter construction, the Fokker D VII had an angular beauty. AUTHOR'S COLLECTION

Captain Edward V. Rickenbacker—forever "Captain Eddie" to the press—looms out of the tiny cockpit of his SPAD XIII fighter. There are a number of noteworthy features here: his confident attitude; the beat-up cowling showing the airplane's hard use; the twin .303 caliber machine guns; the open gun sight; the simple car-type radiator; and the fixed-pitch propeller—all 1917/18 technology and quite enough for any pilot with only two hundred hours of experience to handle.

Pictured above, a somewhat less confident-looking Rickenbacker is shown with "Old Number One," one of two SPAD XIII's that he flew in combat. The round white spots are patches put over German bullet holes. Rickenbacker had them marked with black crosses (not discernable in this photo) to remind him of how close the enemy had come to killing him. The thin airfoil and heavy strut bracing of the SPAD contributed to its great strength. Below, forty-seven years later, and now chairman of the board of Eastern Airlines, Rickenbacker is shown with a restored World War I SPAD VII marked in his colors, but of earlier vintage than the aircraft he flew. U.S. AIR FORCE

Lieutenant Alan Winslow and his Nieuport 28. Winslow would score the first kill for the U.S. 94th Aero Squadron (note the 94th's famous Hat-in-the-Ring insignia). The Nieuport had delicate, almost feminine lines. PETER KILDUFF

Lieutenant Douglas Campbell, another member of the 94th Aero Squadron, is pictured here with his Nieuport 28. Campbell scored his first victory in the same dogfight as Winslow.
PETER KILDUFF

A Nieuport 28 restored to flying condition after World War II is readied for takeoff at Wright Patterson Air Force Base, Ohio. Note the human "brakes" as the engine is run-up. U.S. AIR FORCE

Hubert "Hub" Zemke was not particularly photogenic, but circumstances arranged that he would appear in many USAAF publicity shots. This one is poignant because the signature was affixed just one month before his death in 1994. WARREN M. BODIE

A restored Curtiss P-40 belonging to Sue Parish, flying near Oshkosh, Wisconsin. The P-40 was important because it was available in quantity and was just adequate in its performance if flown correctly. AUTHOR'S COLLECTION

Zemke was even more important as a leader than as an ace. These are some of the outstanding pilots who blossomed under his tutelage: From left front: Francis "Gabby" Gabreski, Robert Johnson, Walker "Bud" Mahurin, and Robert Landry; on the wing are Walter Cook and David C. Schilling. This group achieved more than 104 victories in the air following Zemke's lead. WARREN M. BODIE

This is Zemke's Republic P-47 Thunderbolt shortly after its arrival in the United Kingdom in 1943. Its huge size made it the object of derision by pilots used to the svelte lines of the petite Spitfire, but the P-47 was extraordinarily rugged and proved itself capable in many different types of missions. WARREN M. BODIE

When Eddie Rickenbacker (fourth from the left) visited the U.S. 56th Fighter Group in England in 1943, he was greeted by an old friend from World War I, Brigadier General Frank O'Driscoll "Monk" Hunter, seen here at Rickenbacker's left. On Rickenbacker's right is Zemke, who had his problems with Hunter. Immediately behind Zemke is David Schilling, who had his problems with Zemke. The others are unknown. WARREN M. BODIE

Another marching shot, this time of four tough aces of the 56th Fighter Group. From left, the C.O., Zemke (17.75 victories); Schilling (22.5 victories); Gabreski (31.0 victories); and Fred Christensen (21.5 victories). The photo was taken at RAF Boxted in the summer of 1944. WARREN M. BODIE

The most notorious German fighter of World War II was the Messerschmitt Bf 109G, against which both Zemke and Robin Olds fought on many occasions. WARREN M. BODIE

A captured German Focke Wulf Fw 190 is pictured in flight over Ohio. Many consider the Fw 190 to be the most aesthetically pleasing of all World War II fighters. AUTHOR'S COLLECTION

More versatile than the Me 109, but less capable at altitude, the Focke Wulf Fw 190 was one of the best fighters of the war, excelling at both air-to-air combat and in ground attack work. Olds shot down several of these.
WARREN M. BODIE

A flight of three brightly polished Republic P-47Ns. The P-47N was an excellent aircraft, but like all combat planes, it needed first-rate maintenance. Without that, it was dangerous, as Frederick Blesse found out. U.S. Air Force

A postwar restoration of a Lockheed P-38, shown here in invasion stripes. Robin Olds would become an ace in the P-38, as would the leading American ace of World War II, Richard Bong.

PLANES OF FAME MUSEUM, CHINO, CALIF. AIRPORT

The North American F-86 proved itself in combat and was loved by its pilots. These aircraft are from the 4520th Combat Crew Training Group at Nellis Air Force Base, Nevada. WARREN M. BODIE

What would be called a "glamour shot" today shows young Captain Frederick C. Blesse standing by his North American F-86 fighter after shooting down his first MiG-15, on May 25, 1952.

AIR FORCE ASSOCIATION

A North Korean MiG-15 after a landing mishap—the nose gear is sheered off. The airplane proved to be a worthy opponent to the F-86. WARREN M. BODIE

Rickenbacker (left) and Blesse stand by a SPAD and an F-86 at the Richmond, Virginia, Air Show in 1953. Either man could have flown the other's airplane in the appropriate war, and both would have done well. MAJOR GENERAL FREDERICK C. BLESSE, USAF (RET.)

Blesse (center) is congratulated by Colonel Harrison Thyng (left) and Captain Clifford D. Jolley (right) on September 8, 1952, just after becoming the leading ace of the Korean War with 7 victories. Thyng, who had five victories in World War II and added five more in Korea, and, Jolley, who had five victories at the time and would score two more, were aces in their own right. MAJOR GENERAL FREDERICK C. BLESSE, USAF (RET.)

One war later, and flying a far more sophisticated aircraft, Colonel Blesse stands by his McDonnell F-4C Phantom fighter. He was Director of Operations for the 366th Tactical Fighter Wing, the "Gunfighters," at Da Nang Air Base in South Vietnam. Air Force Association

Colonel Robin Olds (left) and Captain John Stone were two of the principal authors of Operation Bolo, the most successful aerial combat engagement of the Vietnam War. AIR FORCE ASSOCIATION

Olds's success leading the squadron emboldened him to wear a strictly nonregulation mustache, shown here in a photo with other MiG killers of the U.S. 555th Tactical Fighter Squadron. Left to right, Captain Francis M. Gullick, First Lieutenant William D. Lafever, Captain Richard M. Pascoe, Olds, Major Thomas M. Hirsch, Captain Norman Wells, and Major Everett J. Raspberry. AIR FORCE ASSOCIATION

By May 1967, Olds had honed his 8th Tactical Fighter Wing into a killing machine. Here the victors of three kills on May 20th are (left to right) Major Philip P. Combies, First Lieutenant Daniel L. Lafferty, Major John R. Pardo, First Lieutenant Stephen B. Croker, and First Lieutenant Stephen A. Wayne. Colonel Olds is on the ladder, stenciling the three victory stars to the wing scoreboard.

AIR FORCE ASSOCIATION

The McDonnell F-4C Phantom that Olds flew in Vietnam was a far more capable aircraft than the P-38 or P-51 he flew in World War II. The bombs and missiles were all carried externally, and it required the brute power of two engines to push the F-4 to supersonic speeds. U.S. AIR FORCE

The F-4's companion was the Republic F-105 Thunderchief, always called "Thud" by its pilots. This stock publicity photo shows the wide array of ordnance that it could carry. U.S. Air Force

"Going Downtown," the F-105s and F-4s required refueling from the indispensable Boeing KC-135 tankers. AIR FORCE ASSOCIATION

The most modern enemy fighter to appear
in Vietnam was the sleek MiG-21. Small, light,
and very maneuverable, it was a formidable
adversary, especially when equipped with Atoll
heat-seeking missiles. AIR FORCE ASSOCIATION

The value of having an internal cannon on a fighter became immediately apparent in Vietnam. Here an F-105 shoots down a MiG-17 with a 20-mm Gattling gun.
AIR FORCE ASSOCIATION

Later in the war, the 8th Tactical Fighter Wing received McDonnell F-4D Phantoms that were capable of carrying precision-guided munitions. This one carried two laser-guided bombs and two Sparrow missiles. Air Force Association

The SA-2 had a proximity fuse so that it did not have to strike an aircraft to destroy it. Just detonating within lethal range was sufficient to bring about ghastly results, such as this F-4C being shot down on August 12, 1967, over Hanoi. Both the pilot, Lieutenant Colonel Edwin L. Atterbury, and his weapons system operator, Major Thomas V. Parrot, survived the incident, but Colonel Atterbury was murdered by his captors. Author's Collection

The SA-2 guideline surface-to-air missile was deployed in vast numbers by the North Viet-namese and required constant visual and electronic vigilance by U.S. pilots to counter them. AIR FORCE ASSOCIATION

It looks easy, but air refueling is demanding work, especially at night under conditions of radio silence. The heavily laden F-4, shown here loaded with bombs and missiles, required refueling before and after a strike. Air Force Association

Besides raising the standard of the squadron's performance, he also raised the standard of its living conditions, turning Da Nang from a survival area into a comfortable, if not luxurious, base for its officers and airmen.

Blesse's performance in Vietnam revived his career. He was entrusted with the 474th Tactical Fighter Wing, flying the very controversial General Dynamics F-111s, and in the process became a brigadier general. He returned to Vietnam in 1971 to become Director of Operations for the Seventh Air Force and was promoted to Major General, the rank he held when he retired in 1975. At that time, he had 6,500 flying hours, gained in aircraft as widely separated in time and technology as the Curtiss P-40 and the McDonnell Douglas F-15. He flew over 650 combat hours, and is the nation's sixth-ranking jet ace. His decorations include the Distinguished Service Cross (second only to the Medal of Honor), two Silver Stars, six Distinguished Flying Crosses, twenty-one Air Medals, a Purple Heart, a Bronze Star with "V" device, and twenty-one others.

After he retired from the service, he pursued a career with the Grumman Aircraft Corporation. Now fully retired, except from golf and speaking engagements, he lives in Florida. He is still much in demand as a lecturer, and young fighter pilots—and their commanders—still turn to him for counsel.

Air forces are bureaucracies, like any large organization. In times of peace, the lessons learned in war are sometimes forgotten, even lessons put forward so explicitly by Blesse. Another fighter pilot, Robin Olds, learned his lessons in World War II, flying with Zemke. Politics and fate kept him out of the Korean War, but his knowledge and his skills would be invaluable in Vietnam.

★ E I G H T ★
IN ZEMKE'S MOLD

I am a Warrior!

The words ring out over the audience as the speaker, seventy-five years old but still tall and strong, stands square shouldered, his feet spread like a linebacker awaiting an onslaught. Suddenly, his face dissolves from a menacing challenge to a welcoming grin. The crowd is on its feet, applauding wildly, for this man, Robin Olds, *is* a warrior—and one hell of a speaker as well.

Olds had just concluded a forty-five-minute talk to an audience of aviation buffs in Spartanburg, South Carolina. The speech at first seemed oddly rambling, moving from shooting down Messerschmitts in World War II to shooting down MiGs in Vietnam to bureaucracy in the Pentagon to skiing. But as the old fighter pilot went on, it was obvious that he was painting an intricate picture, showing how important it was to America to make young pilots into warriors like himself, not merely willing but eager to fight for their country.

As the ovation subsided, the crowd began to rush the podium, in ones and twos at first, and then in a general mass, all wanting a word with a legend. He had words, plenty of words, for them all.

AN ESTABLISHMENT BACKGROUND

Robin Olds was born on July 14, 1922, in Honolulu, the son of then-Captain (later Major General) Robert Olds, one of the most influential men in the Air Corps.

A flyer since 1917, Robert had been one of the most outspoken instructors at the Air Corps Tactical School. Later he was commander of the 2d Bombardment Group, which pioneered the use of the Boeing YB-17 and led it on the pioneering 1937 goodwill flight through South America. Robert also conducted the Air Corps tests on the Norden bombsight and successfully advocated its adoption as standard equipment. Had he not died in 1943 of sudden illness, he almost certainly would have become a four-star general.

Young Robin Olds grew up at Langley Field, Virginia, surrounded by the men who would become famous as leaders during and after World War II. They included, among many others, Carl "Tooey" Spaatz, Frank Andrews, and an intense, young Curtis LeMay. They were, with his father, the "bomber barons," advocates of the fast, heavily armed bomber. All disciples of Billy Mitchell, they believed that a well-armed bomber force could fight off enemy fighter opposition and reach its target without fighter escort. Young Robin was an apostate; he wanted to be a fighter pilot.

Olds remembers his childhood at Army bases with pride and pleasure. He had no way of knowing that his father and his friends were all slated to become general officers—they were just "regular guys" to him. It was a happy, thoroughly normal time for an Army brat. He recalls that he would amuse his father by identifying any approaching aircraft by simply listening to the sound of its engine. He could tell the rumble of Pratt & Whitney radials in the Keystone bombers, the purring of the Curtiss V-12 in the Curtiss P-6es, and the hacking groaning cough of the older airplanes, powered by aging Liberty engines.

Robin Olds also understood routine military matters. He saw that it took much longer for reserve officers to be promoted and that they were always vulnerable to a force cut. By the age of ten, he had made up his mind to go to West Point, get his regular commission, and then go to flying school. (When World War II came in September 1939 he tried to volunteer for the Royal Canadian Air Force. At seventeen, he was too young to join without parental approval. His dad "went through the ceiling" and insisted that he go to West Point.)

WEST POINT: PLUSES AND MINUSES

Olds the Warrior still has mixed feelings about West Point, the warrior factory. He has the greatest admiration for the motto Duty, Honor, Country, so admirably expressed by General Douglas MacArthur. He still admires the traditions, the beautiful buildings, and the sense of belonging to his class. But he felt that West Point taught very little about fighting, and he knew from personal experience that some of the older tactical officers took a sadistic pride in using the honor code to trap cadets into admissions of guilt about minor infractions. He was caught one evening in March of his final year, after having had a single drink. When asked if he had had a drink down in New York City, he was honor-bound to answer yes. The tactical officer broke him from his Cadet Captain rank. He was made to walk punishment tours until within five minutes of his graduation parade.

Many veterans of West Point share his mixed feelings, but few have had a chance to do as he did later, impose his will on a service academy. Olds was Commandant of Cadets at the Air Force Academy from November 1967 through early 1971. He personally saw to it that the honor code was used as an instrument to ensure integrity and not to levy petty punishments.

Olds entered West Point in September 1941. A natural athlete, if not a natural disciplinarian, he excelled at football and was selected as an all-American tackle in 1942. Today he tells with obvious relish of how his warrior instincts spilled over in one game. A cheap postplay shot—an elbow to his mouth—by an opponent sent him to the locker room minus his front teeth. With thirty-two stitches in his lower lip, Olds insisted on returning to the game, for one reason: to get revenge. Just before the half, he cornered the player who had punched him and threw a completely legal block that broke his ribs. Before the stretcher bearers could cart his antagonist off the field, Olds towered over him. Grinning, he ripped off his helmet and pointed to his lip and missing teeth, then to his opponent's ribs. It was a warrior's response, instinctive but also measured. The same traits would serve him well in combat.

Olds's athletic prowess helped him become a cadet officer, but he really did not enjoy the narrower aspects of military life at the academy. In 1942 he received two great pieces of news. The first was that the course was being cut from four years to three, to provide more officers for the vastly expanded Army. The curriculum was not so much shortened as consolidated; classes were stacked on classes, and there was virtually no free time. Olds did not care, for it meant he would get to war sooner.

The second was that he was to begin primary flight training at the Spartan School of Aviation at Tulsa, Oklahoma, in June of 1942. Primary flight training gave the basics, but it was essentially a screening process to weed out those who lacked the capacity—or the genuine desire—to fly. A pilot's career often depends on the quality of his instructors, and Olds was no exception. He lucked out with his first instructor, John Kostura, who taught him to fly in a Fairchild PT-19, a low-wing trainer powered by a Ranger in-line engine. The two men hit it off at once, and Olds recalls it as a "joyous time." He proved to be an excellent pilot, and Kostura began to teach him aerobatics that were well beyond the conventional primary curriculum.

Olds was less fortunate when he was sent back to West Point, where the flying training was conducted about twenty miles north at Stewart Field. There his instructor, a pompous young Captain, nicknamed "Military Bill," emphasized military drill more than flying the Vultee BT-13 "Vibrator" used in basic training. Worse, he considered the six-foot-two-inches-tall, 205-pound Olds as too big for fighters and assigned him to advanced training as a bomber pilot. Olds was crushed, but duty was duty and he accepted the assignment to fly Beech AT-10s, a twin-engine trainer of all-wood construction. His luck turned, for his new instructor, Lieutenant John Hacker, identified him as fighter pilot material. The two flew the little Beech like a fighter, dogfighting with North American AT-6s, and once flying under every bridge over the Hudson River between Albany and New York City. Hacker would see to it that Olds was assigned to Lockheed P-38s, a twin-engine fighter with a cockpit ample for his size.

Life was hectic at West Point, with academics and flying alternating morning and afternoon. Typically, Olds would spend the morning in the classroom and the afternoon flying, and then would go to the gym, where he would change into his football uniform. All of his spare time, between flights, on the bus, or sneaked in the bathroom late at night, was spent studying to master the tough pass or fail courses.

In April 1943 he was called to Tucson, where his father, only forty-seven, lay dying in the hospital from pericardial disease. Olds remembers confiding, with some apprehension, that he was going to be a fighter pilot. His father smiled and said, "I never went up in the air without learning something new, so never think you know it all." Olds remembers, and honors, these words to this day.

On June 1, 1943, Olds was commissioned a Second Lieutenant in the U.S. Army Air Corps and received his pilot's wings. He would go on to a career in which he would always distinguish himself in war but manage to antagonize his bosses in peace. Ironically, the beliefs that would get him in trouble in peacetime would always prove to be correct in combat.

OPERATIONS

Lieutenant Hacker's getting him assigned to P-38s initially proved to be more of a hazard than a help. He was sent to Williams Field, Arizona, where a consignment of Lockheed P-322s was used for training.

P-322 was the designation given by the USAAF to a series of 143 Lockheed Lightnings purchased by the British and French and then taken over by the Army in December 1941. Outwardly similar in appearance to the standard P-38, the P-322 differed in two crucial ways. Because U.S. export laws prohibited the export of turbosuperchargers, the P-322s used unsupercharged Allison C15 engines. And, while the propellers of the standard Lightning rotated in opposite directions, negating torque effect (the tendency for the rotation of the propeller to pull the aircraft to one side), those of the P-322 did not. The two changes turned the normally tractable P-38 into the very nasty P-322, which Lockheed engineer Willis Hawkins has called the "most dangerous plane Lockheed ever built."

Olds survived the Williams experience, graduating to fly P-38s with a replacement training unit stationed at Muroc Dry Lake, now the site of Edwards Air Force Base. The unit was equipped with standard P-38s, but once again danger loomed, for there was insufficient training, poor maintenance, and a general lack of safety consciousness. Part of the problem was the mixture of aircraft models. The pilots were flying P-38Ds, Es, and Fs, and each one had changes in the control layout. Olds recalls one afternoon when flying was canceled after eleven major accidents, including one in midair, had occurred since dawn.

Olds flew as often as possible, building up his flying time while impatiently waiting for assignment to an overseas combat unit. He waited and waited until he found he was in a Catch-22 situation worthy of Joseph Heller. The unofficial word had been put out that West Point graduates were not going to be assigned overseas unless they went as flight leaders with a squadron that had been trained as a unit. However, commanders of units going overseas did not want green pilots without combat experience serving as flight leaders. As a result, Olds and six other West Pointers were stuck in a cycle of training jobs in California.

Olds and his classmate, Al Tucker, finally went to his current outfit's headquarters in Los Angeles and found an elderly sergeant in the personnel section. The sergeant listened to their complaints and asked where they wanted to go. Thirty minutes later, Olds had orders for himself—and for six of his buddies—to go to England.

This was the first time Olds went out of channels to get into combat. It would not be the last.

COMBAT IN EUROPE

Olds joined the 434th Fighter Squadron of the 479th Fighter Group at Lomita, California, in March 1944 and went to England with the unit. Within a week after their arrival, they were flying combat. His delay in getting to battle had one important benefit: he had about 650 hours flying time. Some 250 hours of this was in the P-38, and he was its master.

The P-38 was a delightful—but complex—aircraft to fly. Its twin turbo-superchargers had to be watched carefully, and the electrically controlled propellers were given to overspeeding. The fuel system required careful management, particularly under single-engine conditions. In a prolonged dive, the Lightning (like the P-47) would encounter compressibility problems that, unless handled properly, could result in either a dive into the ground or the aircraft coming apart in the air. The compressibility problem was an almost crippling disadvantage, for it required that the P-38's diving speed be limited so that it was not fast enough to catch—or get away from—a diving German fighter.

The Lightning handled very well, but it was unforgiving of any mistake and many men made the error of attempting to show off their aerobatic prowess at low level, only to "buy the farm" in the euphemism of the day. Few were immune to the practice; the commander of the 436th Fighter Squadron lost his life on a local flight on May 24, 1944, two days before the unit's first combat operation.

The performance of the P-38Js flown by the 479th was more than adequate. It was faster than its opponents, with a top speed of 425 mph. Surprisingly, its slender elliptically shaped wings made it very maneuverable despite its twin engines and large size. Although often described as unmaneuverable, it was actually able to turn with both the Messerschmitt and Focke Wulf fighters and was not susceptible to spins in even a very tight turn. Turns could be accelerated by varying the speed of the two engines, literally "motoring" the aircraft around in the air with differential power. (Olds has commented that he was not an advocate of this practice.)

The turning ability of the P-38 was used to gain advantage in one-on-one combat. While the Allied air forces greatly outnumbered the Luftwaffe in total aircraft, the Germans were able to concentrate their forces. In most of Olds's fights, the enemy outnumbered the P-38s. The Americans adopted a tactic that had originated in World War I and would be used as "the Wheel" by MiGs during the Vietnam War. Called the "Lufberry Circle," the maneuver required the outnumbered P-38s to fly in two circles, separated by about 800 feet in altitude, with the aircraft in each circle flying in opposite directions. Any enemy aircraft attacking this defensive formation would inevitably have a P-38 on its tail.

Despite its many good qualities, German pilots preferred to fight the P-38 rather than the P-47 or the Mustang. One reason was that the Lightning was susceptible to engine malfunction. German pilots loved to come across a P-38 heading for home with one engine feathered.

The Allison engines did not operate well in the high humidity and cold temperatures of northern Europe, and engine failures were so common that P-38s were limited to altitudes of 20,000 feet and below whenever possible. The lower altitude was welcome for another reason. Without an engine in the nose, the P-38's cockpit was unbearably cold at altitude and at the end of a long mission, pilots often had to be lifted from their seats and massaged before they could begin to walk. Instead of an engine, the P-38's nose contained the excellent armament package of a 20-mm cannon and four .50-caliber machine guns.

An aggressive pilot, however, could capitalize on the P-38's advantages and mask its limitations. Thus it was leadership that was important, and leadership would play a big role in shaping Olds as a combat pilot.

His initial combat sorties over occupied France were too mild for his taste. He and his buddies thought that the squadron commander, Major (later Lieutenant Colonel) James Herren, was too cautious. Herren was undoubtedly correct to be conservative when breaking in new pilots, but Olds wanted to attack the enemy trains and airfields he saw below, and he quietly plotted with a friend to do so.

Their next mission passed as uneventfully as the previous ones until Olds saw the silver steam of a train running across the French countryside.

He called, "New Cross Leader, this is New Cross Blue 3. I have a train down there at eight o'clock. I'm going down on it, will you cover me?"

The word "Roger" came back, and Olds peeled off, exhilarated to be diving to the attack, anxious to fire his guns at a German target. He had made three passes at the train when the whole squadron followed him down to shoot it up. Major Herren's exasperated voice came in over the radio: "Get your asses back in formation; we are going home."

Back in England, Herren stood Olds at attention and blasted him for being disobedient, for breaking formation, and for leading the squadron down on an unauthorized target. Herren went on and on, with Olds standing at West Point cadet attention, eyes focused on Herren's eyes. Then Herren asked, "What have you got to say for yourself?" Olds said, "I asked for you to cover me when I went down on the train, and you said 'Roger.'"

Herren denied saying it, but he knew he was beaten; he would have to put every man in the squadron under oath to find out who had said "Roger," and he let the matter drop.

Olds did not. He had confirmed that to do any fighting he was going to have to break rules—and the prospect did not bother him a bit. Unlike many of his colleagues, Olds was not so much determined to become an ace as he was to do a job. That job included shooting down Germans wherever possible, but it also included damaging them in other ways, and he would continuously develop methods that would assure the success of the squadron. In the course of the next several months, he would both become an ace and develop tactical concepts that would withstand the test of time. They would also damage his career prospects because they bucked current trends.

RIDDLE AND ZEMKE

The 479th Fighter Group was commanded by Lieutenant Colonel Kyle Riddle from its inception on December 25, 1943, until he was shot down on August 10, 1944. Riddle managed to escape and return to Allied lines. By then, France had been liberated, and he was able to return to his own outfit, which, as previously noted, was now commanded by Colonel Hub Zemke of 56th Fighter Group fame. In an unusual, and probably unwise, move, Riddle was designated as Zemke's deputy. The situation resolved itself on October 30, 1944, when Zemke's aircraft broke apart over Germany and he became a POW. Riddle reassumed command of the 479th, a sequence of events probably not found elsewhere in the USAAF.

The effect of these changes of command was profound on Olds and the other members of his Group. Many of them liked Riddle, but after they accustomed themselves to Zemke's stiffer personality, they found out that he was a great combat leader.

Today, Olds finds his impressions of Riddle and Zemke difficult to express. He liked and respected both men, but he and Zemke were on the same wavelength—they both understood how to seek out the enemy and destroy him.

In the brief eighty-two days that Zemke commanded the 479th, he transformed it, and in the process, transformed Olds. Today he recalls with misty eyes the utter confidence they had in Zemke, and the certainty that if there were fights to be found, Zemke would find them. He was so respected at VIII Fighter Command Headquarters that the 479th began getting the more desirable missions, assignments that carried with them the probability of engaging with the enemy.

Olds's first brush with Zemke was not entirely promising. Four days after Zemke assumed command, Olds, age twenty-two, found himself alone after a predawn takeoff from his field. Without hesitation, Olds headed across the Channel to bomb the assigned target, a bridge at Chalon-sur-Saône in France. He listened on his radio to the squadrons that had taken off earlier and realized that they were uncertain of their position—they were lost.

Flying alone over enemy territory was not recommended, but Olds forged ahead and dropped one span of the bridge with two 500-pound bombs. (In 1948 Olds confirmed this on an automobile trip through France.) He then headed for England, enjoying the early-morning flight over the vineyards of Burgundy. Suddenly he spotted two aircraft ahead, just dots in the morning sky. As he tells the story today, his hand moves to the back of his neck and he says, "The hair went up on the back of my head. I knew they were Germans instinctively."

Olds approached from behind, at low altitude, perfect for his P-38, which he had named "Scat III." The two planes were Focke Wulfs, stubby winged, radial-engined fighters that were the pride of the Luftwaffe. He eased behind them, his P-38 swaying in the wake turbulence of the formation. He sighted on the wingman and squeezed off a short burst that sent him down. The flight leader, an obvious pro, stood his fighter on the wing and turned into Olds. A turning fight developed at treetop level, the maneuverability of the P-38 surprising the German. As the two turned together tightly, Olds's bullets struck the 190's fuselage and wings. The German pilot bailed out.

On the way home, he realized that his claims probably would not be confirmed. The camera on the P-38 was right under the 20-mm gun, and when you fired the guns the camera shook so that it was almost impossible to see what was registered on the film.

As he filled out his combat report after he landed, Zemke came over and gave him some curt comments about flying over France without a wingman. Then he congratulated him, for an American outfit flying over the scene of his battle had confirmed both of the kills. As elated as he was, Olds recalls Zemke looking at him with steely eyes that made him squirm.

Zemke, of course, liked aggressive fighter pilots, and he was particularly fond of Olds, who kept morale up in the Officers' Mess with his antics and with his iconoclastic cartoons on service life that were pinned to the wall.

Olds remarked later that the entire group had liked and admired Riddle, but they found in Zemke the leader who could teach them how to fight. In the process, exactly as Zemke wished, the leadership evolved down the group, through the squadron commanders and to the flight leaders. It was a practice Olds would follow for the rest of his career, particularly in Vietnam.

Eleven days after his first two kills, Olds became an ace by breaking the rules once again. A Captain now and a flight leader, on August 24, 1944, Olds was flying in Newcross Squadron to the extreme right of the Group, which was on a fighter sweep over central Germany. Zemke was leading in Bison Squadron and Lakeside Squadron was to the right. The Group flew in almost line-abreast formation, covering as much sky as possible.

Olds detected a swarm of enemy aircraft high and moving right to left across their formation to his right. He signaled to his flight to pull up to investigate.

Flying at full throttle, Olds brought the two Lightnings behind a gaggle of 50-plus Messerschmitt Bf 109s cruising at about 28,000 feet altitude with the nervous twitching movements that characterized Luftwaffe formation flights. Suddenly Olds remembered his drop tanks and jettisoned them. B. E. Hollister, his wingman, was in position, but the other two airplanes in his flight were far back. To a frantic call from "Highway"—Zemke's call sign—Olds responded that he was closing on a gaggle of bandits, approaching a big lake.

Unseen, Olds dropped behind a flight of four 109s and filled his sights with the cockpit of the trailing Messerschmitt. As he was about to squeeze the trigger, both engines quit—he had forgotten to switch tanks. Startled, he nonetheless fired, destroying the airplane, and becoming in his telling "the only fighter pilot in history to shoot down an enemy while gliding."

Unsure how many Lightnings were attacking or where they were attacking from, the Messerschmitt formation erupted into an inchoate mass, destroying their chances to intercept the bombers. A few saw the Lightnings, and the fight developed into a turning, twisting, diving melee. Olds saw that Hollister was in a good position to fire and told him to take the two 109s that moved to the right. In a brilliant bit of shooting, Hollister downed both airplanes.

Olds picked out another 109 and fired; his 20-mm cannon and .50-caliber bullets hammered the enemy fighter, which rolled, inverted, and dived, smoke pouring from its cowling. In the midst of the fight, Olds had seen a German plane attacking a Mustang, far below. He rolled, inverted, and dove straight down, and immediately hit compressibility, his elevator controls locking and his aircraft vibrating so badly that his canopy blew off. Now his troubles doubled, for the airfoil over the horizontal and vertical stabilizers was disrupted and the hurricane of frigid air robbed his body of heat. With the throttles at idle he sat helpless, unable to do any more until the denser air slowed the aircraft enough that he could begin a high-G pull out. Too fast to bail out, he sat, grunting and straining as he pulled back on the fighter's control column, watching the ground hurtle up. The nose began to come up, but the trees and houses were getting bigger faster. He was below the level of the local trees when the P-38, wings creaking, was finally in level flight.

He set course for England again, only to be jolted by gunfire from another Messerschmitt, happy to find a cripple to shoot down. Sheer instinct forced him to break left, and the P-38 shuddered into a high-speed stall. The Messerschmitt pilot overshot. Olds leveled his wings and fired; the 109 rolled over and dove straight into the ground. Preoccupied with keeping his battered P-38 in the air, it did not even occur to him that the last victory made him an ace.

When asked about the wisdom of a lone pair of Lightnings attacking a formation of 50 109s, Olds had his answers ready: "I felt sorry for those poor sons-of-bitches. They didn't know what had hit them." He felt that as the aggressor, he had a big advantage. He knew that the Germans would begin milling around, each man looking for the Lightning on his tail, and unable to find it in the vastness of the sky. Olds had not intended to stick around until they found him; he wanted to make his hit and then leave. When that did not work out, he did what he always did: adjust to the circumstances with an attack.

As time passed, Olds's score increased, as did his confidence. He became respected for his meticulous assessment of German tactics, plotting out the routes to the target areas, and determining where the Luftwaffe would assemble to make its attacks. Like Zemke, he concluded that the best fighter tactics were those that sent fighters out ahead to enemy rendezvous points.

In the process of learning to fight, Olds also learned about courage. He had a member of his flight who slept in the same room with him. Olds won't reveal his name, even today, calling him simply Pilot X. The man was an absolute jumble of fear who endured nightmares every night, crying out in his sleep. Within a few weeks, he was shot down and killed, and Olds had a revelation. Pilot X had been terrified, but he had gone on every flight, never aborted a mission, and flew without complaint. Olds contrasted the man's emotions with his own indifference to fear and realized that Pilot X was far braver than he.

Like Zemke, his goal was to damage the enemy wherever he could, and although he preferred combat in the air, he became skilled in strafing German airfields, always striking the flak installations first, then attacking the planes and hangars. He was credited with eleven and a half aircraft destroyed on the ground in these strafing attacks.

Although he has the traditional fighter pilot's disparaging attitude toward bomber pilots, Olds was sickened by the heavy losses the bombers continued to take from fighters and flak. On one mission, he had seen, at a great distance, the Luftwaffe use its "company front" tactics on a formation of B-24s. By the time he reached the scene of combat, the sky was filled with burning Liberators and para-chutes. It bothered him that despite the sacrifice of so many planes and so many men, most of the bombs that were dropped missed their targets.

The 479th had traded in its P-38s for North American P-51D Mustangs during September 1944. The versatile Mustangs were effective dive-bombers, although their liquid-cooled engines were vulnerable to flak and small-arms fire. As he became adept at dive-bombing, an idea began to form. Olds put forward a proposal stating that the Eighth Air Force would do more damage, more economically, if it sent small groups of P-51s to dive-bomb German targets rather than sending out the huge bomber formations to do area bombing. Instead of 1,000 B-17s, each dropping two tons of bombs in the hope that 2 or 3 percent would hit the intended targets, Olds wanted to send a flight of fifty Mustangs to attack specific high-value targets. He argued that the maneuverability and speed of the Mustang would render it less susceptible to flak damage, and after it dropped its bombs, it could engage in air combat or strafe on the way back.

Olds was in effect calling for the use of "smart bombs" with the pilots per-forming the functions in the P-51s that sophisticated lasers and computers do in fighter-bombers today. As might be expected, given the effort that had been poured into the bomber campaign, the idea from a young Captain fighter pilot that the entire mammoth operation be shelved was laughed off. It was correct in theory, however, and would have worked not only in World War II, but in Korea as well. It was put into practice to a limited degree in the Vietnam War, but it was not until the Gulf War that his concept of using fighters to deliver munitions with precision was brought to full fruition.

This was the first of many papers Olds was to write in the course of his career. Neither he nor the Air Force ever realized the conundrum they presented. Here was a hard-drinking, boisterous fighter pilot, more at home in the Officers' Club bar than the library, writing excellent papers on controversial subjects. The Air Force staff was unable to reconcile the two concepts, and there was an element of jealousy involved. Olds should be content with being a glamorous fighter pilot and should leave the report writing to them. Over the years, his often prophetic papers would be viewed as an aberration and summarily discounted.

No one could argue with him in the air. Using Zemke fan tactics, Olds went on to score eight more aerial victories for a total of thirteen. By the end of the war, flying *Scat VII*, he was a twenty-two-year-old Major commanding an elite fighter squadron, and the future looked bright. He was, after all, the son of a revered general officer. He was a West Point graduate who had been named an All-American, as well as a distinguished ace who had displayed true leadership in the 479th. Olds seemed to have more than enough credentials to be on the fast track to general officer rank. Unfortunately, the fast track would have some bureaucratic and political detours.

BETWEEN THE WARS

Olds's first postwar assignments seemed to be golden. He placed second in the jet division of the 1946 Thompson Trophy closed-course race. The most prestigious of all aircraft races, the Thompson had featured the flying skills of Jimmy Doolittle and Roscoe Turner before the war, and was now the venue for modified World War II fighters. It demanded searing speeds and many low altitude high-G turns and was really too dangerous for jets. The USAAF, however, was proud of its new fighters and summoned its hottest pilots to show them off. Olds flew a Lockheed P-80 at 514.853 miles per hour, just 1.14 seconds behind the winner, Major Gus Lindquist, who was in a souped-up P-80 out of Wright Patterson. Olds turned in the fastest lap at 553.293 mph, about 180 mph faster than the piston-engine racers of the day. The race put his names in the headlines once again, and there were some within the service who thought he was moving just a little too fast.

Olds's piloting skills landed him a place on the USAAF's first jet aerobatic team, the direct ancestors of today's Thunderbirds. This was a dream assignment, for the Army wanted the public to know how important jet aircraft were in the postwar world and saw to it that its jet team got plenty of publicity.

Hollywood embraced the flyers, and at a party Olds met a strikingly beautiful film star, Ella Raines. Olds, bubbling with youth and confidence, stood in sharp contrast to the artificial film personalities she usually met. He invited her to an airshow at nearby Mines Field, where he further impressed her with his daring flying. They began dating, and were married the next February. It was a publicist's dream—the movie star and the fighter ace—and for the first years it was a happy time. Both enjoyed drinking, but when Raines's career began to wane in the mid-1950s, she began to drink too much and the marriage became turbulent. They stayed together, however, traveling the world, until her death in 1983.

On July 4, 1947, Olds became the lead pilot of what was now the United States Air Force's aerobatic team. He did it the hard way. The former leader, Pappy Herbst, flew into the ground during a show at Del Mar, California. He had been married the day before—and had partied with Olds and the other pilots the day before that.

Herbst's death and the growing notoriety of the team's partying antics caused concern. Major General Glenn O. Barcus was Commander of the Twelfth Air Force at March Air Force Base. Barcus himself was no stranger to publicity, and later, during the Korean War, would gain fame by flying his F-86 over Pyongyang and personally daring the enemy to come up and fight. But he saw a pattern emerging and decided to head it off before another person was killed. In March 1948 he pulled Olds off the aerobatic team and gave him a staff job in the Twelfth Air Force Headquarters at March AFB.

Olds suffered—not in silence—for a year before wangling a plum assignment, exchange duty with the Royal Air Force No. 1 Squadron. Flying Gloster Meteors out of the famous Battle of Britain base, Tangmere, Olds once again demonstrated his leadership in the demanding environment of the Royal Air Force's senior squadron. Formed at Farnborough on May 13, 1912, from the No. 1 (Airship) Company, the unit had fought with distinction in both World Wars. Before his year tour was over, Olds was made Squadron Commander, a rare honor, different and in some ways more significant than the two Silver Stars, two Distinguished Flying Crosses, and the British Distinguished Flying Cross he had at the time.

There followed a series of assignments as Operations Officer and Commander in Air Defense Command (ADC) squadrons that would have seemed to provide a perfect career progression except for one thing. The Korean War was going on, and despite all his efforts, Olds could not get assigned to a combat unit. He served for two years as Commander of the 71st Fighter Interceptor Squadron, operating out of the Greater Pittsburgh Airport. He is still furious about this today, for he knew why he was being kept out of the war. His Group Commander told him with a sneer, "No, I ain't going to Korea, and if I'm not going, you sure as hell are not!"

THE CHANGING TIDE

Olds had stormed down to his headquarters to resign but was persuaded to stay in by Major General Frederick Smith, the Commander of Eastern Air Defense Force. Smith had both known his father and followed Robin's career. He gathered Olds into the ADC fold and saw to it that he was moved into jobs with greater responsibility, assuring his promotion to Lieutenant Colonel in 1951 and Colonel in 1953. The new rank would prove to be a fifteen-year plateau during which his career marked time.

There is no little irony in the fact that Olds's progress was adversely affected by changes that occurred within the United States Air Force as the "bomber barons" of his father's time came into prominence. General Curtis LeMay had made the Strategic Air Command (SAC) the single most important component of the USAF, for it countered the vast military strength of the Soviet Union. LeMay had turned SAC into a premier military instrument, admired for its readiness and efficiency, and sought out by ambitious officers anxious to make their way to the top.

SAC's preeminence was based on its nuclear power, and it was inevitable that its arch rival, the Tactical Air Command (TAC), should seek a nuclear mission of its own. Technology had made it possible, for as the power of jet engines grew and jet airframes became more sophisticated, the size of nuclear weapons shrank.

The division of nuclear labor between SAC and TAC was never harmonious, but it was clear that the growing numerical advantage of the Soviet bloc required the use of tactical nuclear weapons. SAC had enough to do with the strategic targets and could not countenance a diversion of its assets for European battlegrounds.

By 1951 tests conducted with Republic F-84 Thunderjets and North American B-45 bombers warranted the establishment of the 49th Air Division within TAC, which was now commanded by a veteran fighter pilot from the 94th Pursuit Squadron, General Joseph K. Cannon. LeMay had not initially opposed TAC's possession of nuclear weapons, but by 1957 wanted to combine TAC and SAC nuclear capability into an "Air Offensive Command," an organization that foreshadowed today's Air Combat Command.

LeMay's idea was rejected and he altered his tactics. In 1961 longtime bomber pilot and former Commanding General of SAC's Fifteenth Air Force, General Walter C. Sweeney Jr., was given command of TAC. There followed what was termed "the SACimcision of TAC," as it was turned away from its conventional role to the pursuit of a nuclear mission. TAC now did only the most limited training for conventional warfare.

This trend of events ran exactly counter to Robin Olds's experience and beliefs. Despite the fact that he continued to be assigned to Air Defense Command units, he believed himself at heart to be a "TAC man" and constantly produced papers that called for a return to the Air Force's traditional skills: air superiority, interdiction, and close air support. These in turn called for training in air combat maneuvering, aerial gunnery, dive-bombing, and other disciplines, which had proved to be effective in both World War II and Korea.

It should be noted that these simple requests demanded genuine effort on the part of all concerned. Realistic air combat maneuvering meant that risks had to be taken. Aircraft were flown in close proximity to each other, as they would be in combat, at high speeds and high G forces. Accidents were inevitable. Aerial gunnery meant that ranges had to be established and maintained and that pilots had to learn the difficult techniques to achieve both accuracy and safety. Dive-bombing practice was perhaps even more demanding, because with the slightest miscalculation—target fixation, failure to allow for the winds, simple inattention—the aircraft would smash into the ground.

Unfortunately, Olds's ideas were mundane when compared to the drama inherent in carrying a nuclear bomb in low and fast to destroy not a target but perhaps a division. His papers were met with a mixture of exasperation and derision, in part because he was considered to be off base by proposing ideas for TAC rather than for ADC. To the people in TAC, it was evident that Olds had not "gotten with the nuclear program." They regarded his ideas on training as outdated, and he was repeatedly assured that there would never be another war in which dogfighting would play a role. The future was to be found in missiles and in nuclear weapons.

In August 1958 he was sent to the last place he wanted to be, the Pentagon, to a job in the basement called the Air Defense Division in the Operations Division of the Joint Chiefs of Staff. He continued to run his private war, offering papers that ran from a demand to upgrade munitions (most of which were relicts of World War II and the Korean War) to bewailing the utter absence of conventional training.

It was a situation that the pragmatic Olds could not understand, for the USAF existed in a real world teeming with examples of conventional warfare. In the Middle East, Israel had confounded its Arab enemies with air power. The

Israelis had used air combat maneuvering, close air support, and dive-bombing to achieve their victories. Conventional air power had been used throughout Africa and on the Arabian Peninsula.

In Asia, conventional air power had been the mainstay of combat, from the British efforts in Malaysia to the Communist takeover in China to the attacks in the Straits of Formosa to France's losing battle in Indochina. On the Indian subcontinent, India and Pakistan had waged bitter air wars and were ready to fight again. No one was using nuclear weapons, and there was growing evidence that nuclear weapons would never be used because their consequences were so earth-shattering.

Perhaps more important than anything else, the Soviet Union was in the constant process of introducing large numbers of new air superiority fighters and new close-support aircraft. Its production was so great that it was able to spread its aircraft and tactics well beyond its European satellites into almost every continent. To Olds, it was self-evident that any future fight with the Soviet Union short of a full-scale nuclear exchange would require the same type of training and tactics that had proven successful in World War II. And he did not believe there would ever be a nuclear exchange.

At the same time, he continued to plead the cause of conventional training. Indomitable, he was not discouraged that his papers were not well received. He continued writing them and expanded the variety of subjects. He became an advocate for the Air Force's acquisition of the Douglas A-1E, the single-piston-engine Navy attack bomber that would prove so effective in Vietnam.

Olds's concepts went well beyond basic aircraft questions. He prepared a revolutionary paper that was both read and approved. Recognizing the Soviet emphasis on ballistic missiles over bombers, it called for a huge reduction in the Air Defense Command. In 1962 he also prepared a study for the military use of space, sketching out what would be called Star Wars during the Reagan administration.

Yet he was a voice in the wilderness, and as years passed, his critics began to regard him if not as eccentric, then at least as hopelessly obsolete in his thinking, unable to understand the progress in technology. The opposite was true: he understood technology very well and he also understood its limitations.

Curiously enough, it was the very advances of Communist technology that created the combat situation in which Olds's ideas would be vindicated—with a vengeance.

BACK IN THE SADDLE—THE NUCLEAR SADDLE

In August of 1963, after a year at the National War College, Olds received a cherished TAC assignment, the command of the 81st Tactical Fighter Wing in Bentwaters, England. There he had the potent McDonnell F-101A and F-101C aircraft whose mission was to carry nuclear warfare into the heart of the Soviet empire. They would devastate the air defense of the Soviet bloc, taking out key airfields, radar systems, and surface-to-air missile sites. SAC would simultaneously be striking the major Soviet cities and the most important military targets.

Olds worked as he always did, at full throttle and with total commitment. He did not let his belief that there would never be a nuclear war slow down his efforts to make the 71st the best instrument for nuclear destruction in the Air Force inventory.

Fortunately, he had the planes and the people to do so. The F-101 was one of the five "century series" fighters the Air Force procured in an effort to cover all bases. Intended originally as a long-range escort fighter, it had been developed as both a nuclear attack plane and an air defense interceptor. Fast and relatively long ranged, it was later developed into a reconnaissance aircraft. An excellent aircraft in its own right, it was perhaps more important in preparing the Air Force to accept the later McDonnell F-4 Phantom II.

Olds had another asset at Bentwaters, his deputy for operations, Colonel Daniel "Chappie" James Jr. James was a perfect foil for Olds, because he was a public relations genius and an excellent manager. The two men were stationed together in Vietnam, where the press, much to Olds's dislike, portrayed them as "Blackman and Robin." James went on to become the Air Force's first black four-star general.

At Bentwaters, Olds took a perverse pride in developing the unit's prowess until they were supremely capable, all the while certain that they would never be used. The effort he made, and the results the 71st achieved led to his being selected for promotion to brigadier general.

Before the promotion list could be approved, his brass-baiting nature got the better of him, and he decided to create his own aerobatic team, flying the F-101s. The Voodoos, as they were called, were not highly maneuverable aircraft, being large and not suitable to low-level acrobatics. Using the aircraft for airshows may have boosted morale, but it cut into their available flying time.

Olds's action gives insight into his character. As he recounts it now, "The war in SEA [Southeast Asia] was heating up. I knew I had to be there, knew that personally and professionally. I could not be a 'baby' general. But I couldn't say 'no' to the pending promotion. Hell, I was not even supposed to know about it. If I said 'No,' they would say 'O.K.—retire.' So what to do? Piss off my SAC (bomber) boss at 3d Air Force. Give him a reason to be so mad that he'd want to punish. Then count on General Gabriel Disosway to read between the lines, let the CO of 3d Air Force give me hell, but *not* let him court-martial me. How to accomplish this? Put on a formation acrobatic show without asking permission. Whoooo! It worked."

Once again, a proactive gesture had put his career in jeopardy, with many of his enemies pushing for a court-martial that would "put him in his place" once and for all. He was saved from court-martial, but his name was redlined off the promotion list. General Disosway, Commander in Chief of the USAF in Europe, let him finish his tour two months later and sent him to Shaw Air Force Base, South Carolina, as the ninth Air Force Assistant Deputy for Operations.

MUTUALLY MISUNDERSTOOD TECHNOLOGY

No two nations had more misunderstandings about each other than the United States and the Soviet Union. During and after World War II, the United States woefully misjudged the intentions of the Soviet Union in regard to the acquisition of satellites and the imposition of the Communist system upon them. The Soviet Union in its turn misunderstood the intentions of the United States in regard first to its will to defend Europe, and then in a typical about-face, in regard to the United States beginning an aggressive war. Yet by some miracle both countries arrived at an understanding about the use of nuclear weapons. The incredible concept of Mutually Assured Destruction (MAD), which reasoned that neither superpower would start a nuclear war, because both countries were known to have sufficient nuclear power to utterly eradicate the other even after a nuclear first strike, somehow managed to work. Had understanding regarding MAD (the most appropriate acronym in history) failed, the world would have been destroyed. Both sides had rational leaders who understood this and who succeeded in avoiding incidents that might have provoked World War III.

The technology that was developed by each side to ensure their nuclear capability also forced the development of hundreds of allied disciplines. Defense against a nuclear strike required the deployment, by both sides, of extensive radar networks, interceptors, antiaircraft guns, and surface-to-air missile defenses. The Soviet Union spent far more on its defensive efforts than did the United States.

The Soviet civil defense expenditure was vastly greater and envisioned protecting not only the governmental leadership but also the great mass of the urban populations. The United States paid less than lip service to civil defense.

In aircraft, the Soviet Union emphasized its interceptors and ground-attack aircraft. It spent much less on its bomber force than did the United States, preferring instead to lay out the greater part of its military budget on intercontinental ballistic missiles.

And, while the United States did have a military assistance program for its allies and for friendly nations, the Soviet Union systematically exported its offensive and defensive weaponry to its client states. Thus it was that many of the Soviet technological advances intended to counter American military might were deployed in North Vietnam.

THE PROBLEMS WITH SUCCESS

The development of the Strategic Air Command, first with bombers, then with the addition of intercontinental ballistic missiles, resulted in the very organic difficulties that Robin Olds had been crusading against. The USAF, in SAC and TAC, possessed a fantastically powerful nuclear striking force, which would achieve its mission only if it were never used.

In creating this force, there was little money—and less inclination—to create conventional forces that could be used in conventional wars. The Soviet Union was known to be strong, having placed into mass production a long series of fighters and attack aircraft. However, no attempt was made to assess how those aircraft would be fought, nor what would be the best means to counter them. The USAF conducted only a limited amount of air-to-air combat training, and this was rendered almost useless by three factors. First, the combat was always between similar aircraft, for example, F-4 versus F-4, and not against aircraft that would simulate the characteristics of Soviet planes. Second, safety was paramount; all mock air combat was conducted under such artificial restrictions of air speed, altitude, and maneuver that it was more like an aerial ballet than aerial combat. Finally, there was very little practice in the delivery of ordnance, and here, too, safety considerations vitiated the utility of the exercise.

Perhaps the most egregious error in thinking was the absolute miscalculation about the skill level of enemy air power. The 10-to-1 victory ratio scored by F-86s over MiGs in Korea had a heady and harmful effect. It was inconceivable that the latest USAF aircraft, including the Republic F-84 and North American F-100, which Olds now considers to be flawed designs, would not be able to prevail in a similar way over whatever aircraft the enemy would put forward. One of the greatest mistakes was the assumption that there would not be dogfighting in any future war.

When reality began to sink in, the Air Force procured the McDonnell F-4 Phantom II. It had been designed originally as a fleet defense aircraft, intended to use its radar and missiles to reach out and destroy incoming enemy bombers. As the aircraft matured, it was found it could accomplish other missions, including bombing, dive-bombing, and reconnaissance. It was not obvious to anyone— except a few people like Robin Olds—that the missiles designed to destroy bombers in level flight might not be useful in air-to-air combat with an agile enemy fighter.

When, in actual combat in Vietnam, the victory ratio proved not to be 10-to-1 but sometimes as low as 1-to-2, it was finally realized that something was terribly wrong. Olds had repeatedly tried to focus attention on the coming problem. Now he would emerge from his exile at Shaw and have the opportunity to rectify it in person, in combat.

★ N I N E ★
BACK IN COMBAT AT LAST

Few men could have been so fully prepared to assume command of a USAF fighter wing in Vietnam as was Robin Olds in the early summer of 1966. He had been personally selected by General William W. "Spike" Momyer, the Seventh Air Force commander in Saigon. A tough Oklahoman who had scored eight victories in Curtiss P-40s in World War II, Momyer disapproved of Olds's flamboyant indifference to discipline. Yet Momyer knew that the 8th Tactical Fighter Wing (TFW) was in desperate straits, and needed Olds's brand of leadership.

Although he still drank with the joyous abandon of a new second lieutenant, Olds had brought himself into perfect physical condition. At forty-four, he was six feet two inches tall and weighed 195 pounds, ten less than when he had played All-American football at West Point. Already well known as an ace, Olds had been given a quick but customized checkout in the McDonnell F-4C Phantom II, and knew that within a few weeks he would be its master.

His morale was good, even though he knew that he was considered a maverick by the regular TAC establishment. Olds was well aware that the assignment to Ubon, Thailand, was the opportunity he had always cherished, the chance to prove his ideas on aerial warfare.

When Olds arrived at Ubon Royal Thai Air Base on September 30, 1966, he walked into a unit that had been through some tough times. The 8th TFW had qualified crews, but they had not obtained much in the way of results. The pilots justifiably felt an overwhelming resentment at the way their talents were being misused and their lives wasted. In the three months before Olds's arrival, the 8th

TFW had lost twenty-two pilots and eleven aircraft and naturally was dispirited. The enlisted personnel were exhausted. Overworked and underappreciated, they labored night and day to satisfy abstract statistical requirements for higher sortie rates per aircraft that were generated in Washington. (An absurd program called "Rapid Roger" had been inaugurated, with the purpose of getting one and a half sorties from each F-4 each day. The program had nothing to do with hurting the enemy—it was simply a statistical gimmick that assumed a troublesome life of its own.)

Olds also knew that all of the things he had advocated and for which he had been scorned—greater skills in gunnery, dogfighting and dive-bombing—were now the only thing that mattered in Vietnam. He also knew that the replacement pilots he would receive would never have flown an F-4 loaded down with live ordnance. They would never have been taught how to deliver a cluster bomb unit, how to evade a surface-to-air missile (SAM), or how to use electronics countermeasures in formation flying. Things were turning out just as he had predicted. There was no nuclear war—just the hard knife-fighting war of bombs against well-defended targets, engaged by pilots not fully trained for the mission.

He was determined to do things his way and try to win the war. It was an easy choice to make, but a tough one to carry out. From the start of the Vietnam War, the exercise of air power was frustrated by absurd political decisions that were the cause of the poor results and poor morale at Ubon.

ARRIVAL AT UBON

When the first Americans had arrived at Ubon Royal Thai Air Base in 1965, they found a runway, screened wooden hooches, and the remnants of Japanese World War II hangars. By the fall of 1966, Ubon was in the process of being transformed by American prefabricated buildings, air conditioned quarters, and an apron filled with the aircraft of a dozen different units. Despite an agreement between the Thai and U.S. governments to control wages and prevent inflation, the Thai economy was in the midst of an unprecedented boom caused by the influx of Americans. The social order was being altered, not least because waitresses at the NCO club made more in tips than Thai generals did in salary. Doctors and lawyers abandoned their professions to set up service businesses near American bases.

Stepping out of the airplane into the sweltering Thai heat, Olds's mind went back to his own youth in a fighter squadron in England, when the guard had changed from Riddle to Zemke. He was now in Zemke's position, coming in to set things right, to introduce new tactics, and to create a new discipline. He remembered the mixture of pity and contempt with which young veterans look at old pilots like himself. Olds knew they thought he was a World War II relic who had not even flown in Korea, coming in from a cushy stateside billet to teach them how to fight *their* war.

The first thing he had to do was gain the confidence of the youngsters he was to command and, in doing so, give them something to fight for. In England in 1944, everyone knew exactly why the war was worth fighting: Nazi Germany was an evil enemy that had to be defeated. American leaders, from the President down, enjoyed the greatest respect. In Vietnam, no one was sure why the war was being fought, or if it was worth fighting at all. American leaders were regarded with disgust for the way they demanded that the war be fought. Olds knew there was but one answer: make the pilots want to fight for each other, to fight for the Wolfpack, the 8th Tactical Fighter Wing. It would not be easy, for too many mistakes had been made for too long.

Olds felt comfortable in the Phantom fighter even though he had not yet mastered the techniques of air combat using missiles instead of guns. He did not wish to be too quick to judge, but he knew immediately that the Wolfpack's tactics were wrong. Olds was confident that he could master the new technology of combat, but he was more concerned about the psychological situation. The pilots were being forced to fight the war on the worst possible terms and were increasingly concerned about the lack of support in the United States for the war.

THE INVERSION OF AIR POWER

Oddly enough, lack of support for the Vietnam War had come first from American military leaders, who had been unanimously opposed to entering into a war in Southeast Asia. When in 1964 the political leadership decreed that the United States was going to intervene, the Air Force Chief of Staff, General Curtis LeMay, submitted a plan for a bombing campaign. The plan called for a sixteen-day attack by heavy bombers against ninety-four targets. In 1964 North Vietnam had fewer than two dozen radar sites; fewer than 1,600 antiaircraft guns, mostly of small caliber and not controlled by radar; no surface-to-air missiles; and only two airfields that could handle jet fighters. The NV air force had about three dozen MiG-15 and -17 jet fighters, but the standard of training was very low. The combined efforts of the USAF and the U.S. Navy could have suppressed these defenses in just a few massive air strikes, and North Vietnam would then have been defenseless. The Vietnam War might have been very different.

Unfortunately, the U.S. political leadership could not muster the courage to execute LeMay's plan, and instead of using air power properly, proceeded to throttle it with arbitrary rules of engagement. The alternative solution, backed by Secretary of Defense Robert McNamara, was a ground war in Southeast Asia. This choice ultimately involved more than 550,000 troops and cost more than 50,000 American lives in a futile war.

The execution of McNamara's strategy required that all concepts of air power be inverted. Strategic bombing was conducted by fighter-bombers, while tactical bombing was conducted by strategic bombers. Some 6,162,000 tons of bombs were dropped in Southeast Asia, more than had been dropped in Europe during World War II. Logic was inverted along with air power, because 90 percent of the bombs were dropped not on the territory of our enemy, the North Vietnamese, but on the homeland of our ally, South Vietnam.

The political leaders of the United States, following the advice of General Maxwell Taylor, elected to pursue a policy of "flexible response" and "gradualism." They professed to believe that they could demonstrate the overwhelming power of the United States in measured small steps, each one a clever signal to the North Vietnamese to be reasonable and negotiate.

ROLLING THUNDER

The most obvious example of gradualism was the "Rolling Thunder" bombing campaign conducted from 1965 through 1968. Rolling Thunder was intended to create a viable state of South Vietnam and simultaneously avoid conflict with China or the Soviet Union. It was also intended to raise the morale of the South Vietnamese by making the transport of material to the Viet Cong from North Vietnam too expensive to continue.

The attacks were to be made initially on the most southern portion of North Vietnam, and then expand northward and increase in intensity if the North Vietnamese did not respond as desired. The idea was self-defeating, of course, because Rolling Thunder gave the defenders time to organize the countermeasures necessary to defeat the next escalation.

Olds had been briefed on the rules of engagement, but it was not until his pilots unloaded that he understood the full measure of the problem. President Lyndon B. Johnson had emasculated Rolling Thunder from the start by conferring effective political air superiority on the enemy. There was no blockade, so the Vietnamese ports were filled with Russian and Chinese freighters offloading everything from SAMs to rice. The ports could have been closed in a week with combined air strikes and mining operations, but they were not. Instead, the pilots had to pick off the supplies as they moved down the Ho Chi Minh trail, one truck—or sometimes, one human porter—at a time.

Just as in Korea, sanctuary areas had been created. One was a thirty-mile-wide strip along the Chinese border, allowing free transit of road and rail supplies across the border. The cities of Hanoi and Haiphong, including their military installations, were placed off-limits to the bombing for most of the time.

The types of targets that could be attacked were severely limited. Only very few attacks were permitted on the enemy's electrical power systems, arms industries, transportation network, oil facilities, and other vital war industries. Even the enemy's agricultural system, with its dams and irrigated fields, was off-limits.

To Olds's utter consternation, enemy airfields, flak installations, and surface-to-air missile installations were off-limits. The regulations against attack seemed almost treasonous. SAM sites could not be attacked when they were most vulnerable, as they were being built. Nor could they be attacked when they were completed. They could only be attacked if their radar was actually targeting the American aircraft and preparing to fire.

Even worse, the MiG airfields, which could have been suppressed in a few hours, were off limits. When the MiGs were in the air, they could not be attacked unless they demonstrated "hostile intent" by turning in to make an attack.

The final absurdity was that target selection was controlled directly by the White House in weekly meetings of the President and the Secretary of Defense. In practice, the combat wings had no say in target selection. The White House chose the targets, the ordnance to be used, and the routes to and from the target. Given the inevitable time delays, this meant that many missions were totally wasted, because the enemy, forewarned, was long gone.

Despite the many restrictions on obtaining effective results, Secretary McNamara's penchant for quantitative analysis resulted in an emphasis being placed on the number of sorties flown rather than on the destruction done to the enemy. During a bomb shortage (one denied by the White House) this sortie-counting mania led to flights of four F-4Cs being dispatched armed with only one bomb each.

North Vietnam responded sensibly by exploiting these rules of engagement to its greatest advantage. It placed its most important facilities in sanctuary areas—

on irrigation dikes, along railways, in hospitals, near temples, and so on. The enemy concentrated its flak and SAMs in areas that might be attacked, not bothering to defend areas it knew to be off limits. In essence, American restrictions had created a sharply defined funnel down which the attacking aircraft had to fly. The North Vietnamese put their antiaircraft, SAMs, and MiGs in the throat of the funnel.

The wistful American hope that the North Vietnamese would see the light and stop their attempt to take over South Vietnam persisted for years, despite its obvious failure. On seven occasions, President Johnson called a "bombing halt" intended to signal U.S. willingness to negotiate a peaceful settlement of the war. The North Vietnamese responded each time by using the bombing halts to move more materials and build more defenses.

Sometimes especially successful North Vietnamese attacks resulted in the Rolling Thunder restrictions being relaxed, and strikes were then permitted against oil facilities, industry, ports, and railroads. While these inflicted damage, heavy bombers were never used, and the strikes were not sustained over a long enough period of time.

An evaluation of the first eighteen months of Rolling Thunder indicated that it had cost the North Vietnamese about $150 million in lost supplies, all of which were quickly replaced by the Soviet Union and China. Unfortunately, it cost the United States $250 million *a month* to inflict that level of damage.

In the end, Rolling Thunder was a monumental failure, despite the courage and the skill of the crews conducting the battle. Almost 650,000 tons of bombs were dropped, most on the North Vietnamese transportation system, but the flow of supplies continually increased. Rolling Thunder was also a monument to the stupidity of the American decision-making process, which H. R. McMasters has correctly identified as a "dereliction of duty" by those who knew better. Robert McNamara inadvertently confirmed this charge in his own memoirs.

OPERATING OUT OF UBON

Olds arrived at a time when the rules of engagement had morale at a low level in the 8th Tactical Fighter Wing. The impact of his arrival at Ubon has passed into legend, with everyone who was there—including Olds—having specific but differing memories of what he said and how he said it. His first act—exactly like Rickenbacker's when he assumed command of the 94th—was to call the pilots together and outline what he expected of them and what they could expect of him. In essence, he said, "You have the experience here; I don't. I'm going to learn from you, flying as tail-end Charlie. In two or three weeks, I'll know as much as you do."

The first talk was one of many. Olds insinuated himself into the very fabric of the Wing, working day and night, as was his custom. His visits did not stop with the flying squadrons; he went to all the units, from the mess halls to the motor pool. He trooped the line, talking to the mechanics and the armament personnel. Within days, he seemed to know everyone by name, and he established that he could be talked to, man to man. He was there to listen, to learn, and to do something about the problems.

Olds was not too surprised when he found how few missions the previous commander had flown in twelve months. He decided that he would lead more "counters"—missions over North Vietnam—than anyone else in the wing. (He did exactly that, ultimately flying 120-odd missions to the North and 42 more in Laos.)

When he started flying, he began as number four in the last flight. Over a period of weeks, he worked himself into the lead position—but only after he had learned everything there was to know about flying it. He gave the briefings, led the flights, and conducted the debriefings. Olds was in charge, but he invited challenges and accepted suggestions when they made sense, whatever the source.

When he was not flying, he did what he had done in England twenty-two years before: study the geography of the enemy's territory to determine the best approach and departure routes and to learn where his defenses were. Within weeks, he could fly over North Vietnam without a map, knowing where the SAMs and flak were supposed to be hidden.

Olds was all business, even socially. Whether he was beating his pilots on the squash court—which he did regularly—or outdrinking them at the club—which he did with equal regularity—he would talk about combat operations. Flamboyant and given to outlandish gestures, his language sometimes grew wild and profane, but it always centered on one thing: hammering the enemy.

Olds extended the same professional consideration to the noncommissioned officers and the enlisted personnel, because he knew he needed to know what they thought. This was demanding ground, because the wise old Master Sergeants had seen many a commander come and go. They did not judge him on his ability as a pilot—they judged him on how he got things done, if he had the supplies coming in on schedule and, most important, if he backed them in their continuing fight with headquarters. When the word got around among the noncommissioned types that Olds was the genuine article and that his word was to be believed, morale and productivity began to pick up.

Within weeks, Olds had destroyed the barriers of rank and apathy and established communication links that began to bind the unit together. Olds did not chase popularity, however, and he took leadership risks to get his point across. On one of his first missions, flying tail-end Charlie at the end of the formation, he noted that the flight leader had logged the mission as a "counter" (one over North Vietnam), when they had actually bombed in Laos.

The next morning he called a briefing and notified the rest of the wing that he had fired the flight commander. The reason was simple: Olds demanded integrity in all aspects of their work. A few weeks later, he walked to the podium to give a briefing, carrying a pack of paperwork, submissions for awards and decorations for missions flown in the previous few weeks. Olds announced, "These award requests only talk about missions flown and bombs dropped. They don't say anything about the damage you did the enemy. Let's get it straight. You are here to destroy the enemy. I'm not approving medals for people who just show up for work." With that, he tossed the paperwork into a wastebasket and went on with his briefing.

Similar actions would have permanently ruined a lesser man; as it was, the pilots loved it. They knew exactly what he meant, and they took a growing pride in the standards of achievement he set.

None of this would have improved the combat effectiveness of the 8th, however, unless Olds had not also proved himself to be a "good stick," that is, a good pilot. It was easy enough for him to demonstrate his flying proficiency, but he knew that his real challenge would be to raise the wing's proficiency to the point that it could accomplish its mission with pride.

The air war in Southeast Asia had grown visibly more intense shortly after his arrival in the theater, and December 2, 1966, became known as "Black Friday" when the Air Force lost five aircraft and the Navy three to surface-to-air missiles or antiaircraft fire. Air Force losses included three F-4Cs, one RF-4C, and an F-105. The Navy lost one F-4B and two Douglas A-4C Skyhawks.

These ground-fire losses were matched by the marked increase in MiG activity during the last quarter of 1966. Because the rules of engagement prohibited airfield attacks, Olds was determined to blunt the enemy's efforts by luring the MiGs into air-to-air combat and then destroying them. To do so, he would have to get official permission from headquarters—not a task he relished.

INTO COMBAT

Both China and the Soviet Union had rallied to support the North Vietnamese, for nothing suited their policies better than the involvement of the United States in a ground war in Southeast Asia. A virtually endless stream of supplies came by ship and rail, along with military "advisers" who were not averse to pulling a trigger if the opportunity presented itself. By September 1966, the North Vietnamese had established an integrated air defense system. It included both acquisition and target radar systems, vastly increased quantities of antiaircraft guns, ranging from 37-mm to 100-mm in caliber, additional jet fighters, and, for the first time, batteries of SA-2 Surface-to-Air Missiles (SAMs). All of these efforts were coordinated by well-staffed command and control centers. Initially, these centers were capable of controlling either SAMs or MiGs, but not both at the same time, but by the time of Olds's departure in 1967, both could be controlled simultaneously.

The high level of sophistication of the command and control centers and SAM sites required direction and often operation by Soviet personnel. Unlike Korea, however, no Soviet pilots were used. The MiG fighters were flown only by North Vietnamese pilots. With extensive Soviet and Chinese training, they became very proficient in their operation. In keeping with Soviet doctrine, however, the MiGs operated under strict ground control.

If the American fighter force had not been hamstrung by President Johnson's rules of engagement, it could have eliminated the North Vietnamese air defense system in a matter of days. The MiGs would have been destroyed on their airfields, and the SAMs would have been blown up in their storage depots. A systematic attack would have eliminated the radar-controlled flak and the command centers.

Instead, the rules of engagement fostered a climate in which the enemy forces could thrive, for the missions of the two opposing air forces were diametrically opposed. The American air forces had to fly long distances over the same routes at the same times to strike small and often mobile targets. The North Vietnamese air force's mission was fulfilled if it only made the bombers jettison their bombs. It did not have to engage in air-to-air combat, nor did it need to shoot down enemy aircraft, as long as the bombs were jettisoned away from the target area.

THE MIX OF FIGHTERS

The two main fighters deployed by the USAF to Vietnam during Olds's stay were the McDonnell F-4C Phantom II and the Republic F-105 Thunderchief. Both were great hulking brutes of aircraft and both were designed for totally different missions than they performed in Vietnam.

The Phantom had originally been designed as a Navy fleet defense fighter, and carried only missiles as armament. With its huge bent wings, drooping tail, and fire-belching, smoke-trailing twin engines, the F-4 worked as well as a bomber as it did as a fighter. Laden with early versions of advanced electronics, it required the smooth coordination of a two-man crew to give optimum performance. Initially, both crew members were pilots, with an experienced man in the front seat and a relatively new pilot in the back, usually referred to as a GIB, "guy in back." Later, navigators were brought in as weapon systems officers (WSOs) to fly in the back seat.

While not the absolute best in any category—air superiority, reconnaissance, bombing, or suppression of enemy defenses—the Phantom was extremely good in all categories and was used by the Air Force, Navy, and Marines. That same versatility gave it maximum exposure in combat, where it suffered the most losses of any fighter aircraft in Vietnam, incurring some 20.1 percent of all fixed-wing aircraft losses in the war.

The F-4's partner, the F-105, had epitomized the TAC craving for a nuclear bomber, and it could carry a huge nuclear weapon within its streamlined bomb bay at supersonic speeds. In Vietnam, the streamlined symmetry of the F-105 was spoiled by hanging bombs on its external racks. Only the throbbing power of its single engine could force it through the air at speeds that gave it a chance at survival. The Thunderchief (a nickname never used by pilots) had thin, short wings that lacked the lift to give it maneuverability, but it still managed to knock down twenty-seven MiGs in the course of the war.

Better known by its nickname "Thud" (for the sound it made in its many early crashes), the F-105 became the workhorse for "going downtown," the pilot's expression for missions to Hanoi. Later in the war, a two-seat version, the F-105F, became an excellent Wild Weasel aircraft. The Wild Weasels used themselves as decoys to goad the enemy into revealing the position of his SAM sites with a radar signal. The enemy could then be destroyed with missiles and bombs. No fewer than 397 F-105s were lost in combat or operationally during the Vietnam War.

If the F-4 and the F-105s were heavyweights, two-fisted sluggers, the opposing MiGs were nimble lightweights, difficult to engage, yet capable of delivering a devastating punch.

The initial opposition was provided by the MiG-17, an updated version of the MiG-15, and considered by most to be obsolete by the late 1950s. Even though it was capable of only about 50 percent of the speed of an F-4, at low altitudes and on the terms on which the MiG fought, its three cannons made it a dangerous adversary. Indeed, the first MiG victories of the war were won by MiG-17s.

A much more modern fighter, the MiG-21 arrived in April 1966. Given the unimaginative NATO nickname "Fishbed," the MiG-21 was a beautiful little delta-wing interceptor, armed with both a twin-barrel 23-mm cannon and two K-13A "Atoll" heat-seeking missiles. The latter were essentially copies of the AIM-9 Sidewinder.

At altitude, the MiG-21 could outfly the F-4 in almost all flight regimes; it had spectacular acceleration and turning capability. At lower altitudes, the F-4s could use their colossal energy in vertical maneuvers that offset the MiGs' turning capability, for like all delta-wing aircraft, they lost energy quickly in turns.

The tactical situation was perfect for the North Vietnamese use of heat-seeking missiles, for the American fighter-bombers approached at relatively predictable speeds and courses. As their confidence level grew, the MiG-21 pilots began to make ground-controlled attacks in which they approached low and from the rear. They would snap up, fire an Atoll heat seeker, and depart the area.

For most of the war, the rules of engagement permitted the North Vietnamese MiG pilots to choose when and where they would do battle. The USAF fighters, in contrast, had no choice but to carry the war to the enemy in the face of a multi-layered defense.

INTEGRATED AIR DEFENSE

Both the USAF and the USN would have preferred that their aircraft operate at altitudes of 20,000 to 40,000 feet, where they would have been out of range of antiaircraft fire. The SA-2 was most efficient in this altitude range, however, and the loss of an F-4C on July 24, 1965, forced a change in tactics. To lessen the effectiveness of enemy SA-2 missiles, attacks were now to be made at low altitudes, about 5,000 feet above ground level. Attacking aircraft were met by intense antiaircraft fire, ranging from mass volleys of handheld weapons to 37-mm,

57-mm, 85-mm, and 100-mm flak. By 1966 the North Vietnamese had more than 4,000 antiaircraft guns of all types plus eighty-five SAM sites.

As the North Vietnamese gained additional equipment, they pushed their flak batteries ever farther to the south, exposing the American aircraft to fire for longer portions of their route. Over the course of Olds's tour, the large-caliber flak became much more numerous and was more often radar controlled. By the end of his tour, the North Vietnamese had deployed more than 7,000 flak batteries, of which about 1,500 were heavy caliber, and had installed some 200 SAM sites. Olds would later remark that he never flew one mission over Germany that was as tough as every mission over Hanoi.

Losses to antiaircraft fire dictated flight at altitudes above the level where flak was dangerous, but this exposed the Americans to attack by the SA-2s. The American response was to employ more Douglas EB-66 electronic warfare aircraft to jam the enemy radar and to bomb the SAM sites more vigorously. Wild Weasel and Iron Hand flights were established to counter the SAMs. The Wild Weasels, initially F-100s, but later F-105s, would loiter near SAM sites to provoke an attack. When the enemy radar was turned on, the Wild Weasels launched missiles that homed on the radar signal, while the Iron Hand flight (usually F-105s) dropped bombs on the site. It was terribly dangerous work, and losses were high, but the tactics were effective and losses to SAMs went down to a sustainable level.

With flak and SAMs to divert the enemy, the MiGs could choose a time and place of their own choosing to attack. They generally lurked on the outskirts of the battle, ready to make a spoiling attack to force the bombers to jettison their bombs, or to make an attack on a straggler.

OLDS MAKES HIS MOVE

Olds took advantage of a formal cocktail party staged in Bagio, in the Philippine Islands, to sidle up to the man who had selected him for his job, General William "Spike" Momyer, Seventh Air Force Commander. Olds noted Momyer's standard cool manner, but after a few polite remarks, he said, "Sir, the MiGs are getting pesky." Olds went on to explain that he had some ideas about bringing the MiGs to battle. Momyer's expression of deep disinterest didn't change. He moved away abruptly, leaving Olds with the uncomfortable impression that he had blown a good opportunity.

In fact he had not. Momyer was pleased with reports he had heard of Olds's progress with the 8th TFW and in a few days called him to Saigon to discuss his ideas on engaging the MiGs. This time Momyer listened carefully and told him to develop a plan, one that specifically excluded attacking North Vietnamese airfields.

Olds's timing was good, for he had arrived at a turning point in the air war. Before the last quarter of 1966, MiG aircraft had not been as great a threat to USAF strike forces as the surface-to-air missiles and antiaircraft fire were. Ironically enough, the introduction of the QRC-160 (ALQ-71) electronics countermeasures pod on the F-105s changed this. The QRC-160 was effective in neutralizing the radar controlling the SAMs and flak, and the resilient North Vietnamese responded by increasing their use of MiG fighters.

Operating under ground control and making maximum use of both cloud cover and the almost benevolent American rules of engagement, the enemy aircraft were adroitly employed. The MiGs, especially the later model MiG-21s armed with heat-seeking missiles, were now trying to score kills wherever possible.

The previous reluctance of the MiG-21s to engage did not mean that the North Vietnamese pilots lacked either courage or skill. At the time, only sixteen MiG-21s were estimated to be in the theater, and the enemy had to employ them selectively to maximize their utility.

By December 13, Olds began working closely with two bright young veterans of the 8th to develop his idea. The basic concept was for F-4s to simulate F-105s, and Olds gave his planners specific guidelines to work by. Central to the concept was that while no airfields could be attacked, any airborne MiGs must be prevented from landing by having flights of Phantoms orbiting airfields and cutting off escape routes to China. Olds hoped to engage the MiGs in combat and destroy them. If that did not work, he wanted to run them out of fuel by denying them access to their airfields. Either way, there would be MiG losses.

The planning group included Captain John "J. B." Stone and Lieutenant Ralph F. Wetterhahn. They worked under the tightest security and even the aircrews that were going to fly the missions were not briefed until December 30. Then and only then were they briefed on the tactics, call signs, routes, and the hundred other data items needed for the mission. Quick practice sessions were laid on to sharpen aircraft identification and review the details of missile parameters, front- and back-seat coordination, and the other techniques that would be required for successful execution.

The planners proved to be a perfect combination, Olds providing the overview and the major decision elements—the "what, when, where, and how" of the attack—with the younger officers, more experienced in the theater, filling in the cracks. The team worked long hours to develop the key details on force structure, refueling points and altitudes, ingress and egress routes, radio communications, flak suppression, and electronic countermeasures—all literally matters of life and death.

The planners determined that if the MiGs engaged in combat, they would have an endurance of only about fifty-five minutes from takeoff to landing. Phantom flight arrival times were set five minutes apart to ensure maximum opportunities for engagement. They planned for a "west force" of eight flights of F-4Cs from the 8th to strike from Ubon RTAFB in concert with an "east force" strike made up of five flights of F-4Cs from the 366th TFW at Da Nang. It was to be an aerial Cannae.

Everything hinged on luring the MiGs into the air, where they could be destroyed. This would not be easy, for the Communists often declined to attack if they thought the weather would seriously impair bombing accuracy. The North Vietnamese had many advantages. All of the targets were sited in the midst of the heaviest integrated air defense system in the world. Their geography and the onerous rules of engagement had severely reduced the F-105s' options during the Rolling Thunder missions. The number of approach routes was limited as were the permissions for targets to be attacked.

Olds took these factors into account. The strike force would imitate the route, speed, and radio chatter of a normal F-105 mission, but instead of bomb-laden Thuds, it would consist of F-4Cs, all armed with four AIM-7E Sparrows and four AIM-9B Sidewinders. Major General Donovan Smith at Seventh Air Force suggested that they carry the QRC-160 electronic countermeasures pod that the Thuds had been carrying, attaching them to the right outboard pylon.

Simply acquiring the necessary QRC-160 pods was a logistic effort that extended throughout Southeast Asia before reaching all the way back to the United States. It was perhaps the first of a series of events that embroiled many disparate elements of the Air Force in Operation Bolo.

On December 22, Olds briefed Momyer in Saigon, and the plan was accepted without a change, with execution planned for January 1, 1967. The force would comprise ninety-six fighters (fifty-six F-4Cs, twenty-four F-105s, and sixteen Lockheed F-104s) and include Boeing KC-135 tankers, Douglas EB-66s (with F-4 escort) for electronic countermeasure support, Lockheed RC-121 Big Eye surveillance aircraft, and rescue forces.

Eight days after briefing Momyer, Olds canceled all leaves at the 8th TFW and postponed the New Year's Eve party. Then bad weather moved in, and it was obvious that the mission would not be flown on January 1, and probably not on January 2. The party was reinstated for the evening of January 1, a mistake, for the mission was laid back on early in the morning of January 2, much to the dismay of those who had partied not wisely but too well. Olds was not among the latter group, for he had spent every night following up on details and solving problems. He was everywhere—at supply, in the hangars, down on the flight line, and in the briefing room. Despite the probability of bad weather, he decided to go on with the mission, in part because the QRC-160 pods were "on loan" to him for only seven days.

BOLO UNDER WAY

Code words assigned to flights, targets, and routes were normally computer-generated at Seventh Air Force. The Wolfpack flights were given the names of cars, with mission commander Colonel Olds leading Olds flight. (Olds was dismayed by this; he felt that the flights should have been given names similar to those used by the F-105 flights. In his premission briefing, he told his pilots to use first names for their radio calls.) MiG base locations were identified by the names of U.S. cities, with Phuc Yen, northwest of Hanoi, being Frisco, and Gia Lam, south of Hanoi, being Los Angeles.

It had required a massive Air Force–wide effort to bring Bolo into being. The entire 8th TFW's energy was thrown into overcoming last-minute problems, with the support troops working all night long. (In a typical last-minute glitch, it was found that the sway braces on the F-4C were located differently than on the F-105. The mechanics worked all night to reinforce the shell of the QRC-160 pod to accept the F-4C sway brace.) But when the aircraft rolled for takeoff, the long days of nonstop planning, frantic accumulation of resources, the intense training of munitions crews, crew chiefs, pilots, and backseaters now began to funnel down into a nine-minute dogfight. In that brief span of time, a historic battle was fought in a slice of sky that ranged from 10,000 to 18,000 feet in altitude within a fifteen-mile radius of Phuc Yen airfield.

WHERE ARE THE MIGS?

Olds carefully emulated the F-105 flight profile, flying a fluid-four formation at 480 knots until reaching the Red River, then accelerating to 540 knots and assuming the QRC-160 pod formation. This was similar to the standard fluid four, but with a separation of about 1,500 feet. The aircraft would weave up and down, and the combined effect of the pods jammed the enemy acquisition radar. The Thud feint was maintained until three minutes after Olds's flight arrived at its TOT—time over target. By that time, Olds expected the North Vietnamese to have recognized the ruse.

Olds was disconcerted when he arrived over Phuc Yen at 1400 Zulu, exactly on schedule, only to find that the MiGs were not airborne. There was a complete undercast, with tops at about 7,000 feet, and the Communist ground controllers had delayed the MiG takeoffs by about fifteen minutes. Olds had no way to know this, and had to contemplate calling the mission off for the inbound flights. He passed over Phuc Yen airfield to the southeast and then made a 180-degree turn to the northwest. The first sign of enemy activity proved sterile when Olds 3 picked up then lost a bogie moving swiftly in the opposite direction.

Seconds later, Ford flight, led by his longtime friend Colonel Daniel "Chappie" James, burst into the battle area exactly on time, just as the MiG-21s began popping up out of the undercast.

Ford 3 called out a MiG-21 closing on Olds flight. Colonel Olds turned to throw off the MiG's aim and attacked another MiG that appeared in his eleven o'clock position, low and a little over a mile away.

It was Olds's first engagement with a MiG. With his backseater, Lieutenant Charles Clifton, he set up for an AIM-7 Sparrow attack. (The Sparrow was a radar-guided missile intended for use against bomber formations.) He fired two Sparrows and a Sidewinder, but none of them guided. Olds sighted another MiG—they were appearing everywhere now—and used the Phantom's power and energy to vector roll behind it. This time he fired two Sidewinders. The first one blew the MiG-21's wing off to score one of the first kills of the mission. The pilot did not eject.

Ralph Wetterhahn, one of the key planners, had been disappointed to be delegated to flying as Olds 2, but in the course of Olds's attack, slid behind a MiG-21. Working with his GIB—guy in back—First Lieutenant Jerry K. Sharp, he salvoed two Sparrows. The second Sparrow caught the MiG just forward of its stabilizer and blew it up. Two down!

The sky was now filled with a mixture of F-4s, using their tremendous energy in vertical climbs and dives, and MiGs circling to take advantage of their greater maneuverability.

Olds 4, flown by Captain Walter S. Radeker III, with First Lieutenant James E.

Murray III in the back, targeted a MiG tracking Olds 3. Radeker experienced some difficulty getting a solid tone on his Sidewinder (the tone of a "growl" that signaled the missile was ready to fire), yet the missile guided perfectly, striking just forward of the MiG's tail and sending it spinning into the undercast. Three down!

The next MiG fell to Captain Everett T. Raspberry and First Lieutenant Robert W. Western in Ford 2. Two MiGs had closed on Ford 3 and 4, overshot, then pressed an attack on Ford 1, overshooting him as well. The MiG broke into a hard left turn, and Raspberry rolled to wind up at the MiG's six o'clock position. He fired a Sidewinder that guided up the MiG's tailpipe, blowing it up. Four down!

Rambler flight had arrived exactly on time, to find itself in the midst of the MiG melee. One of the most important of the planners, Captain John B. Stone, was flying with Lieutenant Clifton P. Dunnegan Jr. as the backseater. Over Phuc Yen, Stone picked up two MiGs, 4,000 feet below and two miles away. Uncertain of his lock-on, Stone fired three Sparrows. The second missile impacted at the MiG's wing root, and the pilot ejected. Five down!

Two young First Lieutenants, Aircraft Commander Lawrence J. Glynn and Pilot Lawrence E. Carry, in Rambler 2 had been on Rambler lead's wing all through its combat maneuvers. Just after Rambler 1 scored, Glynn locked on to a MiG-21 and fired two Sparrows. The second missile blew up the MiG, and its debris damaged Rambler 2 slightly. The enemy pilot's parachute was seen to open. Six down!

The last victory went to Major Phil Combies in Rambler 4, and flying with Lieutenant Lee Dutton in the back seat. After Dutton had locked on, Combies tracked a MiG-21 and fired two Sparrows, the second impacting in the tail section. Combies later speculated that the pilot must have ejected when he saw the missile coming, for a parachute was seen almost immediately. Seven down! Combies and Major Herman L. Knapp in Rambler 3 each claimed a probable as well.

Suddenly the MiGs were gone, and the four remaining Wolfpack flights (Lincoln, Tempest, Plymouth, and Vespa) arrived to find the game gone to ground. Operation Bolo was over.

Olds taxied in at Ubon with his canopy open and hands upraised in a gesture of victory to the cheering crowd of maintenance personnel. After months of hardship and disappointment, Olds had led the 8th to a spectacular victory: seven kills and no losses. Suddenly, there was something to fight for—the Wolfpack itself.

Seventh Air Force was elated with the Wolfpack's results. Twelve F-4Cs had engaged fourteen MiGs and shot down seven of them, with no losses. It is worth noting that of the fourteen crewmembers who scored victories, only one, Lieutenant Lawrence Glynn, had ever seen a MiG in air combat before. (Olds had seen MiGs at a distance.)

Olds had also proved that the F-4C was clearly superior to the MiG-21 in a dogfight. Eighteen Sparrows had been launched, of which only nine guided, but these nailed four MiGs. Twelve Sidewinders were launched, seven guided correctly, and three MiGs were destroyed.

Perhaps more important than anything else in terms of morale and unity, the battle proved beyond a shadow of a doubt the importance of the largely unsung "guy in back," who locked the radar on the target and who, despite the continuously changing G forces, kept his head on a swivel, watching out for enemy aircraft and SAMs. Many of the GIBs would get a reward—flying in the front seat of an F-4 on another combat tour. Olds never doubted the importance of the GIB and unfailingly gave them credit for their actions.

The battle proved Olds to his men for all time not only as a commander who could execute a plan, but also as a leader who took his men into combat, waxed the enemy, and led them out again. Olds made sure that everyone who participated in Operation Bolo, whether in the air or on the ground, was given full credit for their contributions. Bolo gave a lift in morale to the entire Air Force. And it was just a start for Olds.

MORE VICTORIES

Olds continued to lead his unit, flying mission after mission, but did not score again until May 4. Flying with First Lieutenant William D. Lafever, Olds led the second of two flights of F-4Cs, escorting five F-105 flights. From Olds's point of view, it looked like this:

> The MiGs were at my 10 o'clock position and closing on Drill, the F-105 Flight from their 7:30 position. [The importance of situational awareness becomes apparent immediately—three flights of aircraft are involved here, at three different altitudes, in three different positions and on three different, turning, courses.]
>
> I broke the rear flight [Olds's own rear flight of F-4s] into the MiGs, called the F-105s to break, and maneuvered to obtain a missile firing position on one of the MiG-21s. I obtained a boresight lock-on, interlocks in, went full system,

kept the pipper on the MIG and fired two AIM-7s in a ripple. [Unlike a gun, which can be sighted and fired rather directly, the air-to-air missiles had definite limits on their inner and outer firing ranges, and also had to be "locked on" to their target and put through their preparatory routines. These ranges and limits differed for the AIM-9 Sidewinder and AIM-7 Sparrow. Ripple fire is to fire in succession. Firing could not be done under high-G loads.]

One AIM-7 went ballistic. ["Ballistic" meaning flying its own, unguided trajectory.] The other guided but passed behind the MiG and did not detonate. [AIM-7s were notorious for their failures. During Rolling Thunder, of 340 firings, 214 failed (63 percent), 99 missed (29 percent), and 27 hit (8 percent). Such a performance was pretty disheartening to air crews, which had to endure MiGs, flak, and missiles to get a shot in.]

Knowing that I was then too close for further AIM-7 firing, I maneuvered to obtain AIM-9 [heat-seeking Sidewinder] firing parameters. The MiG-21 was maneuvering violently and firing position was difficult to achieve. I snapped two AIM-9s at the MiG but did not observe either missile. The MiG then reversed and presented the best parameter yet. [Parameter meaning shooting position for the missile.] I achieved a loud growl [the noise indicating the Sidewinder has a good lock on], tracked, and fired one AIM-9. From the moment of launch, it was obvious that the missile was locked on. [The Sidewinder was both simpler to use and marginally more reliable than the Sparrow. During Rolling Thunder, out of 187 Sidewinders fired, 105 failed (56 percent), 53 missed (28 percent), and 29 hit (15 percent). Is it any wonder that most pilots wanted guns?]

The MiG then went into a series of frantic turns, some of them so violent that the aircraft snap-rolled in the opposite direction. Fire was coming from the tailpipe, but I was not sure whether it was normal afterburner or damage induced. I fired the remaining AIM-9 at one point, but the shot was down toward the ground and the missile did not discriminate. [In other words, it could not pick out the heat of the MiG's engine from the background of heat emanating from the earth.] I followed the MiG as he turned southeast and headed for Phuc Yen. The aircraft ceased maneuvering and went in a straight slant to the airfield. I stayed 2,500 feet behind him and observed a brilliant white fire streaming from the left side of his fuselage. It looked like magnesium burning, with particles flaking off. I had to break off to the right as I neared Phuc Yen runway at about 2,000 feet, due to heavy, accurate, 85-mm barrage. I lost sight of the MiG at that point. Our number three saw the MiG continue in a gentle straight dive and impact approximately 100 yards south of the runway.

His next victories came on May 20, flying an escort mission for F-105s. This time his backseater was Lieutenant Stephen B. Croker, who would retire years later as a Lieutenant General. Olds liked to rotate his backseaters to give them combat experience. Their call sign was Tampa 01.

On the way up the coast, he had reminisced about the papers he'd written on conventional warfare with Croker, telling him, "Here we are sitting in a Navy airplane, carrying World War II bombs underneath, equipped with a gun sight not as good as I had on my P-51 in 1945. We're going in to drop bombs, and there's going to be flak, SAMs, and MiGs. But don't worry about it—I've been assured by Generals that this was never going to happen again."

Olds took his formation in from the Gulf of Tonkin, just clearing the low-lying hills north of Haiphong, when MiG-17s came in low, from both the left and the right. The MiGs' goal was to attack the F-105s and force them to drop their bombs well before the rail lines that were their targets.

He led his two flights of four F-4s down on the MiGs, beginning what he later termed "an exact replica of the dogfights in World War II."

He was now forty-four years old, and despite his physical conditioning, his reflexes could not match men who were twenty years younger. Yet as he later said, "You are not as quick as you are at twenty-five, but you know what to do and that makes up for it. Younger guys have to think before they start a maneuver. I don't have to think anymore. It is instinct."

Mixed up in the battle were the eight F-4s, twelve MiG-17s, and four F-105s that wandered into and out of the running fight. With that many planes circling tightly, close to the ground, the danger of midair collision was far greater than getting hit by gunfire.

The dogfight went on for about twelve minutes, with the MiGs using new and intricate tactics that suited their style of combat. The MiGs grouped together in small flights of two, three, or four, flying in a wide circle as low as 500 feet. It was their version of the World War I Lufbery, a defensive wheel that put them in their element—sharp turns at low speeds and low altitudes.

When the F-4s tried to engage one of the groups, they were attacked in turn by MiGs from the other side of the circle. Olds finally managed to slide behind one MiG that was about 7,000 feet away, turning in a gentle left turn. Croker got the system locked on and Olds fired two Sparrow missiles. Only one tracked true, and it exploded near the MiG, the Sparrow fragments sufficient to send it down in flames.

The F-4s were going in and out of afterburner as they tried to break up the MiGs' wheel, burning fuel at a furious rate, and hastening the moment when they would have to break off and go to the nearest tanker to refuel. Olds finally had to leave, and as he did so, he saw a lone MiG-17 circling, silver against a brownish field.

The same considerations flashed through Olds's mind as had flashed through Blesse's on the day of his last MiG battle. He was short on fuel; a combat might run him out of fuel, or so low that they would have to bail out. There was no question about what to do. He called to the others in his group and told them to egress. Olds made one circle, to make sure they had all left, then dropped down to the deck to attack, flying just above the trees, the MiG as yet unaware of his presence.

The MiG pilot suddenly saw him, and threw his plane into a series of wild maneuvers, trying to get away. Olds called to Croker, "He's spotted us and doesn't know what to do. He's jinking."

Olds knew that the MiG could run, but couldn't hide. There was a little valley ahead, splitting the mountains. Olds stayed behind, keeping his speed low. He did not want to risk firing a Sidewinder yet, because he knew it was ineffective at 50 feet above the ground.

The MiG turned into a narrow valley that led to a low ridge of hills. Olds chortled to Croker, "Now we've got him."

The MIG pilot had no choice—he had to either fly into the ridge, or pop up over it, and he, of course, chose the latter. Olds was waiting, and when the MiG lifted up, he fired his first Sidewinder. It did not track. The MiG was almost over the ridge now, and made a left turn, giving Olds a dead astern shot. He fired his second Sidewinder. The heat seeker sensed the MiG's broiling exhaust; the missile tracked properly and exploded about ten feet from the right side of the aft fuselage. Pieces broke off and the MiG dived straight into the ground. Olds's gun camera film would show that the enemy aircraft could not have recovered from its dive.

He immediately pulled out of the combat and tore toward the tanker orbit. When Tampa 01 hooked up, it had 300 pounds of fuel remaining—enough for a few minutes more flight.

Olds was now the top scorer of the Vietnam War, with four victories. There was a party in the Officers' Club that night, highlighted when Olds, now sporting a huge and totally unauthorized mustache, climbed a ladder and added four more Red Stars to the 8th TFW scoreboard. He had gained two victories, and two other pilots had each scored one. By now he could do no wrong with the 8th TFW.

THE ELUSIVE FIFTH VICTORY

On June 2, Olds led his flight of four Phantoms into another dogfight. Three victories were claimed, one of them by Olds, but none were confirmed.

Even though the victory was not confirmed, it provided some valuable information to Olds. His friend Chappie James was wired into every grapevine in the theater, and word came that if Olds had scored a fifth victory, he would immediately have been pulled from his command and brought back to the United States. The rationale was obvious: the USAF did not want to risk having its first Vietnam ace shot down—the lesson had been learned in Korea with the death of George Davis.

Olds was furious; his tour was not up until October, and he was not going to leave his troops until then. He went directly to Saigon to confront General Momyer. Momyer protested that he had heard nothing about an order to have Olds brought home if he scored his fifth victory, but Olds did not believe him. Instead, he prowled around Seventh Air Force Headquarters until he met Colonel Louis L. Churchill, an information officer. Churchill confirmed that the instructions had come from Harold Brown, the Secretary of the Air Force.

Olds blew his stack, and swore that he would never claim another victory no matter how many more airplanes he shot down. He went back to the 8th and led them continuously until October, when his tour of duty was up. During that time, he had the opportunity to shoot down several MIGs, but refrained from pulling the trigger and let his wingman do the shooting—most of the time. Instead, he took on many of the toughest missions, including the famous August 11, 1967, bombing attack that at last dropped the notorious Paul Doumer Bridge.

MYSTERY ACE

In recent years, Olds has adopted a more mischievous attitude about his being an ace in Vietnam—the first ace of the war. He is confident that he scored a victory on June 2, even if it was not confirmed, but he goes farther now, and hints broadly that there were other, later victories that he did not claim. He does not say specifically that he shot down a MiG and did not claim it. What he says is that he fired missiles at MiGs—and that he did not usually miss. The inference is clear—he feels that he was the first ace of the Vietnam war but was unable to make the record official because he refused to be called home.

There are mixed feelings about this from the men who flew with him. All of them acknowledge that he was a superb commander who revitalized the 8th

TFW, changing it from a lackluster unit into the Wolfpack. They state unanimously that he was a superb pilot, extraordinarily aggressive, and with excellent situational awareness. They agree that he would have been selfless enough not to claim an airplane in order to stay in combat, leading his wing.

But a phantom kill is something else. Most indicate that it might have been possible, but a few flatly reject the story. They say that it would have been impossible to conceal a kill, because no GIB would have been willing to give up his own claim to a victory. Olds will not argue the point—he just nods wisely, eyes twinkling, content to let the idea surface for consideration.

BACK FROM THE FRONT

In the course of his duties at Ubon, Olds had been called on to host literally hundreds of visitors. One of these was then the Chief of Staff of the United States Air Force, General John P. McConnell. Normally visiting Chiefs get the super-VIP treatment, beginning with a massive base cleanup, followed by specialized briefings filled with statistics showing how great the unit is and concluded with the best dinners the cooks can produce.

Olds took a different tack. He plunged McConnell directly into the hands-on activities of the base, taking him through the hangars, the kitchens, the motor pool, and each time turning him loose to talk to the airmen. In the evening, McConnell liked his whisky neat and Olds matched him drink for drink.

The visit was a roaring success from McConnell's point of view—he felt he was getting the "straight skinny" and had enjoyed every minute with the troops. He admired what Olds had done with the 8th TFW both in terms of combat successes and building unit morale. He also knew that Olds would end his career as a colonel unless he personally took action.

McConnell's solution was simple and brilliant. He ordered that Olds become the next Commandant of Cadets at the Air Force Academy. The assignment carried with it the rank of brigadier general. Olds did not like the idea at first, but it turned out to be good for him and splendid for the Academy.

His next meeting with McConnell symbolizes the old-style Air Force that both men represented. Olds went to the Chief of Staff's office to pay his compliments and get some words of wisdom before assuming his position at the Academy. He went into McConnell's spacious office to find McConnell sitting behind his desk in his shirtsleeves, a Kleenex stuffed up one nostril to stop a nosebleed.

Olds saluted as McConnell lit a cigarette, coming perilously close to setting the Kleenex on fire. Finally, McConnell came around his desk, pointed at Olds's flowing mustache and growled, "Take it off."

That was the end of the briefing.

ACADEMY DAYS AND BACK TO VIETNAM

Being Commandant of Cadets at the Air Force Academy was a far cry from commanding a fighter wing, but Olds knew that it was better than running around the Pentagon, where lowly brigadier and major generals were routinely hazed by the three- and four-star types. His memories of his days there are mixed—pleasure in leading the young cadets, anger with some of the academics, annoyance with outside pressure groups.

He takes far greater pleasure in recalling that in 1971 he was sent back to Vietnam on an inspection trip, flying with every wing but his old outfit, the 8th TFW. He flew twenty-four combat missions and came away with the knowledge that the expertise that had been gained through 1968 had been lost in the intervening three years of the bombing halt.

The problem was not with the aircrews—they were willing and able to fight. The problem lay with the bureaucracy and the myriad levels of staff that had to be accommodated. There were personnel problems as well. The Air Force had established a policy that "no one goes twice until every one has gone once," meaning that you would not have a second tour in Vietnam until everyone else in the Air Force had had their first tour. It was well-meaning, but totally wrong, for it kept experienced pilots from repeating their tours, while it forced people who had long been out of the cockpit into airplanes hotter than they had ever flown. One egregious flaw to the veteran fighter pilots was that it put people with no fighter experience in command of fighter units. The Air Force had, quite simply, got out of the business of fighting a war.

On his return, Olds briefed General John "Three Finger" Ryan, the new Chief of Staff. He gave a concise rundown on readiness, safety, and all the other aspects of his trip, then let the bomb drop, saying, "Sir, there is something else I would like to say. Your fighter forces in Southeast Asia today could not fight their way out of a wet paper bag." The meeting erupted in a series of sputtering protests, and once again, Olds was marked down as a rabble-rouser.

He offered to take a team to Southeast Asia and try to raise combat standards again, but was refused. As a result, he submitted a request for retirement to be effective the following June 1, 1973.

OLDS AS ACE AND LEADER

Olds is unique in that he had leadership roles in two wars that were separated by two decades and a tremendous difference in technology. And, as great as the leaps in technology had been, there were even greater differences in the social and politic‑l fabric of the two eras.

The technological changes were remarkable, due to advances in radar-controlled antiaircraft fire and the introduction of really effective surface-to-air missiles. Jet aircraft performance had improved, and air-to-air missiles were now a factor to be reckoned with. These were significant differences, and Olds had been in the forefront in dealing with them.

He was even more successful in dealing with the political and social changes. Well aware of the effect of anti-Vietnam War sentiment on the families of the men in his unit, Olds took care to inspire them with a loyalty to the 8th Tactical Fighter Wing and to each other. A not surprising by-product of this was the great loyalty they felt to him.

No one better understood the adverse effects that the political rules of engagement had on the Air Force than Robin Olds, yet he complied fully with the requirements and simply sought to fight as hard and effectively within the rules as he could.

It would not have been extraordinary if Olds had concentrated on running up his score of kills. His pilots would have understood his motivation even though his actions might have been condemned by higher headquarters. Instead, Olds sought to fulfill his orders as scrupulously as he could, while punishing the enemy as much as possible. In carrying out this part of his mission, he was not above bending regulations.

As an example of his tenacious desire to inflict harm on the enemy, he refused to add a gun pod to the centerline rack on the later model F-4D Phantoms when they arrived. To do so would have increased his chances—and the chances of his wing—to increase their MiG kills. Instead, he preferred to use the centerline rack to carry six more bombs that he could use for the bombing missions he was ordered to carry out.

In a similar way, when the AIM-4 Falcon missile was delivered for use with the F-4D, he tested it personally and found it wanting. It simply did not work in combat. Olds ordered his maintenance people to remove the Falcons from the D and install Sidewinders. The official technical order for the F-4D had no provision for the Sidewinder, but Olds sat down with his maintenance people to figure out how to "hot-wire" it so it would work. He then altered the launch rail so that the lower inside fin of the Sidewinder would clear the bomb rack sway braces.

Changes like these normally took years of planning and testing and miles of red tape to obtain approval. Olds avoided that by doing it without telling anyone. Now the F-4 could carry both Sidewinders and bombs, and could both perform the MiGCAP (MiG Combat Air Patrol) mission and bomb if the MiGs did not show up. In other words, Olds mastered the technology rather than letting the technology master him. In doing so, he had to master the bureaucracy, instead of letting the bureaucracy master him.

The advent of enough ECM pods to outfit the F-4s provided him with another opportunity. The tech order prescribed that the ECM pod was to be carried on the right-outboard pylon. This meant that the external fuel tanks had to be carried on the centerline shackle and the left-outboard shackle, leaving room for only six bombs.

Olds looked the setup over, directed the ECM pod to be relocated to the inboard pylon, and told the ground crews to remove the centerline external ferry tank, which Olds knew from personal experience to be a hazard in combat. This made room for nine bombs, a 50 percent increase in payload.

This level of leadership, from bomb racks to Operation Bolo, distinguished Olds as a combat commander. He was a warrior, a born ace who enjoyed aerial combat, but he was first and foremost a leader.

★ T E N ★
THE WARRIOR GENE AND HARD WORK

In most previous analyses of the fighter ace, emphasis was placed on everything from hand-eye coordination to inherently pugnacious natures. Other findings noted that many of them were blond and blue-eyed, were powerfully influenced by their mothers, tended to have more daughters than sons as their children, and other interesting but tangential similarities. Curiously enough, no matter how detailed the study, the only common conclusion was that there was absolutely no way anyone could predict who would become an ace from a group of potential pilots.

Given the advances in the science of genetics, this may change. Perhaps the science of mapping the human genome will reveal a "warrior gene" that will at least signal the ace potential.

A close study of the outstanding personalities in the preceding chapters clearly points to the possibility of there being a warrior gene, one that predisposes an individual to success in combat. Yet further analysis makes it obvious that fighter aces are both born *and* made. If a pilot has a natural predisposition to be an aerial warrior and buttresses it with hard work and dedication to the *mission*, he or she has a good chance of becoming an ace. There certainly are other factors involved, including luck, but these three are the key: the warrior gene, hard work, and dedication to the mission.

A more important conclusion to be drawn from this study is that the greatest fighter aces are not necessarily the ones who shoot down the most enemies. The greatest fighter aces are the *leaders* who make their organizations more effective, and thus do more damage to the enemy.

SOME COMPARISONS

Little Edd Rickenbacker did not have much of a chance to play organized sports as a youth, but his natural athleticism found an early outlet in automobile racing. The early racing cars were primitive, but they combined the need for good hand-eye coordination with the ability to estimate speed and distance with life-or-death accuracy. Introduced to flying at a later age than the other three aces in this book, he offset any diminution of his physical ability with his single-minded desire to succeed.

Rickenbacker's definition of success was different from that of many others of his time, but it was echoed by Zemke, Blesse, and Olds. Rick defined his success in two ways: his own personal achievement in scoring victories, but more important, in the success of the unit he first belonged to, then commanded. These were interdependent goals, but he never sacrificed the second for the first.

The degree of Rickenbacker's patriotism and his selflessness can be inferred from the way he paid his service dues. He was an astute businessman, used to living a high-profile life and accustomed to making large sums of money. Rickenbacker knew better than anyone the value of publicity and the impact it would have on his future prospects. He could easily have returned home in the summer of 1918, allowing his troublesome ear to get him invalided out of the service as a war hero. At the time, he could have used his current status as a leading American ace to jump-start his postwar career in a blaze of publicity. Instead, he fought, against medical advice, to return to his outfit and once there, took on the most dangerous missions, including balloon busting and trench strafing.

When the war ended, Rick had accomplished his aims. He was the premier American Ace of Aces, but more important to him, he had made the 94th into the leading American squadron. Of the two achievements, the latter was far more difficult, for he had to overcome the resentment toward his leadership of some of his most gifted colleagues.

In the process of establishing that leadership, Rickenbacker had to deal with two significant obstacles. The first of these was his health; he might easily have succumbed to the weeks-long torment of his ear abscess and stopped flying forever. The second was the momentous shift in technology that came with the changeover from the Nieuport 28 to the SPAD XIII. While the differences might seem small today—another aircraft, another engine—they were enormous at the time, for there was no system of training to ease the transition from one to the other.

The differences in the engine operation and the handling of the two aircraft were sufficient to kill a number of pilots. Rickenbacker had the flying skills to deal with the transition himself, and then smoothed the way for the other pilots by instructing the mechanics in the care and feeding of the 235-horsepower Hispano-S·iza engine.

The ultimate criterion for the success of an ace is victory in the air, and Rickenbacker led here as well, tempering his leadership in the hot fire of combat. When, on November 11, 1918, he had finished his job, he had also pointed the way to the future for men like Hubert Zemke.

As we have seen, young "Hoo-bart" was an athlete, able to express his pugnacious nature openly in the prize ring. When this channel was denied him, his aggressiveness erupted in other ways, some positive, as when he fought the Luftwaffe, some negative, as when he fought his superior officers.

Zemke had studied Rickenbacker's combat tactics and applied them to his early flying career. Unfortunately, there was no way for him to study Rickenbacker's methods of dealing with people, even those he disliked. There were no Dale Carnegie-style "charm school" courses available to him as a young officer, and had there been, he probably would have refused to take them. It is a pity, for with a modicum more self-confidence and just a little human-relations guidance, Hub Zemke might well have become a four-star general.

As things turned out, however, Zemke was simply one of the all-time great combat Group commanders, a model leader for others to follow. He threw himself into battle with zest and sought out the enemy wherever he could be found—in the air or on the ground. He became an ace and tempered his leadership qualities in combat.

Like Rickenbacker, Zemke had a talent for aircraft maintenance that translated into his ability to master changing technologies. He fought during a period of World War II when technology was changing swiftly on both sides. Zemke was able to maximize the utility of the Allied changes while at the same time minimizing the results of enemy advances in technology.

Rickenbacker and Zemke were similar in another respect. Both had to endure seeing far too many young men under their command die an early death. In

Rickenbacker's case, it was because his men combined a thirst for combat with inexperience in a fight against a seasoned enemy. Zemke's situation was slightly different, for most of the losses he endured came not in combat, but in training.

The result of their experience was the same, however. Both men became hardened to losses and came to accept them as a professional cost of fighting the war. Both became role models for those who were to follow.

BLESSE AND OLDS: A NEW ERA

While Rickenbacker and Zemke had similarly Spartan backgrounds, Blesse and Olds came from modestly comfortable middle-class families. Both were well treated by their fathers and were introduced into a clannish service climate that boded well for their future, encompassing, as it did, a service academy education and a familial name that was sure to be recognized by senior officers. The two men were natural athletes, competitive, and filled with the desire to win. Blesse tended to participate more in individual sports, while Olds was a team man.

Neither man rested on his father's laurels, and both pursued careers in different fields. Blesse followed a longer path to both leadership and to fame as an ace. He did not become discouraged even though he was not given an opportunity to score victories or to impart guidance to a squadron until 1952, seven years after his graduation from West Point.

Blesse had prepared well in those seven years, however, and had a clear vision of what was required to use the new technology of jet warfare. He had originated his concepts in peacetime practice sessions, and they differed markedly from those practiced by veteran aces of World War II who were the first air leaders in Korea. He continued to work on them, using his own experiences in MiG Alley.

Blesse elected to codify his findings into written form, providing a tactical manual for others to follow. This is not unusual—many other military leaders had done the same. What was unusual was the degree to which he extended his leadership beyond his unit to the Air Force and indeed, to many of the world's air forces, which soon had copies of *No Guts, No Glory* and were adopting his precepts.

His ideas were so essentially correct for the new age of jet warfare that they were accepted almost by acclamation by one of the most skeptical and difficult-to-convince audiences in the world—the fighter pilots.

Robin Olds was a more prolific writer, whose ideas were broader and sometimes more theoretical than Blesse's. Curiously, the most important of them were doubly anachronistic, being viewed as *behind* the times by his contemporaries when they were in fact *in advance* of the times in practical terms. The truth of his ideas was so obvious to Olds that it caused him immense frustration when his superiors did not understand. He was, and remains, particularly irritated with those who saw nuclear-armed bombers and missiles as the raison d'être of the Air Force.

Olds's combat career was unusual for its length and its variety. He fought as a youth of twenty-two in World War II and as a grizzled veteran in Vietnam in 1967. The two-decade period also encompassed the tremendous technological changes represented by the contrast in *Scat*, his first P-38, and *Scat XXVII*, his last F-4. (*Scat XXVII*, still carrying his four Red-Star victory symbols, can be seen today in the magnificent Air Force Museum at Dayton, Ohio.)

Yet, despite the length and variety, there was at the heart of Olds's career a unifying philosophy on how a war had to be fought. In both World War II and Vietnam, Olds unswervingly saw his mission as being one of carrying out the orders from higher headquarters and of inflicting maximum damage on the enemy. His mission concept, far more than the desire to score aerial victories, dictated his actions.

Because of his youth and junior status, World War II required him to emphasize aerial combat, and he ran up an impressive score of kills. In his maturity in Vietnam, the emphasis was on protecting the F-105s and on delivering bombs. Fighting MiGs, no matter how enjoyable, was a secondary occupation, one at which he still achieved considerable personal success.

Olds's basic philosophy put him in a very different situation from those of Rickenbacker, Zemke, or Blesse. Each of the latter three was able to apply his combat techniques and leadership skills in a contemporary situation. Olds had to advocate combat techniques from the past, ideas that had fallen out of favor, but that he knew were vital to success. To prove them, he had to demonstrate personally the techniques that he had perfected in P-38s and P-51s in the most powerful jet aircraft of the time, the F-4. The physical process of proving the techniques was extraordinarily demanding. Strapping on a twenty-two-ton aircraft and throwing it around in flak-filled skies under high-G forces for hours at a time is tough on young men. Flying the F-4 through the maneuvers needed to evade SAMs, then pushing it down into the teeth of antiaircraft batteries to deliver bombs is hard, gut-wrenching work. Delivering ordnance by peeling off into the pitch-black darkness of the Lao jungle, unable to see the ground or the horizons, time after time, requires a special courage. Olds's ideas worked, and he proved it by leading his men in action.

It was far more difficult to gain acceptance of his ideas from a hidebound bureaucracy, which came around only grudgingly and after repeated demonstrations.

Olds then had to suffer a dual disappointment. Not only was there little recognition of his contribution beyond the customary medals of the time, but also his ideas were dropped. The rigor he had imparted to the air war in Vietnam eroded in the four years of the bombing halt. Not until Operation Linebacker II, conducted in December 1972, would the USAF strike North Vietnam again with the intensity and skill that Olds had advocated.

THE ACES AND TECHNOLOGICAL CHANGE

As has been noted, the speed of combat aircraft rose from less than 100 mph to more than twice the speed of sound during the six-decade period in which aces were made. Curiously enough, the human element was more than adequate at any time for any airplane. Given the training, Eddie Rickenbacker could have flown the Phantom just as easily as Robin Olds would have flown the SPAD. The critical difference is in the duration of training and experience required for the modern aircraft.

In Rickenbacker's day, a man could go from student pilot to Ace of Aces in little more than a year. By 1972 it took many years of training and combat experience to reach the proficiency level required to be an ace. It also took current exposure to combat conditions to hone the pilot's skills to the point that he could be successful in air-to-air combat.

The airplane itself represents just the tip of the pyramid of effort required. In Rickenbacker's day, the pyramid was relatively short—beneath the pilot and his plane stood maintenance and armament sections and perhaps a primitive aircraft detection and warning system. By Vietnam, the pyramid of effort was extremely tall, with the aircraft and its missiles at the pinnacle, supported by layers of intelligence, armament, airborne warning and control systems, maintenance, personnel, and all the other necessary elements of modern warfare.

There is a similar disparity in the quality of the opposition of the times. In 1918 opposing aircraft were roughly equal in capability, although the Allies always maintained a numerical advantage over the Germans. Antiaircraft fire was often intense but rarely dangerous except in low-level attacks. In 1972 the same air-to-air situation applied, but enemy radar-controlled antiaircraft fire had been supplemented by surface-to-air missiles.

The sky became multilayered in its danger. At low level, small arms fire and smaller caliber antiaircraft guns were a constant danger. At middle altitudes, the 57-mm and 85-mm radar-controlled flak grew ever more intense. At higher altitudes, the SAMs came into play, although, as they became more proficient, the North Vietnamese found ways to use them effectively at lower altitudes.

The greatest change in technology came in the electronic war, a veritable baklava of interlayered measures and countermeasures. Now, instead of a flight of bombers launched against a target, escorted, perhaps, by some fighters, a bombing mission took on the aspects of an aerial task force, with chaff aircraft, escort fighters, electronic countermeasures aircraft, tankers, and bombers, all in a fast-moving armada. (See appendix 8.)

Fortunately for the United States, the effectiveness of this massive effort was immeasurably enhanced with the advent of precision-guided munitions, the first generation of "smart bombs." These were the great differentiator, the single weapon that made all of the other developments in offensive aviation worthwhile.

For the prospective ace, however, the adoption of these mass tactics of precision warfare simply reduced the opportunity for battle. Warfare had moved from the certain ascendancy of the Fokker E I over an Allied reconnaissance plane to the bulldozer formations of Operation Linebacker II, in which enemy defenses were crushed by overwhelming superiority in weapons and electronics.

In the years since Vietnam, the technology of aerial warfare has increased even more dramatically, resulting in the kind of austere, almost bloodless warfare seen in Iraq in 1991 and in Yugoslavia in 1999. The advances in technology have now integrated space into the equation, so that information from satellites can guide aircraft or missiles with near absolute precision to the smallest targets. The probability of air-to-air battles on a sustained basis, as found in the four major American wars of the twentieth century, is remote. The situation may change with the emergence of a new superpower such as China or perhaps Japan.

But the technology is changing as well, and there is a clear path leading to a future perhaps fifty years from now when it may be that any aerial combat that does take place will be done by uninhabited aerial vehicles (UAVs), automated fighters remotely controlled.

Automated conflict will be a net loss for lovers of history and for the spirit of humankind. The United States, and indeed, the rest of the world, was a better place for its aces, particularly those of the caliber of Rickenbacker, Zemke, Blesse, and Olds.

They represent the best of that rare breed, the ace. They pushed themselves beyond their physical limits to achieve their victories over their enemies, and beyond their psychological limits to achieve their goals within their own service. They adapted to rapidly changing situations, and countered the technological advantages of their enemy. Each man exposed himself to the rigors of combat, and in doing so established himself as a leader and an innovator.

It may be that we will not see their like again. These four men—Edward Rickenbacker, Hub Zemke, Boots Blesse, and Robin Olds—are the great ace-leaders. They are the true heroes, more than able to represent the past, the present, and the future of aerial combat.

★ APPENDIX ONE ★
COMBAT AIRCRAFT OF THE ACES

DIMENSIONS AND PERFORMANCE

Type	Wingspan	Length	Height	Empty Weight (Lbs)	Gross Weight (Lbs)	Top Speed (Mph)	Ceiling (Feet)	Range (Miles)
1. Fokker E I	31'2¾"	23'7½"	7'10½"	880	1,345	87	11,800	90
2. Nieuport 28	26'3"	20'4"	8'1¾"	1,172	1,631	122	17,060	248
3. Pfalz D III	30'10"	22'9½"	8'10¼"	1,532	2,061	103	17,000	250
4. Albatros D Va	29'8¼"	24'0½"	8'10¼"	1,515	2,066	116	18,700	220
5. SPAD XIII	26'3¾"	20'4"	7'6¼"	1,245	1,863	135	21,815	250
6. Fokker D VII	29'3½"	22'11½"	9'2¼"	1,474	2,112	118	23,000	200
7. Fokker Dr I	23'7"	19'0"	9'9"	893	1,289	103	19,600	220
8. L.V.G. CV	44'9"	26'7"	10'6"	2,280	3,280	97	17,000	350
9. Curtiss P-40N	37'4"	33'4"	12'4"	6,000	8,850	378	38,000	240
10. Republic P-47D	40'9"	36'1"	14'2"	10,000	19,400	428	42,000	475
11. Lockheed P-38J	52'0"	37'10"	9'10"	12,780	21,600	414	44,000	450
12. N.A. P-51D	37'0"	32'3"	12'2"	7,125	11,600	437	41,900	950
13. Mess. Bf 109G	32'6½"	29'7"	11'2"	5,953	6,945	387	38,500	615
14. Mess. Bf 110G-4	53'3¾"	42'9¾"	13'8½"	11,220	21,800	342	36,250	1,305
15. F.W. Fw 190A-8	34'5½"	29'0"	13'0"	7,000	10,805	408	37,400	500
16. Mess. Me 262A-1	40'11½"	34'9½"	12'7"	9,742	14,101	540	36,080	650
17. Republic P-47N	42'7"	36'1"	14'8"	11,000	20,700	467	43,000	800
18. N.A. F-86A	37'1"	37'6"	14'8"	10,495	16,357	630	48,300	785
19. MiG-15	33'1"	33'1¾"	12'6½"	7,170	10,938	640	49,869	882
20. La-9	32'1¾"	28'3¾"	12'0"	5,816	8,104	429	35,400	1,100
21. MiG-17	31'7"	36'11"	12'5¾"	8,664	13,393	711	54,460	1,230
22. McDonnell F-4	38'4¾"	58'3¾"	16'5"	28,000	42,000	1,485	62,000	800
23. Republic F-105	34'11"	64'0"	19'8"	27,500	52,500	1,390	52,000	900

AIRCRAFT DESCRIPTION

1. The *Fokker E I* was such a menace when it appeared that the Royal Air Force was referred to as "Fokker Fodder" in Parliament. It was a single-seat monoplane powered by a 100-horsepower Oberursel nine cylinder rotary engine, armed with a single LMG 08/15 machine gun, synchronized with the propeller so that it could fire straight ahead. This seemingly obvious innovation made it seem invincible in the hands of such notable pilots as Max Immelmann and Oswald Boelcke.

2. The *Nieuport 28* was beautiful but dangerous, susceptible to engine fires and structural breakup. A single-seat biplane powered by a 160-horsepower Gnome 9N rotary engine, it was armed with two .303-inch Vickers machine guns, although some aircraft received Marlin machine guns. The Nieuport 28 was flown exclusively by American units and used with great success, considering its relative fragility.

3. The *Pfalz D III* was a handsome single-place biplane, the product of the Bavarian aircraft industry, and often ignored by historians of World War I. It featured a plywood fuselage and was powered by a 160-horsepower Mercedes six cylinder engine. The Pfalz was armed with two LMG 08/15 machine guns, often called "Spandau" for their place of manufacture. An unusual feature of the Pfalz was the reverse curve of the airfoil of its horizontal stabilizer. Intended to assist in pulling out of a dive, the feature probably cost the aircraft several miles an hour in level flight.

4. The *Albatros D Va* was the aircraft most used by Baron Manfred von Richthofen, who is usually associated with the Fokker triplane. It was the most important German fighter in terms of the numbers produced and remained in service until the end of the war. Its elegant lines concealed an excessive amount of drag, so that its performance never equaled its looks. It was also troubled by structural problems imparted by the use of a single V strut. Powered by a 160-horsepower (some 180-horsepower versions were used) Mercedes engine, and equipped with twin machine guns, the Albatros was a workhorse.

5. The *SPAD XIII* became an icon of the American Air Service, the airplane in which heroes such as Rickenbacker, Luke, Hartney, and others flew. It was a rugged, stoutly built aircraft with a well-deserved reputation for unreliable engine performance. A single-place biplane, it was powered by a 235-horsepower Hispano-Suiza eight cylinder "V" type engine. It was also

the standard fighter of the French Air Force, and was used by the Italians, British, and Belgians as well. The SPAD "had the glide angle of a brick," was tricky to handle at low speeds, and had to be flown with power in landing.

6. The *Fokker D VII* is usually regarded as the finest fighter of World War I. It certainly forecast the future of fighter construction, with its near-cantilever wings and welded steel tube fuselage. Powered by a 160-horsepower Mercedes or a 185-horsepower BMW engine, the D VII was relatively easy to fly and could fight at very high angles of attack. It had the usual German twin "Spandau" machine gun armament.

7. The *Fokker Dr I* copied the general outline of the Sopwith Triplane but used the standard Fokker construction. It could "climb like a lift" and was highly maneuverable, but it was slower than most fighters. Only about 325 were built, but they achieved a fame out of proportion to their worth, because Richthofen was killed in one—and because of Charles Schultz's comic strip creation, Snoopy, whose "Curse You Red Baron" cry caught the public's imagination. Powered by a 110-horsepower Oberursel rotary engine, it carried the standard German two machine gun armament.

8. The *L.V.G. CV* was not a fighter, but is distinguished by an example being the only remaining original German World War I airplane. A good, workmanlike two-seat biplane, it served in light bomber, reconnaissance, artillery observation, and photoreconnaissance roles. It was German practice to have the observer be the officer and commander, while the pilot was often an enlisted man serving as "chauffeur." They were also referred to as "Fritz and Emil," after a popular German comic strip. The L.V.G. was powered by a 200-horsepower Benz engine and had a single Spandau machine gun firing forward and a Parabellum mounted on a gun ring in the rear cockpit.

9. The *Curtiss P-40N* was the American journeyman fighter, not excelling in many respects, but having a good turn of speed and exceptionally rugged construction. The greatest asset of the P-40 was its *availability*. It had reached mass production ahead of all other American fighters, and thus saw service in every theater. It gained fame as the mount of the Flying Tigers and served until the end of the war. The P-40N was powered by an Allison V-1710-81 engine of 1,360 horsepower, and had six .50-inch machine guns. It could also carry a 500-pound bomb.

10. The *Republic P-47D* was, with the Lightning and the Mustang, one of the three most outstanding American fighters of World War II. Powered by the

reliable Pratt & Whitney R-2800 engine of 2,300 horsepower, the "Jug" was a rugged aircraft, ideally suited for the ground support role. It could supplement its heavy eight .50-inch machine guns with up to 2,000 pounds of bombs and rockets. Along with the P-47N, the P-47D served in USAF and Air National Guard squadrons long after the war, being finally phased out in 1955.

11. The *Lockheed P-38* was one of the most beloved designs of all time, primarily because of its distinctive appearance. Designed by Hall Hibbard and Kelly Johnson, and carefully maneuvered into production by Ben Kelsey, the P-38 was most effective in the Pacific theater. The P-38J had two 1,425-horsepower Allison engines and carried one 20-mm cannon and four .50-inch machine guns in its nose. It could carry two 1,600-pound bombs, plus a variety of other stores.

12. The *North American P-51* is generally regarded as the best all-round piston-engine fighter of World War II, although many other fighters have adherents who would dispute the claim. The long range and high speed of the Mustang combined with good visibility to make it a pilot's delight to fly. Powered by a 1,490-horsepower Packard-built Rolls Royce V-1650 engine, the P-51 had six .50-inch machine guns and could carry two 1,000-pound bombs or up to ten 5-inch rockets. The Mustang has proved so popular that there are still hundreds in existence, and many are restored to better-than-new condition.

13. The *Messerschmitt Bf 109* was manufactured in greater quantities—some 33,000—than any other German airplane. It served in every theater in which the Luftwaffe was engaged, and fought from the first day of the war until the last. The Bf-109G-6 was powered by a Daimler Benz DB-605 twelve cylinder liquid-cooled engine of 1,475 horsepower. To reduce weight, armament was limited to one 30-mm or one 20-mm cannon and two 13-mm machine guns. The Bf-109 was notoriously tricky on takeoff and landing, because of the narrow gear tread, but remained a formidable weapon when flown by experienced pilots.

14. The *Messerschmitt Bf 110* was a failure in its intended role as long-range escort fighter, but it was a great success when adapted to the night-fighting role. The Bf 110G-4 was powered by two Daimler Benz DB 605 engines of 1,475 horsepower. It carried a heavy armament of two 30-mm and two 20-mm cannon firing forward and two machine guns flexibly mounted and firing to the rear.

15. The *Focke Wulf Fw 190A-8* is considered by many to be the most beautiful piston-engine fighter of World War II. Its slim, elegant lines endowed it with a tremendous performance, including the fastest rate of roll of all fighters of the period. Powered by a BMW 801D2 engine of 1,700 horsepower, the Fw 190 was the only German fighter to be produced using a radial engine. Armament varied with the subtype, but the Fw 190A-8 was equipped with two 13-mm machine guns in the cowling, two 20-mm cannon in wing roots, and two 20-mm cannon in the outer wing panels.

16. The *Messerschmitt Me 262* was the world's first operational jet fighter, and its introduction into combat was *not* delayed by Hitler's insistence that it be used as a fighter-bomber, as is so often stated, but rather because insufficient time was spent developing the metallurgy for the jet engines. It was clearly the supreme fighter of World War II, and its advanced features—swept wing and pod-mounted engines—were adopted generally after the war. The Me 262A-1 was powered by two Junkers Jumo 004B-1 engines, of 1,980-pounds thrust each. The very heavy armament package consisted of four 30-mm cannon, later supplemented by twenty-four R4M unguided missiles. Some German pilots referred to the Me 262 as a "life insurance policy" because its performance was so superior.

17. The *Republic P-47N* was built as a long-range version of the aircraft, for use in the Pacific theater.

18. The *North American F-86 Sabre* was one of those rare combinations of looks, performance, and an especially apt name. As a result, it captured the hearts and minds not only of those who flew it, but also of those who merely observed its career. Powered by a single General Electric J47-GE-13 engine of 5,200 pounds of static thrust, the F-86A bore the brunt of conflict with the MiG-15 in the early days of the Korean War. Later models were much improved, but the original Sabre was a classic in its own right.

19. The *MiG-15* was a product of the Mikoyan-Guryevich design team, and drew heavily on both German airframe design practice and the availability of the British-designed Rolls Royce Nene engine. It was powered by a Klimov RD-45 engine of 5,952 pounds of thrust. The MiG-15 is truly a classic aircraft, one of the most important jet fighters in history, and can be seen flying at many American air shows today.

20. The *Lavochkin La-9* first appeared in 1944, and was of all-metal construction, unusual for a Soviet fighter of the period. Powered by a 1,850-

horsepower Ash-82FN radial engine, the La-9 was a first-rate fighter that was produced extensively and supplied to Soviet satellite states.

21. The *MiG-17* was intended to replace the MiG-15, and it did so with great success, being faster and adaptable to many missions. Powered by a VK-1F engine that produced 7,451 pounds of thrust in afterburner, the MiG-17 was produced in great quantities, with nearly 10,000 being built, including 2,000 in China and 1,000 in Poland. Armed with the standard Soviet armament package of one 37-mm and two 23-mm cannon, the MiG-17 was the first Soviet fighter to carry air-to-air guided missiles.

22. The *McDonnell F-4 Phantom II* was the supreme Western fighter of its era, with 5,057 being built. Powered by two afterburning GE J79-15 engines, each rated at 10,900 pounds of thrust dry, and 17,000 pounds of thrust in afterburner, the F-4C carried only missile armament, including heat-seeking AIM-9 Sidewinders and radar-guided AIM-7 Sparrows. Every sort of ordnance, from 260-pound MK-81 general-purpose bombs to BLU-1 napalm bombs, could be fitted, including up to eighteen 1,000 pound bombs.

23. The *Republic F-105 Thunderchief,* better known as the Thud, was powered by the Pratt & Whitney J75 turbojet with 24,500 pounds of thrust in afterburner. Armament included a General Electric 20-mm Vulcan "gatling gun," and over 14,000 pounds in external stores, including bombs, napalm, ECM pods, and so on.

★ APPENDIX TWO ★
THE SWIFT GROWTH OF AIR COMBAT

The air war during World War I was never the knightly jousting match that it was reported to be, but it came nearest to that ideal in those early days when Immelmann and Boelcke reigned supreme. The scale of combat was small. At their peak strength, there were no more than forty Fokker Eindeckers at the front. The losses were so slight compared to the daily carnage in the trenches that individual air-to-air combat seemed almost wholesome, a salutary Olympic exercise in contrast with the slogging warfare in the wasteland below.

Despite the glory it brought, downing enemy airplanes was the least-important aspect of air combat at the beginning of the war. Historians have largely ignored the fact that reconnaissance aviation was *immediately* successful in World War I. Despite the few aircraft in service when war began, and the inherent distrust of military high commands of novel new weapons, aircraft affected the outcome of the war in the very first days of battle. Aircraft and their employment were an incomprehensible anathema to many a beribboned general who resented their being flown by young rebels who did not have the sense to join the cavalry.

Germany had entered the war with 230 aircraft, 254 pilots, and 271 observers. They were opposed by about the same number of Russian aircraft on the eastern front and by 141 French and about 50 British aircraft in the west. All of the aircraft on both sides were developments of prewar civil types, and the standard of training of pilots and observers was totally inadequate.

Airplanes, as primitive as the Taubes, Blériots, and BE2cs of the time were, proved immediately and immoderately effective from the opening barrage of the fateful guns of August. They changed the concept of air war from a playboy's side-show to a major consideration in World War I, and the principal condition for suc-cess in World War II.

INDUSTRIAL GROWTH

All of the major nations started World War I with sophisticated industrial systems for the manufacture of rifles, machine guns, cannons, trucks, and other equipment for their armies. These were often vertically integrated industries that ran from coal mines and ore pits to the manufacture of the railway carriages that carried the guns to the front.

In stark contrast, however, not one of the warring countries was prepared in 1914 for the mass manufacture of ever more sophisticated warplanes. The neces-sary engineers to create new designs were not available and could not be drawn from other sources. Nor was there any of the necessary infrastructure—the buyers who would procure parts and raw materials, the personnel people to hire new employees, the staff to train new workers, the mechanics to service airplanes that were produced, or the pilots to test fly them. Land had to be procured, factories built, staffs assembled, even as the demand for new designs and new production mounted. For much of the war, there was little protection for skilled workers from the endless conscription of soldiers for the front. There was even less protection for the poor taxpayer, as companies took advantage of the situation to maximize their profits at every level.

In time, each government was able to establish oversight organizations intended to bring order to the chaos, but the inevitable drawbacks of bureaucratic systems impeded progress. It was not until 1917 that the industries of France and Great Britain, under the forced draft pressures of war and the almost unlimited expen-diture of funds, began to function at the required level of output.

Great Britain was the most successful in its efforts. In 1915 thirty-four firms were able to produce 1,680 aircraft, most of them obsolete types. Soon there were hundreds of firms involved in aircraft production, although some were producing only components. By 1918 the British aviation industry employed almost 350,000 people and delivered 32,536 aircraft, more than twice the 1917 total of 15,814. Most of the 1918 deliveries were of modern types, and more advanced models were on the drawing boards.

German growth had proceeded in a more systematic manner despite being handicapped by a shortage of skilled labor and machine tools. Germany produced

4,532 aircraft in 1915 and over 16,000 in 1918, when the industry employed about 100,000 people.

France's growth had initially been even more chaotic than either Germany's or Great Britain's. Production grew from 4,489 aircraft in 1915 to a remarkable 24,652 in 1918, with 183,000 people employed. French engine production exceeded all other nations.

The convulsive effort involved in aircraft production during the Great War can be shown statistically. Before 1914 no more than 3,000 aircraft of all types had been built worldwide in the eleven years since the Wright brothers flew at Kitty Hawk. From September 1914 until November 1918, in little more than four years, 203,522 aircraft and 263,759 engines were produced by the major warring powers. A great percentage of these was produced in the last eighteen months of hostilities. The breakdown, by countries, is as follows:

Country	Aircraft	Engines
France	67,892	85,316
Great Britain	55,093	41,034
Italy	20,000	38,000
United States	12,000	32,000
Subtotal of Allies:	154,985	196,350
Germany	48,537	40,449
TOTAL	203,522	236,799

The aircraft production of both Austria-Hungary and Russia was comparatively limited; each country produced only about 5,000 aircraft, and even fewer engines.

World War I established the manufacturing base that prepared the way for the use of airpower on a much greater scale in World War II.

The personnel problem was perhaps even more acute than the manufacturing problem. It was accepted in a modern army that a soldier in the trench might require as many as six or seven persons in the logistic train supporting him. In other words, to get 100,000 riflemen at the front, it was necessary to have 700,000 people requisitioning food, staffing hospitals, and doing all the other related tasks. Commanders on both sides found to their horror that keeping a pilot in the air over the front required no fewer than 50 to 100 people in the logistics chain.

Despite the demand for cannon fodder, the importance of airpower had been established forever, and by November 1918, France and Germany had about

2,600 aircraft each at the front, and Great Britain about 3,600. The United States Air Service had built a force of about 700 aircraft.

Losses were high, about equally divided between combat and accidents. At the close of the war, the Royal Air Force was losing about 800 aircraft a month. Some 64 percent of the pilots sent to France were killed, wounded, or missing in action, and only about 25 percent of pilots completed their tour of duty. The average life of a fighter pilot at the front varied, but it was often as short as three weeks.

This was the cauldron into which America would send its totally inexperienced air service.

NEW EQUIPMENT/NEW TACTICS

Aerial warfare was new, and not even those nations most prepared for it had any concept of the scale of industrial effort that would be required. Entire new industries had to be created to manufacture the airframes, engines, instruments, and equipment that were demanded at the front.

Before the war, the companies that were considered to be "mass" production aircraft manufacturers were essentially just turning out larger numbers of hand-built aircraft. The concept of standardized, interchangeable parts, demonstrated first in manufacturing weapons and later by Cadillac, was totally foreign to the aviation industry. Even engines were made on a "file-to-fit" basis, in which a highly skilled craftsman lovingly hand fit parts together. The result was often an excellent product, but one that could not be repaired in the field with the installation of a replacement part. When Rickenbacker later assumed command of his squadron, this lack of interchangeability would be one of his greatest challenges.

Engineering was "By Guess or By God" in many instances, and if aircraft failed under test or in combat, they were often kept in use for months until they could be revised. Unfortunately, as will be seen, Rickenbacker and the U.S. Air Service would be directly affected by this immature engineering process, because it resulted in the unnecessary deaths of many young men in accidents.

AMERICA AND THE GREAT WAR

The United States declared war against Germany on April 6, 1917. (War was not declared against Germany's major ally, the Austro-Hungarian Empire, until December 7, 1917.) The ground war had grown from an assassin's bullet at Sarajevo to a titanic engagement on four fronts—Eastern, Western, Italian, and

Middle Eastern—and two theaters of operation—African and North Atlantic. The numbers of soldiers involved grew to the tens of millions, armed with every kind of weapon. The air war had grown enormously as well, with every nation fielding a wide variety of aircraft.

The United States had declared war possessing a large and efficient Navy, which would see only antisubmarine warfare duty; a small Army, which would be consumed initially with training conscripted troops; and, incredibly for the birth-place of aviation, no aircraft, not one, fit for fighting.

An enormous catch-up process began, in which the Allies optimistically expected the United States to turn out weapons as it turned out Ford Model Ts, rapidly and in endless numbers. Somewhat ingenuously, French Premier Alexan-der Ribot called for the United States to send France an air force of 4,500 planes and to supply the Allies with 2,000 aircraft and 4,000 engines "of the latest type" each month. His call was for the delivery of 22,625 airplanes in the next year—exactly 273 times the previous year's production in America. Newspapers and politicians responded rapturously with enthusiastic promises to "darken the skies over Germany" with American warplanes.

It was not to be, of course. The United States would indeed make a tremen-dous effort, creating a massive aviation industry where none had existed before. The products of that industry, new aircraft of every type of American design and manufacture, would have reached the front by 1919. However, when the war ended on November 11, 1918, the effort was just becoming mature, and a few hundred British-designed, American-built de Havilland DH-4 aircraft were in service in France.

Since the 1909 purchase of its first aircraft, the Wright Military Flyer, the U.S. Army had procured only 224 airplanes, about 30 a year. On April 6, 1917, the Army Air Service had 131 officers and 1,087 enlisted men. There were fifty-five airplanes, most such literal death traps that it was fortunate that only half of them were in commission. None were worthy of combat. And just as the United States had neglected the manufacture of aircraft before entering the war, so had it neg-lected the recruiting and training of pilots.

The failure to procure aircraft might conceivably be attributed to Congres-sional control of the budgets. However, it was unforgivable that the United States Army had failed to *learn* anything from the whirlwind developments of the air war in Europe. It was an incredible situation, given the fact the Army had observers at the front, and that an American fighting unit, the Lafayette Escadrille, had been in combat against the Germans since May 13, 1916.

The United States Congress did not learn much about airpower from World War I. It allowed the services to collapse and kept the aircraft industry in a state of chronic malnutrition. Only a fortuitous series of events, including the purchase of military aircraft by Great Britain and France in 1938, 1939, and 1940, made it possible for the U.S. aviation industry to meet the demands of World War II.

Little more was learned from the World War II equivalent of the Lafayette Escadrille—the Eagle Squadrons of the RAF. Once again, American flyers were fighting in defense of another country, and once again, the American military failed to draw the necessary conclusions from the experience. There was more transfer of knowledge and skill than there had been in World War I, but not as much as might have been expected. In both wars, the United States had to become fully embroiled and learn its lessons the hard way.

★ APPENDIX THREE ★
TECHNICAL NOTES

Few aircraft captured the romance of the air war as did the pretty little French Nieuports, particularly the Nieuport 11, known affectionately as "le Bebe." Although small, it mounted a machine gun firing over its top wing and was effective against the Fokker Eindecker. Its small size and light weight have resulted in it being a popular aircraft for enthusiasts who make replicas of World War I airplanes. It also lends itself to simulation in ultralight aircraft.

The most numerous members of the Nieuport series were sesqui-planes, which had a larger upper wing connected by a V-shaped strut to a smaller, single-spar lower wing. The arrangement made sense aerodynamically, and it provided the pilot with a good view looking down. Unfortunately the V strut was a structural mistake. When stressed in flight by excessive speed or excessive G forces, the lower wing tended to rotate around its single spar, leading to structural failure. In one of the many ironies of the war, the Germans not only manufactured exact copies of one of the Nieuport fighters, but also adopted the V strut for their Albatros series, only to encounter exactly the same problems.

All of the wartime Nieuports were powered by rotary engines, and the Nieuport 28 had a powerful, lightweight 160-horsepower Gnome. Its power output was not governed by a conventional throttle. Instead, the pilot of a Nieuport 28 had a lever with five positions marked on it (0, 1, 2, 3, and 4) that selectively blocked ignition to certain cylinders. At position 4, all cylinders fired, and the engine at full speed provided about 1,400 rpm (revolutions per minute). At position 3, ignition was reduced to some cylinders, reducing power to about 1,100 rpm; position

2 resulted in 750 rpm, about enough power to maintain level flight. Position 1 gave only 500 rpm, just enough to assist in the glide. At position 0, ignition was completely cut off. If the lever was returned to the number 4 position, the engine usually responded immediately with full power.

The engine and structural deficiencies of the Nieuport 28 are covered in the text, but it should be noted that there were many other wartime aircraft that had inherent problems. The Sopwith Camel not only shot down more enemy planes than any other Allied fighter (1,294), but also killed more Allied pilots in flying accidents. The Camel was very tricky to fly, particularly on takeoff, and many a pilot aspirant found himself in a sudden, fatal spin. The problem was the combined massive torque of the rotary engine and propeller and the very small size of the fuselage and rudder. Once mastered, however, the same combination that gave the problem imparted fantastic maneuverability in the air.

The Fokker company had a series of catastrophic quality control problems that made the Fokker Dr I triplane and the later Fokker D VIII high-wing monoplane more dangerous to the Germans than they were to the Allies. Inadequate supervision, poor-quality materials, and in some instances, basic design deficiencies caused the wings of both the Dr I and D VIII to come apart in the air. The Fokker D VII had a series of unexplained catastrophic in-flight fires until it was discovered that the machine guns were so placed that the heat of the engine could cause the ammunition to explode.

The British de Havilland DH-4 was given the nickname "flaming coffin" for the manner in which it burst into flames when struck by German bullets. The DH-4 had a pressurized fuel tank; when struck by a bullet, the pressure forced vaporized fuel out in a highly explosive stream. As mentioned in the text, the 235-horsepower geared version of the Hispano-Suiza engine used in the SPAD XIII had a high failure rate.

Nor were treacherous design faults confined to World War I. In World War II, the Messerschmitt Bf 109 had such vicious characteristics that more than 3,000 flyers were lost in takeoff accidents. The Heinkel He 177 four-engine bomber was so prone to in-flight fires that it was referred to as the "Luftwaffe's lighter," as in cigarette lighter. The British Boulton-Paul Defiant was a fighter without any forward-firing armament. Instead, it had a four-gun turret in the rear seat. The Germans soon learned that the less-than-maneuverable Defiant was an easy target.

The early North American F-86s had a very high accident rate, and so did their counterpart, the MiG-15. In combat, the MiG-15 suffered many of its losses because it lacked the redundant systems of the American fighters, and a small amount of battle damage could bring down the aircraft.

Even so modern an aircraft as the McDonnell F-4, the most important U.S. fighter during the Vietnam War, had plenty of problems. Its engines emitted huge long trails of smoke (unless it was in afterburner) that made it easy to spot by the enemy. Its electrical system was not designed to withstand the rigors of the climate of Southeast Asia, and the potting material that supposedly protected its circuits from moisture simply melted and ran. The F-4s had only a single radio for plane-to-plane communication, and it often malfunctioned. When it did, the repair time was lengthy, for it was located so that the ejection seat had to be removed for it to be serviced.

No country, in the past, the present, or the future, was or will be immune to the errors of design. The marvelous aircraft flying today, and those even more remarkable designs on the drawing board, all have had the benefit of computers to lessen the probability of an error happening. But errors will happen tomorrow, just as they did yesterday.

★ APPENDIX FOUR ★
DROP TANKS AND FIGHTER ESCORTS

The brutal beating administered by the Luftwaffe during the Regensburg and Schweinfurt raids in October 1943 put to rest the last lingering hopes that American bombers could fly long-range penetration daytime missions without fighter escort. The difficulty was that there were no fighters capable of escorting the bombers deep into Germany. The P-47 was then the most numerous fighter in the theater, and frantic efforts were made to extend its range.

Colonel Hub Zemke had long called for additional internal tanks within the Thunderbolt, but his requests had been ignored. Instead, experiments were made with a variety of external fuel tanks and with new tactics that required the American escort fighters to patrol an area rather than accompany the bombers on their route. This required a lot of planning and almost split-second timing to have the right number of airplanes in the right spot at the right time. Bad weather and the difficulty of maneuvering huge formations of bombers and fighters through thousands of feet of cloud cover without the benefit of radar control made exact timing almost impossible. The Germans understood the situation perfectly and would hold their fighters back until the time they knew the escorting Thunderbolts would have to withdraw.

Ironically, the solution had been available for years. It lay in streamlined external fuel tanks that could be jettisoned when empty or in an emergency. The Curtiss P-6E that Zemke had flown after graduation from flying school had an external tank, and many modern fighters such as the Curtiss P-40 and the Lockheed P-38 had employed drop tanks almost from the start.

The P-47 had originally been intended as an interceptor, by definition a relatively short-range aircraft. To achieve top performance, designer Alexander Kartveli had been fanatical about streamlining, and the P-47 was built without consideration for external tanks, omitting the necessary shackles and plumbing to use them. When the mission of the P-47 was changed to escort fighter, a disfiguring 205-gallon "bathtub" tank had been conformed to the belly of the P-47, but it added tremendous drag and could not be pressurized, so it was useless at altitude. It also did not always separate cleanly, sometimes bouncing into the fuselage bottom or the tailplane.

All this was grist for Cass Hough's mental mill. Hough had flown as an enlisted pilot, then moved quickly through the ranks to become a full Colonel in recognition of his genius in solving problems. It was Hough who supervised the creation of the series of drop tanks for the Thunderbolt that flowed from the USAAF depot at Bovingdon.

A drop tank is relatively simple in appearance but is in fact mechanically and aerodynamically complex. It must not cause too much drag, or the benefits of the additional fuel will be greatly offset. It must fall freely away from the aircraft and not bounce into the wing or tail surfaces. It must not upset the stability of the aircraft at any time, whether full or empty. If it could not be pressurized, it was almost useless. Drop tanks had to have the necessary plumbing to get the fuel to the engine or to other tanks. Standard bomb shackles had to be able to hold it. A good drop tank also had to be reasonably inexpensive and not use too many critical materials, because it was expended on almost every mission. It was also important that it not leak, a problem with some of the early paper laminate tanks.

Hough came up with a brilliant series of designs that met these criteria, using both aluminum and a paper laminate for materials. His tanks were pressurized so that they could be used at altitude and were not jettisoned until the last moment. They ranged in size from 75 to 200 gallons, and by mid-1944, two or three tanks could be installed.

With each improvement in drop tanks, the Thunderbolt's range was extended, and the bombers were protected for a little longer. The Germans responded to each increase in range by pulling their fighters back and delaying engagement. Each time they moved back, the Thunderbolts moved forward. With Germany's borders being pressed back by the Soviet Union, and with the invasion certain to come in the next few months, the Luftwaffe would eventually have nowhere to run, and the P-47 would have the range to turn its pilots into aces.

In the abstract, the concept of extending range by adding tanks seems like a straightforward plan. What is missing in such an analysis is the tangible human effects. The extra tanks provided longer missions. The longer missions meant more hours with an oxygen mask strapped to your face, cutting into the skin. Over the long hours, the oxygen dried out the respiratory system and had a side effect that no one had counted on. The oxygen gradually filled the inner ear; hours later, on the ground, the oxygen would be absorbed, causing an earache from the change in pressure similar to that in a rapid change of altitude. As the missions got longer, the pressure on the bladder grew, and it was difficult to use the primitive relief tubes given the low temperatures and layers of heavy clothing. Digestive problems were common, and simply had to be endured. Then there was the sheer fatigue of long-range flight at high altitude in a constant state of apprehension. If there was combat, there was a high adrenaline factor, with the subsequent letdown. Sometimes at the end of a long day of combat, the pilot was faced with a trip home in a damaged aircraft, only to find Great Britain covered with miserable weather, requiring an instrument landing. External tanks did more than extend the range—they extended the pilot to the very limits of his endurance.

★ APPENDIX FIVE ★
TIME AND TECHNOLOGY

World War II had accelerated technology at an amazing rate, as all the warring nations poured unlimited treasure into research and development. The rate of development was greatest where the need was greatest, in Germany. By 1943 it was evident that the balance of power had shifted dramatically against the Axis. Greatly outnumbered in manpower and unable to match the industrial capacity of the Allies, Germany turned to technology as its one last chance at victory. It sought miracle weapons on land, sea, and in air, pursuing multiple avenues and achieving some incredible successes along with many more failures.

Germany was the first to create an air-to-surface missile, the Fritz X, which would be the first—and to date only—missile to sink a battleship, dispatching the Italian *Roma* in September 1943. Besides rocket- and jet-powered fighters and bombers, Germany would be first with cruise missiles, ballistic missiles, advanced submarines, surface-to-air missiles, and many other would-be "miracle weapons."

The rather innocuous looking V1 buzz bomb was potentially the most dangerous of all of the miracle weapons. A pilotless pulse-jet-powered cruise missile, it followed a steady flight path at about 400 mph and carried an 1,850-pound warhead. It could be launched from ski-shoot-like ground stations, or dropped from aircraft, presaging the ALCMs and CALCMS of the 1990s. After the war, General Dwight D. Eisenhower wrote that the V1 could have delayed or even prevented the invasion of Normandy, if it had been deployed as Hitler had demanded: 8,000 a day from January 1, 1944. The V1 was crude and inaccurate, but it was cheap, made of noncritical materials, and required only a few man-hours to manufacture.

Fortunately, the Allied bombing campaign concentrated on its manufacturing and launch sites sufficiently to delay its deployment until June 12, 1944—six days after the invasion.

The second miracle weapon was the V2, a rocket-powered ballistic missile that was impossible to intercept. The forerunner of today's menacing intercontinental ballistic missiles, the V2 was actually a hobby-shop toy designed under the leadership of Wernher von Braun, whose rocket scientists were more space cadets than military men. They quite literally seduced the German military into spending millions of Reichsmarks on a weapon that was intended by its creators to be the first step into space. The V2 demanded enormous resources to plant its 2,000-pound warhead on an area target, and the German war effort would have been better off if it had never been attempted.

There were other less well known, if no less spectacular, products of the feverish German research effort. The Messerschmitt Me 163 Komet was a lethal combination of rocket power and beautiful aerodynamics, and was by far the fastest aircraft of World War II, having recorded speeds in excess of 630 mph. It was also highly impractical, having too short a range to be useful, and carrying a gun that fired too slowly to register enough hits at the closing speeds of combat. The Me 163 scored some successes, with one unit totaling nine victories, but far more German pilots than that lost their lives in test, training, and combat.

Of all the German developments, one weapon, the Messerschmitt Me 262 jet fighter, might have prolonged the war and perhaps have had some effect on its outcome. Had the Germans concentrated their efforts on the metallurgical research necessary to get jet engines into mass production by 1942—as they could easily have done—the Luftwaffe could have been completely rearmed with Messerschmitt Me 262 jet fighters by the summer of 1943. Had this been the case, the Allies would not have been able to attain air superiority over the Reich, and the invasion would have had to be postponed until the arrival of American and British jet fighters in 1945. During this interval, Hitler and Stalin might have reached an agreement, and the Allies might ultimately have been faced with a decision to drop nuclear weapons on Germany to obtain the final victory.

But the inherently faulty Nazi organizational scheme had diffused the German research effort. Absurd security requirements concealed what was going on from loyal scientists who needed to know; as a result, there was both duplication of effort and failure to share necessary information. The first production jet engines were not produced until the early summer of 1944, and although more than 1,300 Me 262s were produced, only about 300 saw combat.

(It should be emphasized here that Adolf Hitler is often blamed for the failure of the Germans to get the jet fighter into operation earlier than they did, because of his insistence that it also be used as a bomber. The real reason Me 262s did not get into combat earlier was because there were no jet engines available for them until June of 1944.)

Fortunately for the world, and unfortunately for the Nazis, their timing was as off for the Me 262 as it was for all of Germany's hoped-for miracle weapons. None would have the slightest effect on the outcome of the war. Instead, the vast amounts of treasure and brains that Germany poured into a desperate attempt to win a war by technology would flow in equal measure to benefit its enemies, the Western Allies, particularly the United States, and the Soviet Union.

THE GROWTH OF R&D

Before the war, both the Soviet Union and the United States had spent only the most moderate amounts of their defense budgets on research and development. Most of the money was devoted to applied, rather than basic, research.

As a capitalist country, the United States used its military research facilities to further the development of requirements that were then fulfilled by civilian contractors. The incentive provisions found routinely in modern contracts were used only sparingly—winning a contract was such a rare event that contract award was considered incentive enough.

In the Soviet Union, the government sponsored both the R&D and the manufacturers, and had a double-edged incentive program. Those who succeeded were given comfortable salaries and decorations. Those who failed could be executed or imprisoned, because a design that did not meet expectations was frequently considered to be the result of sabotage. In the United States, a crash was met with the joking cliché "back to the drawing board." In the Soviet Union, a crash was often met with a prison sentence. A. N. Tupelov designed some of the planes that would fight in the Korean War from his prison cell.

The United States Army Air Forces had its principal research and development agency in Dayton, Ohio, where the facilities at Wright Field had spilled over to nearby Patterson Field. The National Advisory Committee on Aeronautics, operating primarily from Langley Field, was also important and contributed heavily to Army Air Forces planning.

When war came, with its huge defense budgets, the U.S. aviation companies vastly expanded their own research and development capabilities, some going so far as to build their own wind tunnels. The funds flowing from the war effort pro-vided, for the first time, budgets large enough to hire engineers whose task was pure research.

When the war ended and production contracts were canceled across the board, the active pursuit of aeronautical research and development might have been expected to end in the United States. Instead, thanks to the vision of Gen-eral Henry H. "Hap" Arnold, a significant portion of the reduced AAF budget was allocated to research.

Arnold, who was neither a scientist nor an engineer, saw a future in which an independent Air Force would maintain the peace through overwhelmingly advanced airpower. To bring this about, he sought out the services of Dr. Theo-dore von Karman, placing him at the head of what eventually became the Air Force's Scientific Advisory Board. The SAB would have the vision—and the resources—to continue the development of the advances made in the United States, while incorporating the best German developments.

Stalin, with visions of conquest rather than of maintaining the peace, set about accomplishing the same goal of combining the German advances with the robust Soviet aircraft industry. He had four primary instruments to speed tech-nology. The first was his standby, terror. Then there were the TsAGI (*Tsentral'nyi aergidrodinamicheskii institut*), the Central AeroHydrodynamics Institute, and the OKBs (*Opytnoe konstruktorskoe byuro*), the Experimental Design Bureaus of the state aviation factories, which worked together the way Western government research facilities and contractors worked. The fourth instrument was the least expensive and most productive. Stalin relied heavily on the work of leftist sympa-thizers in the Western democracies. One of his greatest windfalls, almost on the level of the continual passage of atomic secrets by Klaus Fuchs and others, was the provision by the British Labour government of fifty-five Rolls Royce Nene engines, beginning in September 1946. These engines were reverse engineered and promptly adopted for production as the RD-45 by the Klimov design office. This single transaction advanced the Soviet Union's jet engine technology by five years and made the MiG-15 and its successors possible.

★ APPENDIX SIX ★

"BOELCKE DICTA" VERSUS
NO GUTS, NO GLORY

There have been many translations of the "Boelcke Dicta." Following is a modified version, with my comments in brackets.

1. Try to secure all the advantages before attacking. Whenever possible, attack from out of the sun. [With the advent of radar, attacking from out of the sun is possibly less important than before, but because it is impossible to determine how a fight will develop, it is still a good idea to do so.]

2. Always carry through an attack once you have started it. [Breaking off an attack has two results: the first is the impression that you are not as aggressive as you might be, and the second is that you are now a good target for attack.]

3. Fire at close range, and only when your opponent is properly in your sights. [The farther away you are from a target, the more chances you have to misjudge relative speed, altitude, and turn rate. The farther you are away, the more effect that gravity has on the flight of your bullets or cannon shells. If, as the great German ace Erich Hartmann advocated, you get close enough that the target aircraft fills your windscreen—you will have a better chance at success. The introduction of air-to-air missiles has diluted the importance of this rule somewhat.]

4. Keep your eye on your opponent and never let yourself be deceived by ruses. [When air fighting was relatively young, an opponent could feign a spin, and perhaps elude pursuit. But pilots on both sides quickly gained experience and it became more and more difficult to conduct an elaborate

ruse. Colonel Robin Olds's famous Operation Bolo is undoubtedly the finest expression of aerial trickery perpetrated in recent years.]

5. Always attack from behind. [This gives you obvious advantages in position, visibility, disposition of armament, and so on. In *No Guts, No Glory* (see below), Blesse advocates attacking *low* and from behind. It is more difficult to achieve in a combat environment with Airborne Control of aircraft, and the advent of supersophisticated missiles makes this rule less applicable today than before.]

6. If your opponent dives on you, do not try to evade his attack, but fly to meet it. [The opposite of this, turning away from the enemy and attempting to flee, obviously puts you at a greater disadvantage. Turning into him increases the closing speed and your turn makes the opponent's deflection shot more difficult. Once you've passed the enemy, you now have the opportunity to turn the tables and attack.]

7. When in enemy territory, never forget your line of retreat. [This does not just mean the direction of your home base; it also includes such factors as your fuel state, the position of tankers, the velocity and direction of the wind, and many other elements that will govern your ability to return.]

8. Whenever possible, attack in groups of four or six. When the fight breaks up into individual fights, take care that more than one from your side do not go after a single opponent. [This still holds true and is perhaps even more important because of the possibility of midair collisions, losses resulting from friendly missile fire, and so on.]

The "Boelcke Dicta" were simple and direct, and have been pertinent for many years. However, the introduction of high-speed aircraft rendered them inadequate and left the door open for Boots Blesse's famous book *No Guts, No Glory*.

No Guts, No Glory is a far more comprehensive manual than Boelcke's simple set of principles and takes in not only the physics and physiology of high-speed, high-altitude, high-G air combat, but also the psychology of the combatants.

Blesse divided his book into three sections: The Offensive; The Defensive; and Related Subjects. The Offensive Section has no fewer than twenty-five basic principles, as follows:

1. The element of two is your most effective basic fighting team. When the fight is over, you'll be coming home in twos about 90 percent of the time.

2. Two elements (four aircraft) represent your most effective fighting element: the flight.

3. If enemy aircraft are anywhere in the vicinity, get rid of external tanks as soon as possible.

4. When in doubt in a dogfight, trade airspeed for altitude.

5. Two good aerial training flights a week are the minimum necessary to stay in practice. If you aren't fighting the enemy, practice among yourselves.

6. Never continue turning with an aircraft after you are unable to track him with your sight. Pull up immediately and keep your nose behind his tail. If he pulls up, you'll always end up on top because of your attacking airspeed.

7. If, by using speed brakes, you can drift into the radius of turn of the aircraft you are attacking, do it in preference to the Yo-Yo maneuver. It takes less time to get your kill and you don't run the risk of being outmaneuvered by the aircraft you are attacking. What you are leary about is slowing down and thus subjecting yourself to attack. You are at your opponent's airspeed either way and for less time if you use your speed brakes properly. Obviously, the combat area is no place to experiment with this theory. Don't waste your flying time—practice! [The Yo-Yo is a vertical maneuver used to defeat an opponent's ability to turn sharply. There are many variations of the maneuver. Blesse deliberately wrote in an informal, collegial manner, to make his material easier to read.]

8. Cruise at high Mach. [Earlier in the war, cruise was maintained at a lower Mach number to save fuel, but the time required to accelerate made engaging the MiGs more difficult.]

9. Look around, you can't shoot anything until you see it. [A lesson true from Rickenbacker's day to this.]

10. Keep the aircraft you are attacking in sight. One glance away is enough to make you kick yourself for ten years. [All combat pilots have marveled at how quickly an airplane can disappear from sight.]

11. Generally speaking, have an element high and fast when you slow down to maneuver. If you are trying to snip one up in the traffic pattern, you'll find it difficult at best with all the flak. Don't make the job harder by leaving yourself open for a bounce by the always present enemy CAP flights. [CAP stands for combat air patrol, to protect the airfield.]

12. Attack from low and behind whenever possible. That's a fighter's [enemy's] poorest visibility area.

13. If you have an enemy aircraft in front, assume there is one behind; there usually is. [The importance of the wingman is obvious here.]

14. Know the performance data on all aircraft you are apt to be fighting.

15. Know your "Big Three." Be familiar with glide characteristics, air-start procedures, and fuel consumption at altitude and idle RPM. If you are attacked on the way home, you may need all three to make it back safely. [Air start means restarting your engine while in the air, either after shutting it down deliberately to save fuel, or after it has malfunctioned.]

16. Assume every pilot you meet is the world's best (you can swallow your pride that long) and maneuver your aircraft accordingly until he shows that he is not.

17. Don't shoot unless you are positive it is an enemy aircraft. When it's time to fire, you'll know if it's an enemy aircraft or not. If you can't tell, you are out of range.

18. There are three distinct phases in destroying another aircraft in the air:
    a. Maneuvering—85 percent
    b. Positioning the pipper—10 percent [The pipper is the gun sight marker.]
    c. Firing and adjusting the burst—5 percent
    75 percent of all lost kills are the result of attempting phase (b) and (c) before (a) has been adequately solved. [Boots learned this the hard way on his first combat mission with Bud Mahurin.]

19. Guts will do for skill, but not consistently. Know your job in combat, or someone else will be flying in your place.

20. Shut up on the radio. If it doesn't concern everyone, get on another channel.

21. Play on the team—no individualists. The quickest way to be an element leader is to be the best wingman in the squadron.

22. When in doubt—attack! [The Warrior Gene speaks.]

23. Learn the value and the proper procedure for harmonization. [He refers here to the alignment of the guns and their pattern of fire.]

24. Divide the enemy and conquer. It is very difficult even for the best pilots to work mutual support tactics in high-speed jet aircraft. If you can split the tactical formation of the enemy, more often than not his mutual support efforts against you will be ineffective.

25. One last word before you set out to be the next jet ace—**no guts, no**

glory. If you are going to shoot him down, you have to get in there and mix it up with him.

The Defensive Section has 19 basic principles, as follows:

1. If you slow down, have an element high and fast for support.
2. Except at extreme ranges, always turn into the attack.
3. If there are enemy aircraft anywhere in the area, get rid of external tanks and get your Mach up. It's too late after you spot him.
4. Keep your attacker at a high angle off. [To make his deflection shooting more difficult.]
5. Keep airspeeds up when patrolling.
6. Don't ever reverse a turn unless you have your attacker sliding to the outside of the radius of your turn. [See No. 7 in Offensive Principles.]
7. If you have a "hung" external tank, leave the combat area. [A "hung" tank is one that will not jettison.]
8. If you lose your wingman, both of you should leave the combat area.
9. Know the low-speed characteristics of your aircraft. If you are fighting aggressive pilots, you'll need all the know-how you can lay your hands on.
10. Have a "last-ditch" maneuver and practice it. (This would be a final maneuver to get you out of an emergency situation.)
11. Keep a close check on your fuel.
12. "Best Defense is a good offense" is good most of the time—but know your defensive tactics.
13. Don't play Russian Roulette! When you're told to Break—DO IT. [Breaking means a sharp turn away from your line of flight.]
14. Avoid staring at contrails or the only aircraft in sight. There are a dozen around for every one you can see.
15. Watch the sun—a well-planned attack will come out of the sun when possible.
16. The object of any mutual-support maneuver is to sandwich the attacker in between the defending aircraft.
17. In any dogfight, the objective for the defender should be lateral separation. When this is achieved, a reverse and a series of scissors will, if properly executed, put your attacker out in front. The rest is up to you. [There are a whole host of scissor maneuvers, which involve turns to gain the firing position on the enemy.]

18. Place yourself in your attacker's shoes. How would you like to find an enemy flight positioned? Be smart and avoid this formation for your flight.

19. Don't panic—panic is your most formidable enemy!

Blesse goes far beyond these listings of principles of offense and defense, and details how to handle a variety of combat situations. His instructions are far more detailed than Boelcke's, because air combat became far more complex.

★ APPENDIX SEVEN ★
SURFACE-TO-AIR MISSILES

The introduction of the surface-to-air missile was perhaps the most significant technological revolution in defensive warfare that occurred during the Vietnam War. While not a wonder weapon, and vulnerable to defeat both electronically and tactically, the addition of SAMs to existing antiaircraft and MiG defense systems gave the air war a level of complexity that taxed U.S. capabilities to the utmost.

The most important SAM was known as the SA-2 "Guideline" to NATO forces and was called the V-75 Dvina by the Soviets. Development began in 1952 under the auspices of the Lavochkin design bureau, and the V-75 was displayed publicly for the first time in Red Square in Moscow on November 7, 1957. The V-75 program was at the time the most expensive ever undertaken by the Soviet Union, probably costing about the equivalent of $30 billion dollars over the life of its production. The Soviet Union deployed 4,800 launchers during the peak period of V-75 use.

The Dvina system had two main elements, the "Fan Song" engagement radar and the missile launcher. (The NATO code name "Fan Song" was derived from the birdlike sound of the radar radiations.) The V-75 missile was a two-stage, command-guided type, fired from a single rail launcher. The design was intended to be easily moved from one site to another.

A typical SA-2 site consisted of a Dvina Regiment, with three launch battalions, each with six missile launchers. Up to seventy-two missiles were kept on hand, ready to launch. The entire complex was heavily camouflaged, but the distinctiveness of its launch sites, connecting tracks, and storage facilities was usually easily identified by aerial reconnaissance.

The Dvina's first significant combat use came on May 1, 1960, when a salvo of fourteen brought down Francis Gary Powers's U-2 near Sverdlovsk. It was the first of more than 13,000 V-75s that would be fired in combat over the next three decades. The missile achieved success again during the 1962 Cuban missile crisis, shooting down a U-2 flown by Major Rudolph Anderson Jr.

The V-75 had been designed to operate against high-altitude bombers and reconnaissance planes. The Soviet Union had designed another missile, the S-125 Neva (NATO's SA-3 "Goa") for use against low-flying tactical aircraft, but did not wish to provide these to the North Vietnamese, who made do with the SA-2s instead.

During its original tests, the V-75 was projected to have a lethal capability of 50 to 80 percent kills. In actual wartime conditions, it had a far lower kill rate, but it was still a significant weapon.

The first V-75 sites were spotted in North Vietnam in the spring of 1965, and the USAF responded by sending six Douglas RB-66 electronic warfare aircraft. The first loss to an SA-2 came on July 24, 1965, when a McDonnell F-4C of the 47th TFS was shot down about fifty miles northwest of Hanoi. During 1965, 194 SA-2s were fired, downing five USAF and six U.S. Navy aircraft, for a 5.7 percent kill rate.

The USAF responded by bombing SAM sites with more vigor and changing bombing tactics. New electronic equipment was created to detect and give warning of the SAMs, and new electronic countermeasures pods were created. The most effective tactic (and the most dangerous type of combat) was the creation of Wild Weasel and Iron Hand flights to combat the SAM sites with radar-seeking missiles.

Pilots devised methods of combating a SAM after it had been fired. The preferred technique was to spot the SAM after launch, then turn into it with a high-speed diving turn, followed by an abrupt pull up of at least 4 Gs. The maneuver required exquisite timing, for the pilot had to stay out of the range of the missile's proximity fuse, which could cause lethal damage at up to a 200-foot distance.

The North Vietnamese improved their equipment and techniques to counter the new U.S. tactics. They increased the numbers of missiles and prepared about six sites per launcher to conceal their presence. As the war progressed, the advantage swung to the Americans. The kill rate went down to about 1.8 percent in

1967 (56 to 60 kills out of 3,202 missiles fired) and by some estimates as low as .9 percent in 1968.

During the last great American air offensive of the war, Linebacker II, between 884 and 1,242 missiles were fired against the attacking aircraft. A kill rate of 1.2 to 1.7 percent was achieved. (Exact numbers are difficult to establish.) During the entire period of their use in Vietnam, the SA-2s fired about 9,000 missiles, to bring down between 150 to 160 U.S. aircraft.

The SA-2 came into its own after the U.S. withdrawal from Vietnam, for the South Vietnamese lacked the necessary countermeasures equipment. However, the general ineffectiveness of the SA-2 against U.S. aircraft gave leaders in the Soviet Union immediate concern about the state of their air defenses.

★ APPENDIX EIGHT ★
ROUTE PACKAGES AND COMBAT FORMATIONS IN VIETNAM

In Korea it had proved impossible for the United States Air Force and the U.S. Navy to conduct true joint air operations. The principal cause was the Navy's requirement to maintain a strong fleet defense, which meant that it had to always retain control of its assets.

The same situation occurred during the Vietnam War, and initially, an informal system of allocating targets had worked reasonably well. However, as the air war intensified, a more formal arrangement was drawn up in which Vietnam was divided into seven areas, each called by the term Route Package. Route Packages I, II, III, IV, V, VIA, and VIB were established. The Air Force was given Route Packages I, II, and VIA (the Hanoi area), while the Navy received Route Packages III, IV, V, and VIB (the Haiphong area). Route Packages were also known as "RPs," "Packs," or "Paks."

Admiral U. S. G. Sharp, Commander in Chief of Pacific Command, made these package assignments permanent in April 1966.

The Air Force target areas required longer flights from bases in Thailand, and thus required more refueling support. The longer flights also exposed Air Force aircraft to longer periods of attack from MiGs, SAMs, and antiaircraft fire.

Missions to RP VIA and VIB were unquestionably the toughest and were referred to as "going downtown," a term made immortal by the title of Colonel Jack Broughton's great book. Robin Olds recognized the greater hazard of Pak VIA by creating a "first team" to fly the missions and bringing newcomers into the battle only after they had become experienced enough to handle it.

As the war progressed in intensity and complexity, the formations of strike aircraft became increasingly sophisticated, reaching their peak during Linebacker II.

In general terms, a well-planned, well-executed strike would include the following.

1. There would be a preparation effort before the main strike, in which the strike force would be preceded by Iron Hand and Wild Weasel aircraft to suppress the enemy air defenses. Chaff bombers would also lay down a screen of chaff over the route to the target. The chaff bombers would have their own fighter escort and be supported by Douglas EB-66s in an orbit. The EB-66s would also have a MiG Combat Air Patrol (MiGCAP).

2. The formation of strike aircraft would follow, flying in such a manner as to maximize the effectiveness of their defensive equipment. The strike aircraft would have a fighter escort to protect them from MiG attacks.

3. Other fighters would be deployed in orbits as MiGCAP formations.

4. Other EB-66s would be in orbit to help jam enemy communications and defenses.

5. Tanker aircraft would be in their refueling orbits, ready to refuel the aircraft both before and after the strike.

6. Command and control aircraft would be airborne to relay warnings about approaching enemy aircraft.

7. Search and rescue aircraft, with their mix of planes and helicopters, would be in the air, on call.

The size and complexity of such a strike force is today the most compelling argument for the use of stealth aircraft, which greatly diminishes the number of required support aircraft.

★ BIBLIOGRAPHY ★

Berger, Carl, ed. *The United States Air Force in Southeast Asia, 1961–1973*. Washington, D.C.: Office of Air Force History, 1971.

Blesse, Maj. Gen. Frederick C., USAF (Ret.). *Check Six—A Fighter Pilot Looks Back*. Mesa, Ariz.: Champlain Fighter Museum Press, 1987.

Boyne, Walter J. *Beyond the Wild Blue: A History of the U.S. Air Force*. New York: St. Martin's Press, 1997.

———. *Clash of Wings, World War II in the Air*. New York: Simon & Schuster, 1994.

Broughton, Jack. *Going Downtown: The War against Hanoi and Washington*. New York: Orion Books, 1988.

Crane, Conrad C. *American Airpower Strategy in Korea, 1950–1953*. Lawrence, Kans.: University Press of Kansas, 2000.

Davis, Larry. *56th Fighter Group, Squadron*. Carrolton, Tex.: Signal Publishers, 1991.

Dorr, Robert F. *Air War Hanoi*. London: Blandford Press, 1988.

Dorr, Robert F., and Thompson, Warren. *The Korean Air War*. Osceola, Wis.: Motorbooks International, 1994.

Farr, Finis. *Rickenbacker's Luck*. Boston: Houghton Mifflin Company, 1979.

Franks, Norman L. R., and Bailey, Frank W. *Over the Front*. London: Grub Street, 1992.

Freeman, Roger. *Zemke's Wolf Pack*. New York: Orion Books, 1988.

Futrell, Robert F. *The United States Air Force in Korea, 1950–1953.* Washington, D.C.: Office of Air Force History, 1983.

Hartney, Lt. Col. Harold L. *Up and At 'Em.* Harrisburg, Pa.: Stackpole Sons, 1940.

Haulman, Daniel L., and Stancik, William C., eds. *Air Force Aerial Victory Credits in World War I, World War II, Korea and Vietnam.* Washington, D.C.: United States Air Force Historical Research Center, 1988.

Hess, William N. *Zemke's Wolfpack, The 56th Fighter Group in World War II.* Osceola, Wis.: Motorbooks International, 1992.

Hoeppner, Gen. Ernest von. *Germany's War in the Air.* Nashville, Tenn.: The Battery Press, 1994.

Jackson, Robert. *Air War over Korea.* London: Ian Allan Ltd., 1973.

Lewis, W. D. "American Hero: A Life of Eddie Rickenbacker," Baltimore, Md.: Johns Hopkins University Press, projected publication December 2001.

Littauer, Raphael, and Uphoff, Norman, eds. *The Air War in IndoChina.* Rev. Ed. Boston: Beacon Press, 1972.

Lowell, Lawrence A. *New England Aviators, 1914–1918,* Atglen, Pa.: Schiffer Publishing, 1997.

McLaren, David R. *Beware the Thunderbolt, The 56th Fighter Group in World War II.* Atglen, Pa.: Schiffer Military/Aviation History, 1994.

Michel, Marshall L., III. *Clashes, Air Combat over North Vietnam, 1965–1972.* Annapolis, Md.: Naval Institute Press, 1997.

Morrow, John H. *The Great War in the Air.* Shrewsbury, U.K.: Airlife, 1993.

Rickenbacker, Edward V. *Fighting the Flying Circus.* New York: Frederick A. Stokes Company, 1919.

Rickenbacker, Edward V. *Fighting the Flying Circus.* Lakeside Classic Edition annotated by Dr. W. David Lewis. Chicago: R. R. Donnelley and Sons, 1997.

Rickenbacker, Edward V. *Rickenbacker, An Autobiography.* New York: Prentice Hall, 1967.

Rickenbacker, William F. *From Father to Son: The Letters of Captain Eddie Rickenbacker to His Son William, from Boyhood to Manhood.* New York: Walker and Company, 1970

Sloan, James J., Jr. *Wings of Honor.* Atglen, Pa.: Schiffer Publishing, 1994.

Stewart, James T. *Airpower: The Decisive Force in Korea.* Princeton, N.J.: D. Van Nostrand Company, 1957.

Thompson, Wayne, and Nalty, Bernard C. *Within Limits—the U.S. Air Force and the Korean War*. Washington, D.C.: Air Force History and Museums Program, 1996.

Tilford, Earl H., Jr. *Setup: What the Air Force Did in Vietnam and Why*. Maxwell Air Force Base, Ala.: Air University Press, 1991.

Toliver, Raymond F., and Constable, Trevor J. *Fighter Aces of the U.S.A.* Atglen, Pa.: Schiffer Military History, 1997.

Zemke, Hubert, as told to Roger A. Freeman. *Zemke's Stalag*. Washington, D.C.: Smithsonian Institution, 1991.

★ INDEX ★